*Interactive Journalism*

# Interactive Journalism

*Hackers, Data, and Code*

NIKKI USHER

UNIVERSITY OF
ILLINOIS PRESS
Urbana, Chicago, and Springfield

Library of Congress Cataloging-in-Publication Data
Names: Usher, Nikki, author.
Title: Interactive journalism : hackers, data, and code /
    Nikki Usher.
Description: Urbana : University of Illinois Press, 2016.
    | Includes bibliographical references.
Identifiers: LCCN 2016012934 (print) | LCCN
    2016023445 (ebook) | ISBN 9780252040511
    (hardback) | ISBN 9780252081989 (paperback) |
    ISBN 9780252098956 (e-book)
Subjects: LCSH: Online journalism. | Journalism—
    Technological innovations. | BISAC: LANGUAGE
    ARTS & DISCIPLINES / Journalism. | SOCIAL SCIENCE
    / Media Studies. | BUSINESS & ECONOMICS /
    Industries / Computer Industry.
Classification: LCC PN4784.O62 U64 2016 (print) |
    LCC PN4784.O62 (ebook) | DDC 070.4—dc23
    LC record available at https://lccn.loc.gov
    /2016012934

*To Brinton Henry Layser*

# Contents

# Preface

This book did not begin as a study of the subspecialty of interactive journalism. Initially, scholar Seth C. Lewis and I began working on what we saw as an "intersection" of journalism and technology in summer 2011. When we started looking into this research area, we were initially surprised by what seemed to be the dawning of a new era in journalism: Mozilla, the tech company best known for its Web browser, had gotten together with the Knight Foundation to sponsor a contest that would eventually place five fellows in top newsrooms across the country. Other movements were proliferating—the Hacks/Hackers group was emerging, with journalists calling themselves "hacks," and programmers, "hackers," working toward the goal of bringing together these two occupations to improve journalism. Columbia and Northwestern Universities had just added computational journalism classes to teach students programming, and Northwestern had a special program offering scholarships for programmers to come to journalism school.

From June 2011 to September 2015, I conducted research for the book, in the early stages along with Seth. But I found that there was less an intersection from true outsiders than a growth and expansion of journalism itself. There were very few people from the programming and tech worlds who were consistently planning to dedicate their lives to news, particularly to traditional journalism. The tech industry had not suddenly become invested in journalism, though there were some outliers; when it had moved in that direction, it was in the service of traditional journalism. But there was a dedication in journalism among some of its most forward-thinking advocates to increase the prominence and importance of programming and data journalism via computation and visualization in news.

Thus, the current project became a study of how traditional journalism was trying to respond to the changes and challenges it faces. We saw that integral to every discussion of code and programming for traditional journalism was the rise in importance of a new type of news: interactive journalism. And we saw that there were changes in staffing—new people with new technical chops who were treated with great respect and authority in the newsroom, amid the hopeful industry discourse about what these journalists might bring.[1] Wider interest in programming and journalism became centralized inside the traditional news industry itself, so I looked to the most obvious and tangible site of its instantiation: inside traditional journalism, the focus you will see here.

Because this book seeks both academic and non-academic audiences, the introduction and chapter 1 serve to define terms and illuminate theories more useful for academics, and of less interest to journalists. However, they may nonetheless orient journalists as I outline the underlying questions and key arguments. Chapter 2 is the first empirical chapter, discussing the rise of interactive journalism as a subspecialty. Most useful to students might be chapter 4, which discusses how journalists work in newsrooms, or chapter 5, which offers key insights into how interactives are changing storytelling, an angle that may be particularly useful for getting students excited about coding and other digital skills.

I know some journalists are going to read this with a critical eye, and some will likely disagree with my arguments, yet such reaction will mean that my work has been the cross-species text between academics and journalists that I intend it to be. Journalists, who are more accustomed to "immediate" data—the kind gathered for stories—should be aware that academic research is much more drawn out over time, often over many years. Change has happened since I began this research, and when possible, I have attempted to document where changes might make for different observational patterns if conducted upon final manuscript submission. But to keep a constant update would be outside my scope, which is to take a snapshot of an emerging sub-profession and attempt to document its origins, norms, and practices, adding a dose of theoretical inquiry into how this might depart from or enhance current understandings about the profession of journalism as a whole and, more generally, about the sociology of professions. Academics ask different kinds of questions and approach our work with different methodologies. The sociological approach to academic research I've taken here has been from the outside looking in, one might say—and it is the job of the academic to use this distance to make observations those in the field might not see, might not be able to see, or might not think of themselves. These assessments will be different simply by virtue of the fact they are thought about and recorded by an outsider. The methodology section toward the end of the book (just after the conclusion) will illuminate this dynamic further. Please note that all professional titles are current as of when the interviews with participants were conducted.

# Acknowledgments

This book could not have been completed without Seth C. Lewis, whose help in the early part of the research and the early stages of the book was invaluable. Indeed, this book was at the proposal stage a joint venture, later taking on its present form as I changed direction. Nonetheless, if you know Seth's work, you are likely to see the influence of his thinking here. I am quite fortunate to have had the chance to work with such a brilliant, generous, thoughtful, and meticulous colleague.

I would also like to thank Danny Nasset for being interested in this project early on (what now seems very early on) and for staying interested in the work as it navigated through various twists and turns to become what it is today. His patience, guidance, and feedback, along with his excellent choice of reviewers, have helped shape this book into its present form.

Wilson Lowrey at the University of Alabama stepped in as my first reader. I was named an "emerging scholar" by the Association for Education in Mass Communication and Journalism, and the program promised a stipend for research support, assistance with getting to the annual conference, and, most important, a mentor. I unabashedly asked to work with Wilson because I knew he has tremendous experience writing about emerging subfields. Wilson was busier than ever working as an administrator, but he stepped in to be a reader for every single chapter of this book and provided extensive feedback. So thank you, Wilson.

I have to thank also the people who can only be described as my compadres in the journalism studies world, especially: Matt Carlson, who read parts of this book and also dealt with some new-parent freak-outs; Chris (C. W.) Anderson, who was always on hand for a question and ready reply for my insecurities, methods reflexivity, and impostor syndrome; Sue Robinson, who convinced me I could write the history chapter and provided advice without which my child may have never gone to sleep; Nick Diakopoulos, who never laughed at me except when he did, and answered ten million questions; and Matthew Powers, who asked me why any of this was interesting at all and who gave me a chance to look at this question because he had grown tired of this specific research. I extend additional thanks to: Lucy Morieson (for reading the entirety of this book while nine months pregnant and sick), Mark Coddington (for reading the entirety of this book at the very last minute and providing a much-needed gut check), Daniel Kreiss, Avery Holton, Josh Braun, Valérie Bélair-Gagnon, and Rasmus Kleis Nielson; also to the 750-word Facebook fist-bumpers: Karin Wahl-Jorgenson, Katy Pearce, Julia Himberg, Erin Sheley, James Losey, Julia Sonnevand, Lauren Delacruz, and Patrick Merle (and also to Buster Benson, for creating 750words.com).

A number of senior scholars have just been bar-none awesome throughout. I'd like to thank Jay Rosen for his insight and his contributions to the debate we are having, and for his encouragement and support. Pablo Boczkowski, Steve Reese, and Michael Schudson may not remember the meals and the drinks they have had with me while I babbled about this project, but I do. Thank you for your patience. Jeffrey Alexander helped me make it through a major meltdown. Thanks also to Rod Benson, Tim Vos, and David Ryfe for their support and collegiality, and to Terry Flew and Jay Hamilton for their feedback. Bob Franklin's emails are ones I actually print out and post on my walls because of their sage advice. Thank you to Emily Bell for mentorship and the Tow Center for Digital Journalism at the Columbia School of Journalism for support. As always, thanks to Herb Gans for his amazing, wonderful thoughts. And I am tremendously lucky to have Larry Gross as my mentor, with the full support of USC Annenberg always ready if I needed it, even as an alum.

I am fortunate to have the best colleagues ever at the George Washington University. Matt Hindman is not only an amazing colleague but also someone I am delighted to consider a dear friend. I am forever thankful for his incredible contributions to this book and to my general sanity. Special thanks to Silvio Waisbord for his willingness to drop what he's doing and brainstorm with me, especially over cappuccino and, if I am lucky, dark chocolate; to Catie Bailard for cocktails and girl talk; to Will Youmans, primarily for his couch but also for his company; and to Emily Thorson for letting me bug her next door. This book would absolutely not be possible without the support of Frank Sesno and Kim Gross and the School of Media and Public Affairs, who facilitated my research, gave me time to work, helped fund my work, and gave me encouragement and support. And Maria Jackson might be responsible for pretty much everything I've done and can do, as she always is. Todd Kominiak did much of the early work on this project as a research assistant, and Phillip C. Waller did all the horrible manuscript-completion tasks with Southern gentility. Thank you.

Finally, I should thank the people who played some of the most important roles when it came to access and introductions to make the fieldwork possible, some of whom were also instrumental informants for this book: Naz Kahn, Mohammad Haddad, Aron Pilhofer, Jonathan Stray, Michelle Minkoff, Jon Keegan, Simon Rogers, Ted Han, Scott Klein, John O'Keefe, Claire Wardle, Andrew Leimdorfer, Bella Hurrel, Geneva Overholser, David Boardman, Rick Hirsh, Mindy Marquez, Rick Green, Simon Rogers, Kat Downs-Mulder, Brian Boyer, Cyna Alderman, and, of course, others. Thanks also to people in the industry who helped me think through ideas and who answered many questions—Alex Howard, again Michelle Minkoff (who read my most difficult chapter), the emergency email speed-dial crew of Aron Pilhofer, Brian Boyer, and Scott Klein (who deserve the double thanks), Derek Willis, Chris Amico, Alberto Cairo, Sisi Wei, Jeremy Bowers, Andrew DeVigal, and really, truly lots and lots of others with whom I checked and rechecked quotes and facts and ideas, and who helped make this book better. I realize it may be nontraditional to thank informants, but "studying up" and researching in a traditional newsroom during precarious times requires unique cooperation.

This book took a lot of support from friends and at home, particularly as we welcomed our first child. Thanks to the Cabin John crew of ragtag paddlers and the Team Z crew of triathletes, as well as my lovely friends in D.C. and elsewhere. Particular shout outs to: Chuck Thornton (for letting me co-work, for feeding me lunch, and in whose house half of this book was written), Suzy Khimm, Eleanor Morrison, Helen Springut, Erica Smith, Meredith Waters, Ieva Augstums, Matt Springer, Carolyn O'Reilly, Abraham Parker, and Susan von Thun.

Last but very much not least, I thank my wonderful, amazing wife, Shelly Layser. Thanks for letting me wander the globe, for listening to me talk about the travails of fieldwork and empirical research, for enduring my pre-tenure stress over and over again, and for making charts and other academic wifely duties. And of course, you did some pretty hard work with that little dude we have now. To many more files named "Ice Cream" and to one day getting flamingo on 750words.com!

*Interactive Journalism*

# Introduction

## Interactives in the News

"Snow Fall: The Avalanche at Tunnel Creek," a 2012 interactive feature in *The New York Times*, won a Pulitzer Prize for what the judges complimented as a work "enhanced by its deft integration of multimedia elements."[1] This was a new way to tell a story. With a 3D rotating view of the Cascade Mountains, maps that allowed users to point and click and explore of their own volition, videos that were revealed as users scrolled over areas on the page, and integration of audio,[2] this was truly an immersive storytelling experience, one that almost felt like a video game.

*The Times'* first bold leap into an experience-based feature, wholly separated from the rest of its site, received an overwhelmingly positive reception online, with people on Twitter calling it both "beautiful" and "brilliant." The online news site Quartz noted that "Snow Fall" had prompted whispers: "Is this the future of online journalism?"[3] The traffic to the site was substantial: 2.9 million visits for more than 3.5 million page views. According to *The Times'* executive editor at the time, Jill Abramson, at the peak of the story there were twenty-two thousand people on the site, with one-third of them new users to nytimes.com.[4] To make this new story a reality, the old skills of a narrative journalist were combined with new storytelling abilities that relied on knowledge of code and a deft understanding of how to think about creating content for the new capacities of the Web.

"Snow Fall" is but one example that underscores one of the most notable changes to journalism today: the rise of a new form of news—interactive journalism. Traditional journalism faces the growing reality that the news business model remains an unsolvable problem. Audiences can go anywhere at any time. Advances in technology and computing offer opportunities to

# Snow Fall
## The Avalanche at Tunnel Creek

### By JOHN BRANCH

T he snow burst through the trees with no warning but a last-second whoosh of sound, a two-story wall of white and Chris Rudolph's piercing cry: "Avalanche! Elyse!"

The very thing the 16 skiers and snowboarders had sought — fresh, soft snow — instantly became the enemy. Somewhere above, a pristine meadow cracked in the shape of a lightning bolt, slicing a slab nearly 200 feet across and 3 feet deep. Gravity did the rest.

Snow shattered and spilled down the slope. Within seconds, the avalanche was the size of more than a thousand cars barreling down the mountain and weighed millions of pounds. Moving about 70 miles per hour, it crashed through the sturdy old-growth trees, snapping their limbs and shredding bark from their trunks.

The avalanche, in Washington's Cascades in February, slid past some trees and rocks, like ocean swells around a ship's prow. Others it captured and added to its violent load.

Somewhere inside, it also carried people. How many, no one knew.

"Snow Fall," *The New York Times*

explore on the Web and from mobile platforms beyond what has ever been possible before. There are now vastly greater amounts of data being produced than at any time in the past. The infrastructure and experience of information delivery has evolved to seemingly erase time and space boundaries.

This evolution matters to the future of journalism. If traditional journalism is to secure its continued relevance and claims to authoritative knowledge, it must provide some response to these changes. The traditional institution of journalism is at a precipice, and how it will respond ultimately may determine its very survival. This larger setting for news, bound up in changes to economics, technology, and culture, has created the conditions for a new subspecialty of the journalism profession to emerge: interactive journalism. This form of journalism is defined here as *a visual presentation of storytelling through code for multilayered, tactile user control for the purpose of news and information*; and its practitioners, though they have varying backgrounds, skills, and position names, are classified as interactive journalists.

You will find interactive journalism in a variety of forms: multimedia, immersive storytelling, data visualization, data-driven stories, explanatory graphics, or interactive features that combine some or all of these components. Just as interactives vary in form, they vary in subject as well, from the serious—income inequality or campaign finance—to the fun—March Madness brackets, maps of bar crawls and drink specials, and even Oscar ballots. Undergirding their creation is software, requiring programming that is distinct from the foundational functioning of the online or mobile news site. The goal at hand, though, is not to focus solely on the products to understand what is *new* about interactive journalism [5] but instead to understand just who the practitioners are, what work they actually do, and what knowledge they bring to the practice of journalism.

Interactive journalists have now become regulars in almost every major Western newsroom. It is the story of the emergence of a new occupational identity: a new subset of the profession of journalism. Thus, this book is cast in a larger discussion that probes the conditions for the emergence of this subspecialty and its intersection with traditional journalism. What interactive journalists bring to news, then, offers insight into how news work is changing. Interactivity has existed within journalism in many forms before: letters to the editor through mail, faxes, comments, and social media, for example. And the story of data in journalism, a major source of inspiration and raison d'être for interactives in some newsrooms, is one that may have existed since the 1800s, if not earlier. The claim presented here is that the application of code to journalism is qualitatively different now: code enables journalism to be expressed through software—as interactives—on a scale previously unseen and unlike what has come before.

The late 2010s represent a constitutive moment for interactive journalism: a turning point where interactive journalists and the content they produce have truly arrived into the mainstream of traditional newsrooms, while still being novel enough to contribute innovative people, practices, and thinking to the industry. At this time, interactive journalists find themselves showered with professional accolades from Pulitzers and inspire an almost hero-like reverence in the news industry, their skills so highly prized and considered essential to the future of journalism that journalism schools are literally rewriting curriculums to include courses in programming and even joint degrees in computer science; indeed, newsrooms laying off other staff will still hire interactive journalists. Interactive journalism and words associated with interactive journalism have gone up from almost no mentions on Twitter in 2009 to more than six hundred thousand mentions per month.[6] With all this in mind, a consideration of interactive journalists as a distinct occupational subspecialty within journalism is warranted, and the conditions that brought them to this point need to be examined.

The story begins within traditional journalism, in part because this is the heart of the biggest expansions and some of the most noteworthy experiments in interactive journalism, though traditional newsrooms are not the only site for its growth. Here, you will find a study of interactive journalism based on immersive field research and extensive interviews. The book offers examples from traditional institutions like *The New York Times*, *The Wall Street Journal*, the BBC, and beyond, as well as new journalism nonprofits like *ProPublica*, which creates journalism and often partners with these staid institutions to produce journalism intended to supplement the declines in watchdog work. Interactive journalism has a history in earlier journalism developments, but there are also facets of the subspecialty that are indeed new to this moment.

There is of course no monolithic journalism; the god-term "journalism" may be especially misleading today in light of the proliferation of nontraditional models of journalism, from online journalism outlets and mobile platforms to microblogs and social media. But in the case described here, I use journalism to mean the kind of work that is most threatened—and may need to change the most—in the context of the evolving digital environment: traditional journalism. As C. W. Anderson, Emily Bell, and Clay Shirky have argued, "The effect of the current changes in the news ecosystem has already been a reduction in the quality of news in the United States. On present evidence, we are convinced that journalism in this country will get worse before it gets better, and, in some places (principally midsize and small cities with no daily paper) it will get markedly worse."[7] This is a key rationale for a focus on the biggest source of original content for news—traditional journalism—which is explored here.

From the broadest perspective, the argument offered here can be distilled into this: Interactive journalism is a new subspecialty of the journalism profession. It emerges out of a variety of cooperative, contested, external, and internal pressures on the larger profession—from the need for relevance to the particular claim it offers to public knowledge. Empirically, I will show how interactive journalism is essential to understanding news production in the digital age. From a theoretical perspective, I will trace the subspecialty's emergence through a discussion of how people, work, and knowledge shape the development of interactive journalism. Interactive journalists have different backgrounds and emerge at a particular contextual and historical point such that some of the difficulties that arise when new entrants to the field emerge are less visible; though they are not always seamlessly integrated into newsrooms, their story as a subfield in journalism is one of acceptance and welcome rather than threat and fear. And due to their particular backgrounds and perspectives, interactive journalists bring new ways of thinking and doing journalism, such as incorporating openness, offering both near and far perspectives to journalism, self-directed discovery, and a focus on building and making. To begin, though, it's critical to offer some context about the nature of what the news industry is facing right now, which may be quite familiar to some readers. Less familiar, perhaps, may be the significance of other pressures challenging journalism's authority as a dominant source of knowledge: the speed of the Web, the increasing sophistication of user demand, and the expansion of data.

## The Context for the Crisis of Journalism

One way to think about interactive journalism is as a forward-looking innovation in news that comes from the recognition of the new capacities for news creation enabled by advances in technology. Another way to think about interactive journalism is as a defensive industry response to make sure that journalism keeps up with advances in technology as a way to make sure it remains culturally relevant. My perspective is that interactive journalism emerges as a result of both of these cultural influences, but it would not have the increasing power it does in the news industry and in news organizations were it not for the present problems in journalism.

There is a crisis in traditional journalism, particularly in newspapers. The evidence of a real crisis is across earnings statements (down across decades, but accelerating at a pace not seen before); in layoffs and employment numbers at levels lower than they have been in fifty years; in declines in coverage of political institutions like state houses and Washington; in the sale of century-old news buildings as newsrooms visibly downsize away from grand downtown historic spaces into smaller, nondescript offices;[8] in the inability to secure reliable online advertising rates and of most newspapers to convert readers into paying for online news; in the unbundling of company debt that isolates newspapers; and in the general and widespread failure to find any real way to monetize journalism. Consider this single statistic from the Newspaper Association of America: from 2000 to 2014, newspaper advertising revenue fell from a peak of $67 billion to $19.9 billion (including online ads). That's more than $47 billion fewer dollars in just fourteen years.[9]

Digital journalism and online and mobile-native journalism are bright spots. Venture capital is flowing into digital journalism in millions of dollars. Digital news startups are responsible for thousands of new journalism jobs. Digital news nonprofits are providing a critical supplement (and enhancement) to traditional journalism. And some older digital news outlets have held on for more than a decade as niche blogs or tabloids; think of the legal blog *Above the Law* or gossip news blog *Gawker*, both ancient by Web standards. New ecologies for journalism emerge: in the United States, Supreme Court watchers turn in droves to the upstart *Scotusblog* for breaking news for major decisions, and even some hyperlocal journalism outlets do actually get traffic.[10] But these digital efforts are supplementary, unlikely to fill a void left by their traditional counterparts; they are often specifically targeted to niche audiences, and their futures may be equally uncertain. Digital journalism is exciting, but it is by no means a solution to the very real problem that the major sources of original content creation in most major metropolitan cities in the United States are struggling—badly.

The newspaper crisis is certainly not exclusive to the United States; the crisis in journalism is raging in Western Europe as well. I often speak as an invited guest at newsrooms in Europe and to European journalists who come to the United States, and the executives I speak to are quite concerned about the challenges facing the continued survival of their organizations. While Scandinavian countries are generally in OK shape due to government subsidies, German, Dutch, Austrian, and French newspapers are facing serious declines.[11] In the United Kingdom, despite a vibrant and competitive press culture, the largest newspapers, such as *The Times of London*, are losing money. *The Financial Times* has even managed to insert a line of code into online content so that when you copy and paste an online article into an email, text appears that reads "High quality global journalism requires an investment. Please share this article with others using the link below." The link, of course, leads to a paywall. This serves both to induce guilt in a would-be copy-and-paster and to direct a user to pay for an article.

Journalistic authority, what Matt Carlson defines as "journalism's right to be listened to," is also facing a crisis.[12] Traditional journalism—particularly the traditional news organization—faces fresh challenges, thanks to the rise of new media technologies. From social media to cell phones to the Web, ordinary people now have access to capture, tell, and spread news stories about critical events of the day. The barriers (and boundaries) between the paid journalist working for a news organization and the armchair journalist seem more permeable, at least in the sense that the ordinary person now may perceive that he or she has more access than ever before to journalists and to creating content, even if this may not really be the case. Add to this mix the rise of a richer digital ecosystem for news with more choice, leaving any single outlet with a potentially diminished authoritative voice. And the public simply doesn't think journalists do much for society; a 2013 Pew Research Center survey found that just 28 percent of people thought journalists contributed "a lot" to society, compared with 72 percent for teachers and 66 percent for doctors.[13] These factors, combined with a decline in trust in journalism via a number of recent and high-profile scandals, alternative ways to communicate or receive information, and the economic distress facing journalism in general, vastly diminish any authority traditional journalism had previously amassed as a truth-teller and communicator of what is to be known about the world.

This crisis in journalism, then, frames the context for innovation today, including areas such as interactive journalism. Newspapers get a bad rap when it comes to innovation more generally. A common refrain is that newsrooms simply didn't see the internet coming, but that's just not true: most newspaper chains had some sort of early experimentation with either videotext or some sort of early proto-internet news-delivery vehicle delivered to what looked like future personal computers. For instance, Knight Ridder and *The New York Times* had small departments charged with creating and organizing content for these machines, which looked like televisions or computers connected to a phone line. In the case of *The Times*, the product was targeted to businesses and hotels. In fact, between 1983 and 1986, *The Times* was even delivering the newspaper via this early internet with original content—in an experiment that was then killed off due to lack of interest (there were only 250 subscribers).

As Reuters media columnist Jack Shafer dug up, some journalists *had* predicted the importance of the rise of the Web and the importance of capitalizing on digital advertising.[14] In 1992, Robert G. Kaiser, former managing editor of *The Washington Post*, penned a memo articulating the rise and promise of the coming Web revolution. Writing from a conference he had just attended, he noted:

> No one in our business has yet launched a really impressive or successful electronic product, but someone surely will. I'd bet it will happen rather soon. The Post ought to be in the forefront of this—not for the adventure, but for important *defensive* purposes. We'll only defeat electronic competitors by playing their game better than they can play it. And we can.

I was amazed how often the subject of electronic classifieds and electronic Yellow Pages was raised with me at this conference. Smart people are convinced that both make enormous sense.[15]

Kaiser understood that *The Post* had to be preemptive, and he predicted that electronic classifieds were something newspapers had to move on. McKinsey and Company, advisors to *The Times*, made a similar suggestion.[16]

Amazingly, in 1994, the Knight Ridder Research and Design Newspaper Lab "invented" the iPad—years ahead of the first Microsoft prototype that began in earnest the movement toward the creation of the tablet.[17] Well, not *exactly*, but the R&D team envisioned a portable tablet device where one could get the day's news, along with a selection of personalized classified advertisements. The tablet would be touch-responsive and thin, and would feature video and interactive content. Its designers missed some pretty key ideas, assuming, for example, that a stylus would be our interaction with the touch screens of the future, and imagining little discs rather than wireless for information transmission—but the essence of tablet future was there. One year later, Knight Ridder shut down the lab, ostensibly to focus on the emerging Web.

In short, the larger story of technological change within its social context has always been bound up in the story of journalism's progress. The story of journalism's adaptation to more recent technological change is mixed. News ethnographies have devoted considerable attention to this question. In the late 1990s, Pablo Boczkowski researched how organizational, technological, and communicative practices helped create new forms of journalism and new journalistic practices—including some of the earliest forms of multimedia and participatory content.[18]

More recent empirical work has chronicled a failure to adapt to change and to the Web. David Ryfe found, in his analysis of newspapers going through change, that regional newspapers were basically hostile to the idea of adapting to the Web. C. W. Anderson, who looks more broadly at news ecosystems, found that while we could see evolutions in journalistic form from outside journalism, newsrooms had uneven patterns and practices of working with these new actors, and equally uneven approaches to thinking about adapting to the challenges of the Web—from thinking about metrics to thinking about the daily practices of news work.[19] My own ethnographic research on *The New York Times* documented extensively the frenetic split inside the newsroom between Web and print. The emergent practices of immediacy in the digital age, interactivity, and participation were incredibly contested by traditional journalists. And four years after my work, in 2014, a leaked "innovation" report revealed that the newspaper was indeed still stuck in an inability to innovate culturally inside the newsroom, and from the business side, the paper had not yet begun to think proactively about a changed business environment.[20]

In the context of this contest over whether newsrooms have innovated enough, though, a new narrative of experimentation has been this appropriation of code into journalism, one that is an importation of new technology practices that may serve to make a case for the relevancy, importance, and economic stability of traditional journalism. Interactive journalism today is a new form of news and a new way of telling stories, and its practitioners are a new kind of journalist. This brand of news is bound up in a hope for journalism's transformation as the industry attempts to innovate in ways that respond to the reality of a more complicated digital environment.

Interactives are critical to the success of traditional journalism today. As Raju Narisetti, senior vice president for strategy at News Corp explained to me:

> The dramatic increase in the use of interactives follows the great reshaping of modern-day journalism, from a top-down periodic dissemination of relatively static news and information to audiences—primarily through print and television, into a two-way, real-time, engaging digital experience for engaged audiences across computers, tablets and phones.
>
> If the famous and path-breaking *New York Times* interactive, "Snow Fall: The Avalanche at Tunnel Creek," were a news story that others quickly copied, the "experience" of consuming that same story elsewhere would be far less satisfying or engaging, perhaps, to most readers because of the highly interactive presentation that the Times created. **And it is that interactive experience that made this piece of Times journalism both engaging and defensible. This is another reason why smart newsrooms will continue to produce more interactive journalism and create a new competitive advantage that doesn't just rely on unique content alone.**[21]

As *The Washington Post*'s executive editor Marty Baron explained at the South-by-Southwest Interactive Festival in 2015, the combination of programming and journalism "has been absolutely critical to our transformation. . . . It's not your father's newsroom." He noted that the goal was to "transform storytelling," and he gave examples to the panel's audience—interactives such as the search for the missing Malaysian airplane MH370 and more amusing interactives like the "Bad News Beards" of baseball.[22] But what were the pressures that led to transforming storytelling? Why does it seem so critical to newsrooms to have these interactives? To answer this, it's important to understand what specific pressures are facing the press.

## The Demands on Journalism Today

Traditional journalism faces many major challenges from technological change. These changes are not independent or causal factors alone but are bound up as part of larger social conditions, such as how people use the technology and its social functions. Technological challenges derive from the material conditions that influence the way that people adapt, create, and innovate, but these technological innovations and challenges are the direct result of how people have created the technology in the first place. Given the crisis in journalistic authority, the ability to explain the world in ways that are fast and navigable, and that help make sense of what can seem like an ever increasing flow of information becomes critical. And speed and information abundance, user experience, and the rise of big data are challenges afforded by advances in digital technology that journalism needs to adapt to in order to maintain its claim of truth-telling authority.

Journalism has to deal with an infrastructure environment that is simply faster and faster, with the result of an information ecology that churns out more and more content. And, today, the content on the internet travels literally at the speed of light; a 1-kilobyte email travels close to 670 million miles per hour.[23] Though by mid-2015 average broadband speed across the United States was about twelve megabits per second (for an international rank of nineteenth and posting an internet speed of less than half that for South Korea),[24] in the 1990s most modems had a capacity for only fifty-six kilobits per second. Speed for content has gotten extremely fast, especially in the context of how long it takes to transmit information from a daily print newspaper: from the start day's news cycle early in the morning until what might be a print deadline of midnight, and then between two and three hours for a newspaper press run.[25] Incredibly fast online speeds mean two things: that information can move incredibly quickly—a news story, word of a disaster, a photo, some form of public knowledge can spread across the Web in a matter of seconds—and that journalists (and ordinary people as well) are in a constant instant-information environment such that inside newsrooms, journalists feel the pressure to have something new available to the audience at every moment.

David Weinberger writes about information abundance as a paradox because it speaks to "epochal exultation of knowledge"[26] whereby there has been a fundamental change in the infrastructure of what we know and how we know it, but also presents new challenges. This puts tremendous pressure on newsrooms, as I have noted in my book on *The New York Times*. At *The Times*, journalists feared becoming irrelevant if they could not keep the Web site up to date, fearing they might not be a comprehensive and all-inclusive source of information at all times to all people. This is tremendous pressure, but perhaps not unrealistic: If anyone can go anywhere for information, what keeps someone loyal to *The New York Times*? If information is moving with such tremendous speed, and a newspaper or news outlet needs to keep up, then if it isn't up to date, doesn't it appear irrelevant?

But there is another way of looking at this speed and this churn. We live in a world where information appears to be overwhelming (whether it is or is not is an empirical question, but the *perception* of speed and abundance has been widely documented).[27] If journalism can cut through the fog of the incredible amount of information available to modern readers and create something lasting, something helpful, or something that can guide and orient—or perhaps make something good enough that delights and entertains in a way that stands out from the myriad content available from so many different places online—it makes a case for its relevance. These kinds of lasting, distinguishing contributions can come in many forms: from long-form digital journalism to documentary-style journalism, and, significantly, interactive journalism.

But there is another challenge that journalism faces to being a destination for information—and this simply comes from a user-experience perspective. Journalism has traditionally lagged behind other industries when it comes to technological adaptation, and as Boczkowski has chronicled, the move online has been no different and, in fact, often reactionary.[28] User expectations for an online experience have grown in sophistication from a time when broadband did not exist, and if journalism is to be part of people's contemporary (and future) digital experience, it has to respond to these developments with a better product.

User expectations have changed in part due to speed, in part due to user design enhancements (aided by coding advances and better understanding of how people move through the Web), and in part due to a sophisticated online environment offering a rich, interactive environment for user exploration. News organizations fight the battle of load or lag time—how long it takes for a site or an element to appear onscreen (called network latency).[29] Swedish internet provider Ume Net illustrated this by strapping a virtual-reality headset called Oculus Rift on participants. The disruption caused by a lag time of even a fraction of a second was clearly illustrated as headset wearers tried to cook, dance, and go about daily life.[30] Google's research shows that page load times above one second interrupt user flow of thought.[31] And some news Web sites are notoriously slow—the effect of which can be a serious interruption for user experience. Though *The New York Times* has vastly improved its load times, in a 2009 "Meet the Interactive News Team" Q&A on *The New York Times* Web site, the frustrations users can face with load times are clear. Slow speeds are the enemy. One reader said, "Why does it take so long to load the first image of a video piece as I try to scroll down the paper's page? It is starting to be a real frustration." Another said, "I am aghast at how much handshaking . . . my browser has to do while loading Page One. It takes forever!"[32] Many (if not most) newspaper news sites still have these problems.

Jakob Nielsen, an early user-design expert, writes in *Usability Engineering* about the key principles of response time.[33] Though the basic response time expectations have not changed in twenty years, what has changed is the expectation of interactivity. For instance, he writes that in 1991, 0.1 second was the limit for a user to feel that a computer was responding instantaneously. But in 2014 he noted that 0.1 second had become a limit for users to feel that they are "directly manipulating" objects in a user experience—in other words, there is an increased demand for interactivity. One second previously represented (in Google's research) the limit for a user's flow of thought to be uninterrupted; today, this refers to the "limit for users feeling that they are *freely navigating* the command space without having to unduly wait for the computer." Or, users demand free navigation to choose their own way around the experience of an online object before them without an obviously preordained pattern. And ten seconds used to be the limit on keeping users' attention focused on a particular piece of dialogue; now, this refers to the amount of time a user will spend on a specific active *task*.

What this means for journalism is that the profession must respond with some sort of usability design that takes into account demand for user engagement. Static text may not be enough when the demand for actual interactivity and user control has evolved. The expectations for instant manipulation and free navigation need to inform what news sites offer. Certainly, existing sites can offer this through browsing, but news sites also need to find other ways to capitalize on this expectation of direct and instant engagement. News sites are starting to recognize the problems with various user design issues; *The New York Times* went through a significant effort to cut the amount of time it takes for its site to load, requiring a major rewrite of underlying code.[34] Some argue that newsrooms can begin to innovate only if they can offer responsive design, and news organizations are struggling to get out of their fixed and rigid home-page structures.[35] Interactive journalism provides a solution to frustrations with static pages and poor engagement, combining responsive design with user-driven experiences that take advantage of the best of what the Web and mobile experiences have to offer, from data visualization to visual storytelling.

Similarly, journalistic authority faces a new challenge—and a new opportunity—with the rise of big data. "More data" is a constant, surely, but there also exists the opportunity to help people as an authoritative information source for dealing with all of this new data. Seth C. Lewis argues that two major things have changed: the "overwhelming volume and variety of digital information produced by and about human (and natural) activity" and the "rapid advances in and diffusion of computing processing, machine learning, algorithms, and data science."[36] There is simply more data available in the increasingly digital, electronic world, where it is easier to gather information—and at least on some level, to distribute it. In 2012, *Mashable* put it into concrete terms: Each day, there was enough new information produced to fill 168 million DVDs, with each DVD containing roughly 4.4 gigabytes of information.[37] In the entire digital universe of things that we have stored and shared, the GovLab at NYU estimated that the "number of exabytes (1 billion gigabytes) created every day in 2012" was 2.5, with that number doubling every month.[38]

However, by 2014, market research firm International Data Corporation estimated that the "digital universe" had grown to 4.4 zettabytes of data. By 2020, IDC estimates that number will grow by a factor of ten to 44 zettabytes, or roughly as many stored bytes as there are stars in the universe. This dramatic increase in data production can be represented by the huge growth in data storage that has become central to many of the world's top economic drivers.[39] According to a 2014 release, Wal-Mart, for instance, has databases that hold more than 30 petabytes of shopping information.[40] Amazon operates Web servers that have consistently led the cloud services market in both size and processing power. In July 2015, Amazon held 29 percent of the cloud services market, as compared with the 25 percent that its top three competitors—Microsoft, IBM, and Google—held. This market alone is worth more than $20 billion each year.[41]

On the consumer side of data production, an increasing web of internet-connected smartphones and devices have contributed to the massive increase. The growth is represented in the one billion hours of video streamed via Netflix each month of 2014 and, in 2015, the three hundred hours of video uploaded *every minute to YouTube*.[42] And arguably, from the perspective of many reporters, the U.S. government has more data on people than ever before (consider the NSA revelations)—with more data on EACH person in the United States than the Stasi of East Germany ever had in its entire files.[43] Newsrooms frequently use government data, in part because one can file a request for federal government information through the Freedom of Information Act. Beyond that, though, the newsrooms can collect, search, compute, visualize, and organize data in ways that have never been done before.

The rise of data collection means more data to sift through, more potential stories, and more places to search for accountability by institutions. Computer-assisted reporting has existed in some form since the 1950s (as I will explain in chapter 2), but at this point one can "interview the data" (a shorthand for a process of inquiry offered by *New York Times* data journalist Derek Willis)[44] in entirely new ways. Programming can offer a way to sift through databases more easily to find information, to render this information searchable, and to present it to the public. With this in mind, newsrooms have turned to a new era of data inquiry, and while they are not like many giant companies or government sites, which collect and might analyze terabytes of data, newsrooms' programming capacity facilitates access to "bigger data" than ever before. For example, there are larger government and consumer behavior datasets available—with software that can handle it now, as Terry Flew and his colleagues point out.[45] As I will explain, the rise of interactive journalism is concurrent with the rise of data journalism.

There's also a broader story about how the development of the history of programming and the rise of the sophistication of the Web and mobile technologies explain how we got to the point where interactive journalism has become an occupational identity with the prestige and power it has today—and why journalism needs interactive journalism. But this part of the history more deeply intersects with the daily practice and development of journalism and is less part of the overall context for the specific material technological challenges it faces as external pressures. Reckoning with speed and information abundance, user experience demands, and Big Data gives traditional journalism a chance to reassert its relevance at a time of uncertainty, but it also poses new challenges. Interactive journalism is but one way to approach these challenges, and it was not an inevitable result of a march toward innovation; rather, it emerged from myriad influences and choices made in the newsroom. Interactives, then, as Mary Lynn Young and Alfred Hermida note, arise from "existing social, organizational, and material contexts, as well as mutually reinforcing access to new technologies."[46]

## A Look Ahead

Interactive journalists have been praised as bona fide heroes. A *New York Magazine* article heralded *New York Times* interactive journalists as bringing the newspaper into the future. The article, titled "The New Journalism:

Goosing the Gray Lady," had a provocative subhead: "What are these renegade cybergeeks doing at *The New York Times*? Maybe saving it." This, then, is the promise of this emerging subspecialty of journalism. In the following chapters, I bring together a comprehensive portrait of this subspecialty from a theoretical and empirical approach. Chapter 1 defines interactive journalism and explains the underpinning theoretical argument of the book (practitioners may find this less applicable, though the themes discussed here appear throughout the book). Chapter 2 discusses the history of interactive journalism, and chapters 3, 4, and 5 are then organized around the themes of people, work, and knowledge, with a final chapter that suggests where we may be headed as interactive journalism expands.

The first of the empirical chapters, chapter 2, looks at how interactive journalism began. Through oral history and a dive into old blogs and the internet archive, I have attempted to reconstruct the beginnings of how programming and journalism were first being used to tell stories and bring us through this history to the contemporary setting for interactive journalism. I offer insight as well into the history of information graphics and computer-assisted reporting, which are also progenitors of interactive journalism.

Chapter 3 focuses on the *people* behind interactive journalism, beginning with a discussion of how these journalists understand the rise of the subspecialty and its new importance in the field, how they see themselves, and what they bring in terms of unique perspectives and skills as they adopt practices from programming cultures. The messy delineations and difficulty in defining the many types of skills and specialists within the subspecialty are revealed.

Chapter 4 discusses the *work* these journalists do. Through vignettes that move across the world, from an in-depth look at *Al Jazeera English* interactive creation to NPR, from *The Guardian*'s data desk to *The New York Times*, we see the work products of these interactive journalists. We learn also how these desks and their work is incorporated into the larger newsroom efforts. In some cases, there is isomorphism across each newsroom, but in other ways, particular organizations seem to have specific ideas about what unique offerings they provide to the overarching news-production process. The chapter is rooted in a look at production and work.

Chapter 5 explores *knowledge*, or the special abstract knowledge that interactive journalists add to the profession at large. This goes beyond the special skills they have, speaking instead to the different ways their work and expertise informs thinking about journalism more generally.

Finally, chapter 6 offers a bigger picture for what interactive journalism means to journalism as a whole, underscoring how the findings demonstrate the evolution of a profession and reviewing how the new kinds of abstract knowledge inherent in interactive journalism creates new conceptual considerations for the field. Interactive journalism is far from perfect, and limitations—from a fetishization of code to lack of skepticism about data—are discussed. I encourage anyone interested in the methods of this book—from the interviewing and field research to the choices for people's titles and my proposal for "hybrid ethnography" (a particular approach to short-term case studies) to look at the separate chapter on methodology, near the end of the book.

Across all these chapters, you will discover how interactive journalism is changing the profession and gain insight into where it is going—suggesting a dynamic role for the subspecialty in the future of journalism. From a more practical perspective, interactive journalists are changing the form, content, and practice of journalism. From a more theoretical perspective, interactive journalists offer an example of the development of a professional subspecialty—in this case, journalism—and quite significantly, despite some minor daily struggles, are not seen as a threat to journalism by more established types of journalists, but as a welcome addition who can work side by side with others in the newsroom. Their new ways of thinking about journalism prepare it for the advances in digital technology and present potential for experimentation that is flourishing in the fourteen newsrooms studied here, and beyond.

# 1   Interactive Journalism

## *A Budding Profession*

I remember the first time I came across interactive journalism and realized there was an aspect of this kind of news content that was different than anything I had seen before. I had just started what would become this book, and I'd begun thinking about the intersection of "hacks" and "hackers," or programmers and journalists, from a cultural perspective. I was one step away from digging into the interactive content itself, but it was an accidental discovery that showed me how important interactive journalism would be to the future of news.

A *New York Times* interactive made a deeply personal impact on me that influenced one of the biggest decisions I've ever made. We were searching for a home to buy in 2011 in the Washington, D.C., area, and we were feeling quite disheartened. After all, median home price in the district is close to $500,000—and when you're on a professor's salary after years of a pitiful grad school stipend, that seems kind of nuts. At the same time, rents were and still are also out of control—a two-bedroom in a neighborhood we deemed safe with good access to the Metro, shopping, and entertainment could cost close to $3,000 per month, if not more. So, we began trying to figure out whether it was a better idea to rent or buy, yet we didn't know what factors to consider. Then we found *The Times'* Rent vs. Buy calculator ("Is it Better to Rent or Buy").[1] By entering a few bits of personal data unique to us—our monthly rent vs. our potential down payment and the cost of the home, plus the property tax and mortgage rate—we learned that it made much more sense to buy than rent if we were planning to be in the D.C. area long term.

This interactive tool did not constitute breaking news; rather, it was a well-researched piece of journalism that required learning about the financial impact of home mortgages and renting, and then took into account personal data and offered an individualized result. The journalists had to research all the key factors relevant to buying a home, weigh how those factors related to each other, and then (using skills I was now seeing as critical to the newsroom) use programming not only to create the code behind the "rent or buy" calculation but also to present a visually enticing and easy-to-use display of this information. There were spaces to enter numbers and then a graph to show results. Over the years, the tool has only gotten better and easier to use, with more features that can be toggled, dragged, and displayed (even on your smart phone, should you need to think about a home purchase on the go).[2]

After we bought our home, I reflected a bit—this single piece of journalism was responsible for one of the biggest decisions of my life. It wasn't a Pulitzer Prize story that had changed my worldview about a social issue, but it had nevertheless literally changed where I lived. And anyone I knew anywhere could use this calculator—it would be personal and useful to them—and it would simply not have been possible before without a quick, responsive Web, an understanding of programming, and reporting about real estate. The kind of journalism *The New York Times* was offering was changing with content like this calculator, and it was time to think about how, why, and who was changing it.

## Defining Interactive Journalism

Interactive journalism is defined here *as a visual presentation of storytelling through code for multilayered, tactile user control for the purpose of news and information.* Its practitioners, though they have varying backgrounds and skills, are classified as interactive journalists. Interactive journalism is a subspecialty—a new form of journalistic work—but it is certainly one among many; subspecialties include photography, graphics, videography, blogging, copyediting, layout and design, online-exclusive content, and others. Some of these subspecialties have been part of journalism for decades or even centuries—consider photography from its early days to present—while others have emerged in the online era. As a whole, interactive journalism is an all-encompassing term that refers to the *people* who work in this area, the *practice* of doing the work, and the work *product* that results.

Interactivity, though, is a confusing term at best. Interactivity has been called an essential if not defining property of the internet.[3] Scholars in the late 1990s and early 2000s wrote articles trying to define interactivity in the context of human–computer interaction, each one with a familiar refrain: interactivity was a messy concept that the author would make clearer (which often failed to happen). People have proposed a number of ways to think about the concept, the first as primarily an interpersonal relationship whereby interactivity can be measured through how closely messages relate to each other.[4] Others argue that interactivity means that users can modify and participate in controlling a mediated environment in real time, but what "modify" means is unclear.[5] Jennifer Stromer-Galley suggests a way to think about both computer and person-to-person interaction: interactivity as product and interactivity as process.[6] Interactivity as product is defined as the control users have over what they see through some sort of computer experience. Interactivity as process is person-to-person or human interaction. Others define this divide as user-to-system and user-to-user.[7]

In my view, then, and given the subject and form of news discussed here, interactivity has a much simpler definition, one that Stromer-Galley supports and Erik Bucy describes as the "control that users exercise over the selection and presentation of online content, whether story text, audiovisuals, or multimedia, and other aspects of the interface."[8] What is important here is that users have the perception that they are engaging in a two-way exchange, where factors such as time, speed, content, and pathways for discovery create the experience. Ultimately, the predetermined architecture of the interactive creates a structured experience of content.

In an earlier era of interactivity, as I have shown in *Making News at The New York Times*, journalists saw multimedia *as* interactivity. Multimedia was the most compelling way users could engage with multiple forms of journalistic content, the type Bucy suggests.[9] This "multimodal" journalism, or journalism presented through visuals, stories, text, audio, videos, and photos, is one part of interactive journalism—journalism as a multisensory experience.[10] In fact, interactivity may be said to be one of the defining principles of digital journalism.

Journalists recognized that more sophisticated multimedia, coupled with better Web integration, heralded a new capacity to do interactive work. Interactives are even more sophisticated than they once were, building this content as *software* with programmers working inside the editorial process. Small newsrooms even five years ago were unlikely to have an interactive journalist—but today, even those without them are taking risks and trying out new ways of bringing interactives into their work: for example, *The Star-Telegram* in Fort Worth, Texas, uses an off-the-shelf program to upload photos and graphics to help create interactive elements for their most important projects.

With this energy behind interactive journalism, let's look at this definition I've offered in order to get a clearer picture about what the phenomena at hand actually *is*:

*Interactive journalism is defined here as a visual presentation of storytelling through code for multilayered, tactile user control for the purpose of news and information.*

By *visual*, I mean that the product is not a text-based story. Some may think that this applies specifically to a data visualization or a video-laden interactive, but it does not: rather, this visual aspect ought to be considered on a scale. On the most basic side of this, one might consider a database that users can search through—this doesn't look like a story, and it isn't particularly visually pretty. And its product is text you can read. But the user-design is intended to lead you visually through to the elements of the story you ought to click on and explore. The point is that you are not getting a traditional textual element found on every single Web page for every single online journalism presentation—the traditional text, written story—but instead are being offered something that looks different. On the most extreme version of visual presentation, you might place fully immersive and responsive story pages replete with visual stories, maps, animated graphics, annotation via commenting, and beyond.

*Storytelling*, too, operates at a variety of levels. A sports interactive showing the trajectory of a pitch may depict how the ball moves, but it provides new information and insight in some way. A calculator may generate a number or a quiz may generate a silly answer. A collection of movable graphs may not have a direct narrative, but this may offer information that allows the user to put the story together. On the other hand, interactive journalism may tell a self-contained narrative—for instance, an interactive that brings together reported text, images, maps, and beyond to offer greater insight into, say, a conflict zone. Styles of this interaction can be the user telling the computer to do something; having a conversation as if there is a dialogue with the graphic; manipulation, where the structure of the story is changed via appearance; and exploration, where the user is put in charge.[11]

Everything in online journalism requires *code*.[12] But interactive journalism goes above and beyond the code that enables sites to function. Certainly, content management systems are incredibly difficult and complicated, but interactive journalism means layering on top of this content management with particular, specialized coding language built as an expansion to a Web site with additional functionality. *It is code created with the intention of a visible output*. Not all journalists who work with interactive journalism know code, but they use tools that apply an extra layer of coding to journalism. Code in the service of interactive journalism means specialized knowledge, either of code or of tools that use code to make interactive journalism. On perhaps the most coding-heavy side of this scale, we may consider computational journalism, whereby journalists go about finding stories with or by using algorithms.[13]

And at the core of interactive journalism is the idea of *tactile, user-directed, multilayered control*: in other words, a user is directly interfacing with a computer to select and make choices about the pathways through content. A user has always been able, to some degree, to select his or her own content. The difference now is that there is a self-contained experience of manipulation, though nonetheless this experience is within a set, bounded universe devoted to a single, concrete topic for exploration. As Alberto Cairo, a major figure in interactive and news information graphics, points out, these can be linear and nonlinear, and while there is user control, the designer does impose some limits on what users can do.[14] Yet the content has multifaceted areas to explore but no predetermined pathway. The user has the ability to tell himself or herself a story.

By *multilayered*, I mean that the navigation occurs through the experience of multiple elements at once. The user does not have to refresh a page or do anything on his or her own to make the new insight available. While interactive journalism may produce a new version of an image upon a request for new information, the user has not navigated on his or her own away from the original request for the specific experience contained within the interactive.

And *tactile* offers a key way to describe the user experience. Tactile suggests an element of play—that the user is able to do something. There is something almost physical to the experience; the entire experience requires touching via the experience of clicking. Interactive journalism has a plasticity and mobility built into its form. According to user interface and design expert Jenifer Tidwell, this tactile experience can include the ability to scroll and pan, zoom, sort and arrange, search and filter, and go close and far.[15]

The last part of the definition is the most challenging: *for the purpose of news and information*. Through interactive journalism, we know and learn something that orients us to the world—in the classic way that Robert Park talked about the function of news in society: "news as a form of knowledge."[16] As I contend, there is no one journalism, particularly as the definition transforms, changes, and adapts. But I do think there is an essential "newsthink," what Silvio Waisbord defines as a "a way of apprehending the world that distills bottomless amounts of information into news."[17] For me, this offers a generous way to think about journalism—it can be fun, silly, or even entertainment, and it can also be hard-hitting, investigative, public service, and/or the kind of breaking news that makes an editor's heart sing.

Sometimes, the work product of interactive journalism is described as a news application or, in short, a news app—or often *software*. A major leader in this field, Scott Klein of the investigative journalism nonprofit *ProPublica* explained this as "doing journalism by making software instead of words and pictures." Often, though, this definition is just limited to the artifacts that produce data-driven products and does not refer to immersive or less-data-specific work. Similarly, the focus on the news app itself does not help explain the people involved or the type of knowledge created. And calling it "data journalism" is too narrow: there are other kinds of interactive journalism, such as interactive storytelling that provides an immersive digital journalism experience, like "Snow Fall," or interactive features that bring together elements of mapping, data, and multimedia storytelling; further, there are interactives that have nothing to do with data at all but still employ news apps. A BBC interactive called "The Secret Life of Cats," for example, might not fall under this definition,[18] nor would the interactive Oscar ballot put out by *The New York Times*, nor many sports interactives, and potentially not even immersive storytelling like "Snow Fall," and certainly not quizzes that are not directly related to traditional journalism but are associated instead with news events (*Slate* is particularly good at these, such as mocking John Travolta's butchering of a star's name at the Oscars).[19] Thus, interactive journalism is an all-encompassing term that refers to a category of journalism created as, or through, software, and its practitioners are interactive journalists.

Data journalism is an important source of inspiration, expertise, and content for interactive journalism. The term itself is quite slippery to some practitioners: Does it mean the act of actually just using computation to create data findings? Or does there have to be something visual or even interactive in presenting the findings? Journalist Alexander Howard, in his report for the Columbia School of Journalism, gave one of the clearest definitions of data journalism so far: "[The] gathering, cleaning, organizing, analyzing, visualizing, and publishing data to support the creation of acts of journalism."[20] He adds that this means the application of data science to journalism, which he defines as the "study of the extraction of knowledge from data."[21] Data journalism is a combination of sources, the application of statistics, and visualizations to present it all. From my perspective, data journalism is a key part of interactive journalism, but not all data journalism is *interactive*. My focus here is how news and programming have come together to create new forms of journalism, and so the data journalism most relevant to this project is data journalism rendered in interactives, as it relies on new technical expertise to extend code into journalism in ways that inspire new modes of thinking about journalistic work.

Thus, to sum up, the type of work that is being done may be called interactive journalism: *a visual presentation of storytelling through code for multilayered, tactile user control for the purpose of news and information*. But interactive journalism is what we call the *product* and the *process* of creating this product. We need to remember that interactive journalism is more than

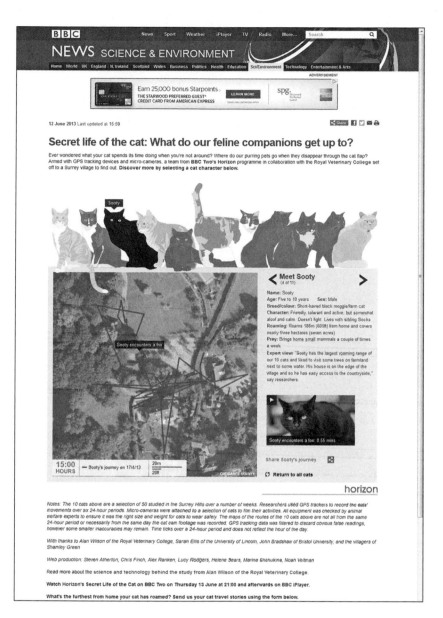

BBC

NEWS SCIENCE & ENVIRONMENT

News    Sport    Weather    iPlayer    TV    Radio    More...    Search

Home  World  UK  England  N. Ireland  Scotland  Wales  Business  Politics  Health  Education  Sci/Environment  Technology  Entertainment & Arts

12 June 2013 Last updated at 15:59          Share

## Secret life of the cat: What do our feline companions get up to?

Ever wondered what your cat spends its time doing when you're not around? Where do our purring pets go when they disappear through the cat flap? Armed with GPS tracking devices and micro-cameras, a team from **BBC Two's Horizon** programme in collaboration with the Royal Veterinary College set off to a Surrey village to find out. **Discover more by selecting a cat character below.**

Sooty

Sooty encounters a fox

### Meet Sooty
(4 of 11)

Name: Sooty
Age: Five to 10 years     Sex: Male
Breed/colour: Short-haired black moggie/farm cat
Character: Friendly, tolerant and active, but somewhat aloof and calm. Doesn't fight. Lives with sibling Socks
Roaming: Roams 186m (600ft) from home and covers nearly three hectares (seven acres)
Prey: Brings home small mammals a couple of times a week
Expert view: "Sooty has the largest roaming range of our 10 cats and liked to visit some trees on farmland next to some water. His house is on the edge of the village and so he has easy access to the countryside," say researchers

Sooty encounters a fox: 0.55 mins

Share Sooty's journey

15:00 HOURS — Sooty's journey on 17/4/13    20m / 20ft    ORDNANCE SURVEY

Return to all cats

horizon

Notes: The 10 cats above are a selection of 50 studied in the Surrey Hills over a number of weeks. Researchers used GPS trackers to record the cats' movements over six 24-hour periods. Micro-cameras were attached to a selection of cats to film their activities. All equipment was checked by animal welfare experts to ensure it was the right size and weight for cats to wear safely. The maps of the routes of the 10 cats above are not all from the same 24-hour period or necessarily from the same day the cat cam footage was recorded. GPS tracking data was filtered to discard obvious false readings, however some smaller inaccuracies may remain. Time ticks over a 24-hour period and does not reflect the hour of the day.

With thanks to Alan Wilson of the Royal Veterinary College, Saran Ellis of the University of Lincoln, John Bradshaw of Bristol University, and the villagers of Shamley Green

Web production: Steven Atherton, Chris Finch, Alex Ranken, Lucy Rodgers, Helene Sears, Marina Shchukina, Noah Veltman

Read more about the science and technology behind the study from Alan Wilson of the Royal Veterinary College.

Watch Horizon's Secret Life of the Cat on BBC Two on Thursday 13 June at 21:00 and afterwards on BBC iPlayer.

What's the furthest from home your cat has roamed? Send us your cat travel stories using the form below.

"The Secret Life of Cats," *BBC News*

a material object: it is also bound up in social and cultural contexts. C. W. Anderson talks about data journalism in the context of an assemblage—as having "interlocking material, culture, and practice-based underpinnings"— and while I do not use these terms here, the interactive itself, the assumptions built into its creation, and the larger sociotechnical culture inform its use, design and reception.[22] This is why the people who make interactives and how they work are at the center of this study.

An important tie-in to interactive journalism is the larger academic association with computational journalism. The two ideas are related but not the same thing; interactives often use code and algorithms to help journalists improve the process and practices of their work beyond just outward presentation of content to the public. The term "computational journalism" originated in 2006 at Georgia Tech, where Irfan Essa, a professor in computer science fresh from a meeting at CNN, came back wondering how computers could be used to better help journalism. He and student Nick Diakopoulos began teaching a course focused on how computer algorithms might help solve some of the problems of journalism. Computational journalism is now associated with efforts to teach journalists how to code—both to program and to apply computer-science thinking to news.[23] This more academic approach generally considers how code can enable better forms of watchdog journalism. Terry Flew and his colleagues, along with Jay Hamilton and Fred Turner, consider the new potential of these algorithms to help enable watchdog journalism in a time of distress. In fact, James Hamilton and Fred Turner define computational journalism as "the combination of algorithms, data, and knowledge from the social sciences to supplement the accountability function of journalism."[24] Diakopoulos has pushed further, arguing that journalists need to make algorithms actually accountable too.[25] This larger connection to watchdog journalism helps remind us that interactives dually serve the purpose of contributing to the public interest and larger goals of journalism writ large. Now, computational journalism is being considered as a "construction," or "articulation" within the profession, suggesting that it is more than a form of newswork, but also a constellation of people and practices.[26]

## People, Work, and Knowledge

### People

Who are these people behind interactive journalism? Extensive field research and interviews marshaled here probe specifics of the backgrounds of these individuals and what they bring to the newsroom as well as the perspectives that they offer. We meet journalists who have come from programming backgrounds, journalists who have taught themselves code, those who know how to use programs to take advantage of code, designer journalists, and "developer" journalists. Bold lines between each type of journalist are hard to draw, but the backgrounds and journalists' own sense of what they do help bring together an underlying sense of who these interactive journalists are. There is not just one type of interactive journalist; rather, there are those with even more specific skills that are united by the overarching goal of presenting interactive journalism.

Not all of these people would call themselves "a journalist"—indeed, that label is certainly contested—and to discuss this negotiated term takes the book into a vast territory that detracts from the project at hand. I offer a few simple reasons for using the term "journalist" to describe this group of people. First, they contribute to acts of creating journalistic work product—what they do results in journalism and how they work is directly related to creating opportunities for new insights. Second, the word "journalism" has a shared common understanding that speaks to those who work in industry and in-stitutional settings. Third, their work is journalism for public consumption relevant to the public interest. And finally, these individuals share what are accepted as dominant news norms and have the ability to communicate with a news sensibility, thereby contributing to overarching editorial projects. If they are connected in a direct pathway to new insights, or help form this backbone, then these individuals, by my definition, may be wrapped together within the term journalist.

Some familiar with this area might immediately think of the professional group of journalists who belong to NICAR, or the National Institute for Computer Assisted Reporting. This group hosts an annual conference, which over the years has moved increasingly to understanding how to use data with computing technology and offers many sessions and workshops dedicated to the basics of programming. The conference is one of the biggest international events for those involved with the intersection of computing and journal-ism, though the international journalists I interviewed here were often not members. Certainly, the NICAR listserv brings together a diverse community of those involved in interactive journalism.

But the interactive journalists discussed here should not merely be con-sidered NICAR journalists; this book is not an account of this group or these people specifically. There is far more to interactive journalism than just this group of professionals. The strong focus on data journalism is not inclusive of journalists who may spend more time specifically working with program-ming aspects of interactive journalism rather than the parsing of data. Not all interactive journalists will be directly involved in investigating data or asking questions about a story; some may be instead building tools to make it easier to help other journalists find stories or may be the visionaries behind the programming and design. What you will find in interactive journalism is a variety of backgrounds and an array of specific skills and approaches to doing journalistic work—but the subfield has a unity and coherence because the ultimate goals and outputs of creating an immersive product are consistent across each sort of interactive journalist.

## Work

The next key step for understanding interactive journalism is examining the actual work product and system and processes of work production. As we will see in the discussion of professionalism, this may be considered the specific form of jurisdiction that this subspecialty occupies within the larger practice and output of journalism. The field visits offer insight into how journalists do their work and what kind of work it is specifically that they do. Each of the newsrooms I visited has particular perceptions about its work process relative to the rest of the organization, and these insights are critical for understanding how interactive journalism fits into the larger journalism process and profession more generally.

Understanding the jurisdiction of interactive journalism, or the work that is done, begins with acknowledging the need for these specialty desks or staff sections (in smaller newsrooms, this may be just one journalist, or even just someone who is not specifically assigned to this work, but dabbling in order to help the organization be more technically astute). In larger newsrooms, these desks have various names: interactive news technologies, news applications, visual team, news specials, data journalism team, data news team, etc. These "desks" within the newsroom have specific journalists assigned to produce interactives with designated editors. Within the news workflow, these teams may create original standalone content or work in a more service-desk arrangement, taking direction for assignment from other journalists. Some of these teams still remain shuttered off to the side of newsrooms, in the boondocks, away from the main production area; others are close to the center of work. In smaller newsrooms, single journalists may labor on interactive journalism, and the goal of their work is to produce these interactives.

These teams have specific functions and produce the kind of work that no one else in the newsroom is creating. In some cases, the team responsible for creating data journalism interactives (and who work on data journalism) are different from the people who create more encompassing interactive work that relies on more sophisticated code. And, in some cases, graphics teams combine with interactive journalists. Because this is an emerging subspecialty, the divisions between the desks are not always clear, but the overarching movement toward people having specialized skill sets charged with specific and specialized tasks has clearly come of age because they produce recognizably different work.

As these journalists talk about their work processes in this book, they do so in a way that explains their work through their work products. They offer detailed examples to highlight their sensibilities toward journalistic work, how they approach stories, how they work with other journalists, how they collect data, and what they consider to be an effective output of what they do. The specific examples discussed are often what journalists consider some of their best work, though they do address some failures. So looking at work tells us about the emergence of the subspecialty and what it is these journalists indeed create.

### Knowledge

There are two ways to think about the kind of special knowledge these interactive journalists offer: special skills and more abstract knowledge about how to do journalism. On the most basic level, these journalists have a specific skill that other journalists do not: special knowledge about code. They are able to communicate, use, and manipulate specific coding languages to create, modify, and improve on interactives, which often allows them to contribute back to a larger programming journalism community with new insights. However, knowing code is just one skill, and it's not a definitive skill; other interactive journalists do not know code but have expert experience using programs that input the data to create interactives. Still others have specific talents in design that are not necessarily shared by the rest of the newsroom because these journalists have a special understanding of software (and specifically Web and mobile) development.

Interactive journalists have a particular knowledge about how to work within the dynamics of the Web to tell engaging, immersive stories. The ways of thinking they come to adopt are in many aspects distinct from what we find across traditional journalism. These include concepts such as "build-it journalism," whereby journalism is facilitated through the creation of computer-enabled tools to make it possible to perform computationally enabled journalism. The purpose of journalism in this case is an approach to building products for work rather than just stories, and it suggests a different kind of ethic. Interactive journalists offer news that provides a see-it-for-yourself approach to journalism, whereby users are able to find stories of their own accord, exploring news independently rather than being offered a specific, time-bound, and ordered narrative. The near/far view built into interactive journalism offers for the first time a way for users to focus in on their neighborhoods and to thereby personalize news, but they can also get a far view of the larger journalistic story. For the first time in journalism, news organizations do not compete with each other for knowledge, practice, and tools across interactive journalism; instead, we see an ethic of openness that helps advance the output of interactive journalism. However, we do still witness a commitment to narrative, expressed in a different way. These kinds of approaches underscore the abstract knowledge interactive journalism provides to the profession.

Interactive journalism has a larger public impact: the rise of interactives means that stories can be told in different ways—perhaps ways that were never before possible. Thus, journalists may help people understand stories through code-enabled multimedia in a way that offers enhanced understanding of a social phenomenon discussed in a story. Or journalists may present and render data in new ways that advance understanding, beyond just the static presentation of information through traditional graphics or through the text of a story. So interactive journalists help change the output of journalistic work and provide a new opportunity for people to receive information.

To be an interactive journalist is to move away from the demands of everyday constructions of textual narratives. It depends on a specific and special claim to abstract knowledge. Chapter 5 in this book focuses on the larger claims to knowledge—knowledge about journalistic work—that emerge from interactive journalism. Their underlying claim is they can do something that others cannot. But there is another way of thinking about this—as alternate ways of constructing knowledge for the public. Journalistic expertise, then, takes on new forms for the digital environment.

## The Professionalization of a Subspecialty of Journalism

Much of current journalism studies has been focused on journalism and change. The rise of interactive journalism is no exception, particularly as it is bound up in a context of economic, technological, institutional, and professional pressures. And throughout history—from the actual professionalization of the field itself, as Michael Schudson traces from printers to an adversarial press—the boundaries of journalism have been continually redrawn as new kinds of journalism and new practices emerge.[27] Within this larger context, we've seen the importance of the development of new skills, such as the very creation of the interview, as well as the expertise of page design, specialty journalists, beat writers, and those, like photojournalists, who work with specific, designated equipment.

The threat to the continued survival of professional journalism comes from economic, technological, sociological, and institutional forces. Traditional journalism has faced recent challenges to its claim to professional authority. Though journalism has always had a continuum of scandals that contest its claim to authority,[28] it is the expansion of the platform for journalism with the rise of digital culture that has created perhaps the greatest challenges of all. Blogging seems to suggest an emergent potential for the development and expansion of the profession within its existing boundaries and self-definition. As Wilson Lowrey shows, blogging exposed a number of vulnerabilities within professional journalism that actually prompted discussions leading to a rethinking of traditional journalism. [29]

Similarly, Seth C. Lewis talks about the changes to professionalism with the rise of participatory content, arguing that the profession has expanded from fearing user-generated content as an assault on authority to embracing an ethic of participation, which privileges "adaptability and openness."[30] Within the context of a "systems of professions" approach, then, the external challenge created a response to new forms of work jurisdiction and change.[31] Additional pressures have emerged as nontraditional organizations are creating news products, such as nongovernmental organizations such as Human Rights Watch issuing news reports from the front lines,[32] potentially reshaping journalistic work.

Despite changes and challenges, traditional journalism outlets can make a claim to a particular kind of expertise. Journalists have the ability to report on complicated events, drawing on methods that are "not easily analyzed and taught."[33] They are, as John Hartley argues, the sense-maker for modernity.[34] And in the past, Lewis maintains, journalists have had claims on the exclusivity to being able to create, produce, and distribute this work.[35] Fundamentally, while journalism may be a "permeable" profession without formal boundaries for entry, according to Andrew Abbott, journalism has "extraordinary power" and has been "founded on providing current 'factual' information to the public since the turn of the [twentieth] century."[36]

Nonetheless, journalism is a difficult occupation to consider as a profession. Often, traditional sociology has generally evaluated professions based on traits, such as barriers to entry, like licensing or tests or mandated education, clearly defined ethical codes, professional organizations, legal frameworks, and the like. Journalism has some but not all of these traits, creating significant debate over whether it "counts." As Michael Schudson and C. W.

Anderson explain, journalism has been considered a trait-based profession with specific claims to authority over a body of a social function.[37] In Silvio Waisbord's tome on professionalism, journalism has often been looked at as "an occupation with professional aspirations" and, within the context of the "ethical dimension of journalism in democracy," as having particular normative practices of doing work.[38] There is substantial literature on professionalism in journalism, including rich comparative work that attempts to assess these normative differences between professional cultures.[39] And there is also substantial literature that debates whether journalism is a profession at all.[40] What I'd like to do here, though, is to think a bit differently about journalism—as a profession, but as a process of knowledge construction and as continuous creation and recreation of practices and jurisdictional claims.

Waisbord and Schudson and Anderson argue that professionalism has too often been equated with these ethical preoccupations—for instance, a belief in objectivity. Professionalism has also been talked about in terms of method, how a profession specifically pursues its service for the public good. Within journalism, this might be considered the method of objectivity, but this idea of a method becomes complicated when applied to professions—what, after all, might count as a method?—and so the boundaries are therefore blurry.[41] Others, such as Eliot Freidson, help further the definition of professionalism by noting that professions develop an occupational identity when they can dominate a specific market role, a convincing way of thinking about the importance of the influence of knowledge on financial gain.[42]

However, if we move beyond this discussion, which has existed for decades,[43] it's more interesting to see how journalism *works* within the contours of a profession. As Abbott, who theorized the "system of professions" approach, maintains, "Whether journalism's inability to monopolize makes it 'not a profession' is not particularly interesting."[44] Abbott's system of professions sets forth ideas about how a profession must adapt to change, and in this regard, the theory offers an excellent framework for considering journalism in transition, moving away from trait-based assessments of a profession to considerations of the social functions of a type of occupation. According to Abbott, professions "seize new problems,"[45] which suggests that professions continue to be in flux as they adapt to economic, social, political, and cultural changes—in this case the specter of the need to adjust to technical, economic, and cultural demands for sophistication online.

The main thrust of his argument examines professions through the work they do, or the "jurisdictional" claims that professions make over a particular, defined expertise—abstract knowledge and skills. Internal and external pressures shape a profession, which competes among other professions for "jurisdiction" over work. For instance, accounting defines its boundaries from law based on the work produced and its specific knowledge. Understanding the people and their skills, the work they produce, and the knowledge they offer is fundamental to this case for the relevance of journalism.

I am focusing here on a professional *subgroup*: interactive journalists. There is far less attention paid to the rise of subspecialties, subgroups, or occupational groups, and particularly subspecialties within newsrooms. Within the professional context of journalism, I argue that a subspecialty emerges from forces that Abbott predicts: technological, economic, and social pressure. The claim for relevance also matters, which typically emerges from clients (in this case, users/readers) and the need of the profession to respond to interprofessional competition and organizational needs.

Subspecialties offer a distinct claim to knowledge within their profession, and their relative emergence/success may be evaluated through external and internal measures. Geoffrey Bloor and Patrick Dawson argue that "the ability for professional subcultures to shape organizational culture is not static but develops over time and reflects a complex interplay between the cultural constituents of an organization and the external environment."[46] In the case of interactive journalism, there is pressure within journalism and outside of journalism for the profession to change. Interactive journalism cannot speak to all subspecialties, and not even all subspecialties that have emerged in journalism, but the case suggests the need for a broader and more robust discussion of subspecialties.

When the formation of occupational subgroups is discussed in the literature, scholarship generally focuses on the idea of threat. Many argue that one of the reasons for this threat may be new technological practices. As with professions more generally, scholars argue that these occupational domains try to assert control over specific areas of work. This desire for expertise in new areas can create tension in journalism, as Barbie Zelizer outlined with the emergence of photojournalism. In 1935 the adoption of wire photos threatened traditional journalists. Traditional journalists viewed changes in technology, and thus photographers, with a "reactionary character" that, according to Zelizer,[47] still affects journalism's integration with technology. It was only when the external pressures of World War II forced changes in the need for news photography that photographers began to be accepted formally as a subgroup.[48] More recently, the early adopters of online journalism were regarded as a distinctly different group with specific skills not found in the rest of the newsroom and were treated with suspicion;[49] though this has dissipated in the United States, online journalists are still treated as a lesser subspecialty in Germany, for example.[50]

However, as Wilson Lowrey argues elsewhere, that differentiation due to external pressures into subgroups may actually help maintain the professional claims of an occupation. Lowrey's study of Russian journalism in the late 2000s with colleague Elina Erzikova showed that the rise of authoritarianism had created a split between "political" reporters and nonpolitical reporters (for example, purveyors of soft news). This article, which chronicles this specialization, also talks about the changes in the jurisdictional acquisition of skills and knowledge with nonpolitical reporters developing skills akin, for instance, to librarians or counselors. Yet the scholars argue that "successful differentiation can help maintain occupations, allowing the continuing practice of core areas of work, as well as strong relations with a wide range of clientele at the profession's boundaries."[51]

Thus, despite threat, subspecialties are quickly subsumed into the over-riding practices of the larger profession. The dominant group tends to define what is "normal"[52] and to set the precedent for norms, values, and practices within the organization. In other words, new occupational subgroups come to share the values of the larger occupational group. Lowrey also studied the rise of visual journalists. He argued that there was the potential for an "invasion" of nonjournalistic norms.[53] Some of these visual journalists were coming from the art world and had nonjournalistic backgrounds. But instead of finding that there was significant conflict between these values, he discovered that visual journalists tended to align with overarching journalistic norms. This is significant because interactive journalists, while offering distinct contributions in forms of knowledge, do not offer an entirely new value system or contradictory way to do work.

Within the profession, subgroups are said to compete for control over work within the larger profession. Subgroups emerge, according to Abbott, around new technologies.[54] A few results may surface: the subgroups may have direct conflict with the larger profession, or they may have unstated conflicts with the larger profession, thereby "stunting"[55] the productive conversation that could contribute to the extension of the profession. However, if the subspecialty is given respect and authority within the context of the larger profession, they may be able to effect real changes in how work gets done. As Lowrey found in his study of visual journalists, they greatly influenced journalism norms only when these journalists were accorded an authoritative presence in the newsroom.[56]

Similarly, Matthew Powers examined early Web developers and computer-assisted reporters and argued that "technologically specific work" can be seen in three ways: "(1) as exemplars of continuity; (2) as threats to be subordinated; and (3) as possibilities for journalistic reinvention."[57] The question remains in this work as to whether interactive journalists submerge conflict and don't change or challenge journalism norms, or whether they are given enough power to expand the profession and provide "possibilities for reinvention"; findings suggest they are powerful enough to make an impact and do not have much contest with traditional journalism because of the affinity for their ability to innovate in the newsroom. Contest between the subgroup and the larger profession is not always present, and it isn't to any large degree in this case, though issues of translation predictably emerge.

Notably, the rise of interactive journalism has not resulted in serious cultural backlash from inside newsrooms either. A case can be made to other journalists that it is important to make a space for people with these skills, and the profession can certainly allow room for such growth. This suggests the need for a nuance within the literature of the professions to recognize that occupational subgroups may emerge peacefully without intraprofessional contest and perhaps add to the existing norms rather than having their contributions muted by dominant normative values. While a dominant normative system may govern the contributions of the subspecialty, the subspecialty can continue to offer its own claims to distinct and unique contributions that expand the domain of professional journalism. For the most part, if not overall, interactive journalists do not find themselves unwelcome; in fact, they are welcomed for what they can do and the new forms of journalism they bring. Despite what can be some daily practical translation challenges, there is no looming question about whether interactive journalists were welcome in the newsrooms I studied—they were, and were at times seen as heroes or saviors.

Journalism is expanding as a profession in part because of the development of this new subspecialty of interactive journalism. How and why the profession expands is the underlying theoretical grounding of the book and is the starting point for examining how interactive journalism can create new ways of thinking about journalism. Thus, through a desire to examine the conditions for how and why interactive journalism emerges as a subspecialty, I've set out some key factors that explain the rise of interactive journalism, some of which have a clear legacy in literature about the formation of occupational subgroups and others of which do not. They include:

1. Subspecialties may emerge uncontested, rather than out of contested competing professional claims.
2. Sociocultural external pressures, such as technology, economics, and culture, influence the rise of subspecialties.
3. Subspecialties emerge out of a need to reclaim relevance.

4. Subspecialties emerge when they can make a claim to external and internal measurements of success.
5. Subspecialties offer a distinct claim to knowledge within a profession's larger jurisdictional aspiration.

These five elements of the development of interactive journalism as a subspecialty sketch the conditions for its rise to prominence today.

SUBSPECIALTIES MAY EMERGE UNCONTESTED, RATHER THAN OUT OF CONTESTED COMPETING PROFESSIONAL CLAIMS. The emergence of subspecialties may be distinct from the larger notion that professions are contested. In the case of interactive journalism, what the subspecialty draws on from other professions or occupational groups does not threaten the programming profession it "takes" from. This may be in part because the skills are being appropriated from a profession that in no way stands to lose its dominance when the new subspecialty emerges. In the case of interactive journalism, programming becomes a key skill and is critically important for some journalists, though not all.

However, *skills are just the beginning.* Interactive journalists are combining these skills with what they know of journalism to produce a distinct form of knowledge about how to do journalistic work online. The creation of this subspecialty is not challenging the authority of programming but expanding journalism, and so it does not reflect a key premise of the system of professions, which suggests that change arises out of contest.

SOCIOCULTURAL EXTERNAL PRESSURES, SUCH AS TECHNOLOGY, ECONOMICS, AND CULTURE, INFLUENCE THE RISE OF SUBSPECIALTIES. As noted in the introduction, the technological forces influencing the need for interactive journalism originate from a few key areas: infrastructure, user design, code sophistication, and data. These technical pressures are coupled with economic pressures. Plainly put, the external economic pressures mean that journalism has no real business model through which to make sustainable profit online. One solution to this problem has been to create value online—but how? Interactive journalism is one foray into this attempt to create value. The conditions for its emergence inside journalism derive from a favorable environment for experimenting with new forms of journalism with the hope that interactive journalism will bring more users or keep loyal users. If there are people with special skills or special knowledge about how to help create value online, there is space within the profession of journalism for them. Thus, we see support for such departments, hiring, and expansion—as well as the interest in experimenting with interactives and data. The economic imperative has created a need for a particular kind of journalism, which is met through interactive journalism.

SUBSPECIALTIES EMERGE OUT OF A NEED TO RECLAIM RELEVANCE. Relevance helps explain the emergence of interactive journalism, reflecting both external and internal pressures on the profession. Traditional journalism, especially today, needs to make a relevance claim, to offer something special that cannot be found elsewhere. On a more micro level, this means that organizations must show that they have the best claim to providing public knowledge that people cannot live without, particularly in a diminished-attention economy online.

This external pressure has resulted in an actionable response: the creation of a viable, visual, and tangible assertion of new sites of public knowledge. Through interactive journalism, from the fun to the serious, journalism outlets are suggesting that they have something to share, that news is still relevant to people's lives in a digital culture. This claim to special knowledge implies that journalists know something that others do not: how to manipulate data or to render information in a visually meaningful and easily understood way, or how to create something entertaining and informative that ordinary people cannot. Journalists must respond to user demands, or what Abbott calls more generally the needs of "clients," in order to retain the profession's larger jurisdiction. Thus, there is an incentive to develop special skills and knowledge to react to these pressures.

SUBSPECIALTIES EMERGE WHEN THEY CAN MAKE A CLAIM TO EXTERNAL AND INTERNAL MEASUREMENTS OF SUCCESS. Interactive journalism has space to expand as a meaningful subspecialty in part because it has both external and internal measures of success within the profession. External measures are literally returns on investments of interactive journalism that are measured outside the actual boundaries of the newsroom. One of the most prominent ways of underscoring importance, success, and relevance is through Web traffic measurements. Web analytics offer a compelling case of the validation for interactive journalism that comes from outside the profession. From an internal perspective, interactive journalism makes its own case as an emerging subspecialty through measurements of its own success.

In the case of a subspecialty, indication of its strength may be through professional organizations and their membership count. NICAR, the main professional organization associated with this field (though not exclusively), has grown from 216 members to 4,500 in just twenty-five years. The annual conference, which now features a preponderance of sessions on interactive journalism, brings together an international audience. This internal measure of success within the profession helps validate the growth of the subspecialty. There is clearly a distinct group of people within journalism who have a specific skill set and a specialized interest that others do not, and who have particular concerns that can be addressed in a dedicated environment.

SUBSPECIALTIES OFFER A DISTINCT CLAIM TO KNOWLEDGE WITHIN A PROFESSION'S LARGER JURISDICTIONAL ASPIRATION.  Finally, the key reason that interactive journalism has become a subspecialty is because it has a jurisdiction of work that no other aspect of the profession can offer. The special skills and special knowledge required are simply not found in other areas of journalism, and we will see in chapter 2 what kind of special knowledge emerges in this field as it takes its cues from programming. Interactive journalists are *the specialists* who are likely the only ones who can claim to be familiar with code or programs that use code. Certainly not all journalists on interactive teams have all the same skills, but the emphasis on the product as software or as journalism expressed through code is simply not a project being undertaken by any other part of the newsroom. Thus, there is a specialized claim to a specific form of work that emerges through the rise of interactive journalism as those with these skill sets come together to articulate their importance to the larger professional project of journalism.

Throughout the book we will see an illustration for how interactive journalism articulates the development of a subspecialty of journalism. While the case may not be entirely generalizable to every subspecialty within journalism, the additions to existing theory suggest the importance of considering this particular case, specifically within the context of the current state of the news industry and these unique pressures on journalism. Specific knowledge and skills play a significant role in establishing this subgroup. More generally, this subspecialty forms as a response to larger sociocultural forces, which in this case stem in part from economics and technological change. These aspects of occupational subgroup development become clearer throughout the book as we explore interactive journalism through *people, work, and knowledge*. But before moving on to the jurisdictional claim that interactive journalists have, we need to investigate the origins of this type of journalism.

# 2 The Rise of a Subspecialty

## Interactive Journalism

NPR's media columnist David Folkenflik delivered a breezy report in 2005 from Lawrence, Kansas, home of the University of Kansas. He narrated his lead-in:

> So here's The World Company at work. It's got a daily newspaper, *The Journal-World*, a local cable TV channel, and, of course, several Web sites, including one with video games. That's right, one of the Web sites goes to the trouble of staging an Xbox version of every University of Kansas men's basketball and football game.

*Video game replays* of every basketball game in the Jayhawks' history. This was interactive journalism at work. And this was *three years* into the online experimentation at *The Lawrence Journal-World*. By the mid-2000s, the newspaper with circulation of a mere twenty thousand had caught the attention of the national media, such as NPR, and big media companies were drawing inspiration from *The Journal-World*'s innovations, including the likes of *The New York Times*. So many news organizations were visiting and taking tours in order to learn about online innovation that, as a *Chicago Tribune* article described, "the interest grew so intense and so disruptive to the workday routine that *The Journal-World* had to schedule visiting hours."[1]

*The Lawrence Journal-World* had been busily doing interactive journalism, with staff journalists who could program creating new features for the Web. For example, as early as 2002, a major news effort intended to examine drought in the state was accompanied by a vibrant interactive experience. As Rob Curley, head of the Web site in Lawrence, explained to Folkenflik:

We put together a map of the state of Kansas where you could mouse over any county in the state, and we would show you what their normal rainfall total would be and what their current rainfall total would be and what that meant in millions of dollars to the local farmers. Then we had our nerds work with the nerds at the state of Kansas, and we built a database of every well in the state of Kansas. So you could see how irrigation was affecting the well water supplies.[2]

*The Lawrence Journal-World* was not the first place or the first time in the brief history of online news that interactives were created, but the special combination of people and the types of projects that emerged solidified the scene as a defining moment in the history of interactive journalism. For the first time, journalists in the newsroom were actively using programming language to render data and information in visible and interactive ways, not just across isolated projects, but woven into the core fabric of the Web site.

Adrian Holovaty, a former staffer at *The Lawrence Journal-World* and now a recalcitrant developer of music software after deciding to quit working in journalism, was at the time a programmer-journalist wunderkind who helped solidify a small community of other journalists interested in the possibilities of programming and journalism on his blog and who became a model of the future of the subspecialty. What happened in Lawrence was nothing short of remarkable and prescient, and it is for this reason that Rob Curley, now the executive editor of *The Orange County Register*, doesn't go a single day without thinking about Lawrence. He explained to me, "We were building things that people really wanted; people had never seen Internet behave this way before, and it just worked really well."

Almost no one had seen an interactive in 2002. In fact, a bare majority of Americans had the internet in their homes, and the vast majority of those only had slow dial-up service. The modern history of interactives doesn't begin with Lawrence, but it is the most dramatic example of the kind of innovation that would come. In the rest of this chapter, I'll outline some of the history of interactives based on interviews with key figures, as well as discuss key technological developments I've identified over the course of my research and reading. This history of interactives is not intended to be exhaustive; the goal, rather, is to underscore the rise of interactive journalism so we can understand how a subfield comes to be.

## The Early Rise of Interactives

Inasmuch as interactive journalism can be attributed to the rise of sophistication in code and computing technology, and draws power from the vast amounts of data present today as never before, it nonetheless has a long history and evolution in news. The rise of the subspecialty emerges from a fusion of photography, graphics, data visualization, and computational journalism. These aspects of journalism all intersect in different ways, merging together to help form interactive journalism.

The form of news itself—its presentation—has evolved throughout history, and the study of it yields some insight into the rise of interactive journalism. Kevin Barnhurst and John Nerone chronicled some of these changes, arguing that the persistent visible structure that repeats day after day, which includes layout, typography, and illustration, presents the look and feel of newspaper, which in turn structures the relationship between it and the public.[3] They categorize newspaper presentation into four formats: printerly, partisan, Victorian, and modern. The printerly newspaper, with its bookish appearance, was for the gentleman; the partisan newspaper had a larger format and suggested the rise of mass politics and a market economy; the Victorian newspaper reflected imperialism; the modern newspaper expressed bureaucratic production and offered expert explanation. Interactive news today builds on this legacy, offering user-guided experiences of news and information that may structure the relationship between press and public as demanded by the previously outlined pressures on journalism today.

The history of images in journalism, particularly graphics, also contributes to the rise of interactives. Mark Monmonier, whose *Maps with the News* represents the most comprehensive account of graphics in news, argues that the beginnings of images in news can be seen as early as the arrival of block printing in the sixth century, where raised images were produced by a roller.[4] John Grimwade, a former graphics editor at *The Times of London* and then *Condé Nast Traveler* between the 1960s to the early aughts, is an amateur historian of infographics in the news. He suggests that the earliest infographics appeared in the early 1800s and mainly focused on battles and murders. According to Grimwade, the first news infographic was published in 1804 in *The London Times* and showed a house that depicted a murder scene as the crime progressed. "It was one of the first narrative news graphics. It a pretty straightforward idea with the rooms of house showing where different things occurred," he recalled.[5]

Charles Minard's graphic depicting Napoleon's march to Moscow is often incorrectly credited as the first news infographic, as it was produced in 1859 but depicted an event that took place in 1812. The first weather map didn't appear in news until the end of the nineteenth century. Other major leaps in infographic expression, though, did not happen until the twentieth century, when the sinking of the *Titanic* and World Wars I and II offered ample opportunity (and desire from readers) to use infographics to depict ongoing news events. *Time* magazine was considered the leading source of news infographics during this era. Grimwade argues that advances in information technology—not necessarily the technology to make infographics, but the speed to communicate information and better data—improved infographics greatly (for instance, real weather data).

Graphics specialists were essentially like draftsmen and had technical drawing skills. They used French curves, ellipse templates, compasses, airbrushes, knives, and, of course, pens. In Grimwade's time (the early 1970s), to trace lines, these graphic journalists had to cut down on acetate plates to prepare for publication. He reminded me that there was no easy way just to fix a graphic—no computer "erasing" to adjust angle or correct an error. A graphic journalist had to have everything essentially perfect. As Monmonier tells it, the 1970s and 1980s saw many innovations in newspaper design that actually led to a more prominent role for photographs and graphics. He argues that graphics accelerated in part due to technological factors and in part due to competitive factors. By 1979, with the founding of the Society for News Design, the field had become a subprofession of its own.

Part of the rise of the graphics department as a distinct specialty within journalism came with the ability of newspapers to use color. As technology improved, both in printing presses and layout, newsroom executives began to look more favorably on the possibility of incorporating more sophisticated graphics in news. Broadcast journalism had begun incorporating graphics in news much earlier (with the advent of TV weather forecasting), and print newspapers began to catch up. Monmonier argues that in the 1970s and 1980s, newspapers began to form full-on art departments that would make the newspaper "attractive and informative"—such that there would be a variety of illustrations: maps, editorial cartoons, business graphics, color photos, and illustrated layouts for special sections (Food or Travel, for example).

Early computer graphics came into the newsroom in the mid-1980s. Monmonier noted that "the programmer and the artist collaborated,"[6] producing charts and graphics. The mouse-controlled arrow allowed for easier online creation, and software (Microsoft's Chart, for example) made it easier to make hectographs, time series graphics, and data charts. And the newspaper's editorial front-end word processing became linked to the typesetting, making it easier for computers to transmit graphics. The Associated Press began moving graphics over its electronic bulletin board, and Knight Ridder and Gannett put Macintoshes for graphic design into newsrooms. In addition, graphics departments were even more formalized according to newspaper structure. He notes that in 1984, graphics officially became a specific unit in the AP under its own editor. And some of those who came to the graphics desk had backgrounds in art rather than journalism. *USA Today*'s founding in 1982, though controversial, elevated the prominence of graphics as a significant aspect of the marketing of journalism.

Monmonier leaves off in 1989, but he makes some cogent predictions about the state of interactive graphics that he believes will emerge in journalism. He writes about the promise of videotext for interactive capacities that will allow user-directed control over information:

> Electronic display makes possible map symbols that blink and move, and computer graphics systems can generate animated maps. Video display technology and modern telecommunications offer the potential for linking highly dynamic cartographic display software with large geographic databases. . . . Should electronic news databases ever emerge as a mass-communications medium, dynamic news maps would become commonplace.[7]

In turn, a dynamic map would give users a "menu of choice" to make selections through a keypad—or even a touchpad, he predicts—whereby computer coding would offer promising ways to focus attention of the user on new kinds of information. From a practical and philosophical perspective, the ideas of interactive Web design were predicted as a fundamental way to engage the computer user of the future, and, for news, the way forward would be user direction through electronic news.

In news, the rise of multimedia capacities and the improvement in Web sites led to early innovations in interactives by the 1990s. Michael Friendly argues that Fortran in the 1970s ushered in highly interactive capacities for the creation of interactive graphics,[8] but it is only in the mid-1990s that we start to see Web-based presentation of interactives in the news. Friendly points out that advances in computing languages made it possible to develop sliders, selection boxes, lists, graphics and tables, and user communication through messages.

Interactive graphics in news may have been born in 1995 at *The Chicago Tribune*, though it is hard to for any one paper to claim to be first. But a conversation at *The South Florida Sun-Sentinel* is indicative of the innovation taking place at the time. In 1996, *Sun-Sentinel* editor Leavett Biles recruited Don Wittekind, a journalist who had some programming background, to help create what Biles called "multimedia informational graphics"[9]—though Wittekind said he had no idea what they were. Their first effort was a graphic on fire ants, which interactive news journalist Alberto Cairo described as "uncharted territory of play buttons and moving around rather than plan old ink, paper, and still pictures."[10] At this point, these newsrooms were experimenting with the beginnings of human computer interaction—with feedback between readers and computers soliciting an actual reaction, be it through visuals, sound, or an onscreen response.[11] So, what was it like, then, at the dawn of the electronic, computer-enhanced interactives? The next section offers some vignettes from the era.

## The Start of Modern Computer Interactives

In the late 1990s, newspapers and news organizations more generally came to the overarching and seemingly obvious conclusion that they needed to invest in robust Web sites. Major newspapers had been burned by early attempts at innovation. As you'll recall, Knight Ridder and *The New York Times*, for example, had invested in Videotext technology, a precursor of the modern personal computer with information transmission facilitated by a modem. But home adoption had been slow, and there were few commercial returns on the service. Pablo Boczkowski provides perhaps the best chronicle of how the print daily newspaper came online. According to his research, economic motivations spurred investment in the Web; as consumers moved to nonprint alternatives, newspapers were already beginning to see declines in profit. And by the end of the 1990s, more than 40 percent of the adult population was online.[12]

Andrew DeVigal, now a professor at the University of Oregon but a former longtime *Chicago Tribune* and *New York Times* interactive journalist, described to me the early days of interactives. He was part of the team that built the first interactive at *The Chicago Tribune*, if not one of the first interactives ever, and he also helped build the newspaper's first Web site. "It was six months from start to finish before we launched. It was one hell of a ride setting up templates. There were no technologies that developed templates for the first year or so [1993–1994]; *The Chicago Tribune* had to do it by hand." He explained that there was "this staff of about twelve young people in this room on the fifth floor, and people in the newsroom called it the 'dorm room' . . . there were all these kids in this room putting together this thing, with music blasting and it was as fun as hell and it was sort of renegade."[13]

At first, *The Chicago Tribune* was only experimenting with video. But for what the Web was capable of in the early to mid-1990s, their video efforts were unsatisfying—they came out small on the page (150 pixels, about 1.5 inches) and there was no professional staff devoted to video work. But a major breakthrough came with what DeVigal claims was the first news interactive, though this is hard to confirm. In 1995, *The Tribune* launched an interactive that tracked every homicide in Chicago, a project that continues in a different form through to today.[14] The team working on the project had to figure out how to make the map interactive without having any obvious technology tools to do so if they were to achieve their goals of enabling people to look up homicides by zip code.

They relied on CGI, or the Common Gateway Interface, which was an early (though still used) script that enables a user to send a request to a Web site and retrieve the output (a pre-programmed map, for instance) without the output having to be shown on the Web page. Essentially, this script was a way to create a sense of a dynamic Web page, even though every request for a homicide had been preprogrammed and hand coded. The team literally had to type in zip codes and build the graphics GIF by GIF—all by hand. This kind of tremendous effort would become seemingly effortless (with no hand coding necessary) as programming and the Web more generally evolved. There were signs that the specialty of interactive journalism was beginning, even in these early days. DeVigal and his staff enjoyed the status of having special skills—including the ability to program and use programs—that no one in the newsroom was using. Their mission was different, too: to tell stories in new ways using new technology.

This special mission was beginning to be articulated by higher-ups and the teams in newsrooms in Chicago and elsewhere. DeVigal emphasized to me that interactive storytelling was interesting to *The Tribune*, to him, and to others, then and now, because it gives users a chance to "truly control the power of their interaction and gives a choice of how to experience a story," a theme we will see elsewhere. Interactive journalists began to develop a specific way of thinking about journalism that would later quite possibly change journalism norms, or at least offer disruptive ways of thinking.

An occupational identity started to come together during this period as well. DeVigal participated in an early panel on interactives in 1995 at the COMDEX conference in Chicago. The conference is now no longer in existence, but it was known as "geek week" and at the time was the one of the largest computer trade shows in the world.[15] There, DeVigal began meeting others working on similar projects related to interactive storytelling, learning about new techniques and projects that, as he recalls, " . . . blew my mind. I saw people doing things I want to do." A professional network was beginning to coalesce, one that would later emerge as a key sign that interactive journalism had come into its own, as it could be measured by internal and external signs of influence, including the number of practitioners.

The field, though, was still disconnected, and there was little isomorphism between newsrooms about tactics, strategies, and forms for interactives—unlike now, as interactives tend to have the same underpinning normative approach to journalism and, despite varieties in subject matter and presentation, have much consistency across newsrooms. But one factor of interactive storytelling was clear: it was laborious no matter where you went, and it required specialized skills and the ability to "hack" within the confines of existing Web and programming limitations in order to get the projects to work.

Elsewhere, building interactives was just as laborious. Geoff McGhee, an early pioneer in interactives who would go on to lead *The New York Times'* first iteration of its interactive team (the online graphics desk), began rudimentary efforts starting in 1997 and into the early 2000s. At the time, though, ABC News, McGhee's employer, had a reputation for innovative Web design and a robust team fueled by significant investment from the network. He recalls that it "took forever" to download a single image on the page, and monitors were at the time still tiny—eleven to twelve inches. With the size of these monitors, and the fact that the predominant browsers of the time, Netscape and Internet Explorer, had so many rows of search buttons and marketing offerings, visual presentation was difficult.[16]

At ABC, McGhee couldn't figure out how to create an interactive with a unique URL. He explained that the only way he could enable an interactive was to code JavaScript in a way that created a pop-up window (like a pop-up ad today) that made it possible to put images on top of each other on the same page. He created maps by putting transparent gifs on top of each other, perhaps first a map, then numbers, then text, and it was possible to click on the numbers or text so they would reveal still further images. "It did give you the sense that you were clicking on an interactive, it was a way to deal with things visually and get a story that went beyond search and scroll," he said.

McGhee explained that these "magical pop-up windows with no links" still "really did go beyond episodic journalism." He and his team created polls, quizzes, backgrounders, and a specific project, he remembers, that got significant attention: individual pages for each Supreme Court justice with a drop-down menu that would allow a user to see the Supreme Court docket and further information. Although the interactives weren't fancy, these developments were solidifying how interactives could provide alternative ways of presenting the news and telling stories to people. DeVigal and McGhee were both journalists who were blending their journalism skills with programming. But other newsrooms were doing interactive experiments, challenging perceptions of storytelling, and redefining occupational identity, but they had not quite realized the vision of a programmer journalist.

Boczkowski offers insight into how journalists were also having trouble with programmers, as many journalists interested in interactives had not quite become programmers and programmers had not quite embraced journalism. He recalls this in a section of *Digitizing the News* that examines *The Houston Chronicle*'s online division.[17] From the late 1990s to 2000, a team of journalists, paired with a programming team, worked on an ambitious project called Virtual Voyager. The effort began when a businessman and a nurse contacted the newspaper to see if it had interest in covering their three-year circumnavigation of the earth. The print travel section passed on the project, but the online division was interested. "At Sea" came to log over one thousand entries and included photos, audio, videos, and a map that automatically updated with the voyagers' location.[18] This was but one Voyager project. Boczkowski, too, argues that this effort went beyond just episodic journalism, telling a story in a different way.

Programmers worked apart from the editorial staff and had demands beyond just working on the Voyager site. While eventually the Voyager and design/programming staff began working together well, the project was more a process of translation between editorial and technical, requiring the coordination of a variety of occupational identities: editorial, programmers, designers, and production staff.[19] Journalists weren't programming yet; the head of the project observed that there were cooperation difficulties between programmers and journalists that could have been solved if he had known more about programming: "Part of it is my fault. I should learn Java."[20] There were other precursors that suggested both the differences inherent in interactive storytelling and the formation of a new professional identity. As that same journalist remarked, "In print journalism, we wanted to go out and experience something and then come back and put it on a sheet of paper. We didn't notice the movement [or] hear the sound except in terms of something we could translate into a printed product. I think Virtual Voyager is making us open our eyes to a form of journalism we didn't need when we were print people."[21] Here, we see the development of a consciousness of both the difference of interactives as well as the proto-formation of an occupational identity distinct from the "print people." This kind of recognition—as being able to provide different contributions—was critical to the rise of interactive journalism.

Other early examples of projects that were less visible to those outside the newsroom were the interactives that were being built as tools just for journalists to do their work—databases, searchable maps, and other versions of interactives for internal rather than external audiences.[22] In the early 2000s, Tom Torok of *The New York Times* (and formerly of *The Philadelphia Inquirer*) demonstrated a tool at a NICAR conference that, as *ProPublica*'s Derek Willis writes, "would make your SQL Server database searchable. Any database, no matter the type of information contained in it." He called it "Shboom."

Willis open-sourced the code for Shboom in 2014 and, in this accompanying post on the online repository GitHub, also noted, "It was a remarkable piece of software for those of us who had no idea what software really was. It is one of the first examples of web development in the newsroom that spread beyond it."[23]

Developments in Europe may have begun slightly later, as most of the journalists I spoke with there pointed to the development of Macromedia's Flash (around 1996) as critical to beginning their interactive career. In Spain, at both *El Pais* and *El Mundo*, journalists began transforming infographics into interactives. Alberto Cairo recalls that the September 11, 2001 attacks were what convinced him (and perhaps the rest of the newsroom at *El Mundo*) that interactives were going to be part of the next wave of the development of online journalism—and certainly the next iteration of infographics. In the United Kingdom, the BBC was an early pioneer of interactives, launching initial efforts in 2000 and 2001. But, as a number of the journalists I spoke with and Boczkowski also suggest, many early adopters were "print people" adapting to online contexts and innovating from a print perspective. A more fluent, online-focused and/or computer-literate journalist would later dominate the specialty. Nonetheless, these early days set in motion what would come to be a way of thinking about interactives that would coalesce industrywide and help lay the groundwork for establishing a professional occupational identity as distinct from the rest of the newsroom.

## Lawrence's Many Contributions

The online team at *The Lawrence Journal-World* worked in the basement of the newspaper building, which was itself located in a rehabbed old Post Office building. Instead of the subterranean space being dingy or smelling musty, the floors were a warm, inviting wood, and visitors were surrounded by red brick walls. Rob Curley described the space as "gorgeous, as if you were walking into the coolest bar and grill you had ever seen." His team crouched around Macs and, thanks to the wide latitude given by the Simons family, benevolent owners, and a flexible print staff, Curley's online group was given the opportunity to innovate.

Projects included a tracker for the state legislature, a database for professors' salaries at KU, a database of every statistic in every box score for every KU football game since the 1890s, a statistical database for every high school player in Kansas, automatically updated weather maps, bar/beer/restaurant specials and guides, interactive and searchable music listings, and beyond. A major innovation was thinking about journalism as structured data—

Adrian Holovaty later wrote an essay about the idea, where he explained, "An obituary is about a person, involves dates and funeral homes. A wedding announcement is about a couple, with a wedding date, engagement date, bride hometown, groom hometown and various other happy, flowery pieces of information."[24] In other words, journalism was made of bits of component pieces, and with the right programming, people could search of their own accord to find the pieces they wanted.

"Adrian opened my eyes to the idea of a relational database," Curley explained. "We didn't know what you should do or not do. We thought, wouldn't it be cool if you had a database with drink specials in Lawrence? Yeah, that's totally cool, so let's build that. How about let's build a bar database with a calendar of events? What about layering photos? What about making all shows searchable and then having downloadable mp3s of the band?"

Curley described a typical Lawrence project. The University of Kansas announced in 2003 that it would no longer honor alumni season tickets as it had in the past, assigning instead a lottery according to a different set of criteria. Reporters got ahold of the new criteria, which included alumni status, giving rates, and length of time the seats were held, among other factors. The online team created an interactive map of the stadium along with a database that would enable users to sort where their new seats might fall based on the data they entered. They could then click on the predicted seat and get a view of the stadium. This sounds perhaps unremarkable for today, but the Lawrence team combined programming, data, and photos and then built interactives in step with traditional reporting to give people a chance to experience a story in a way that was personal to them. Nothing like this had been done before.

Other Lawrence projects included innovations in election coverage. *The Lawrence Journal-World* hosted live online chats with candidates. Holovaty described on his blog an early interactive: "[We made] interactive 'candidate selectors' for the city-commission race and school board race—click on the candidate quotes you agree with, and the script will tell you which candidates you agreed with the most. It's intended mostly as a guide, but it is, without a doubt, useful in that 'Hey, that really made me think about the candidates' sort of way." Here, election information was being retold in ways that gave readers a direct, user-navigated experience of learning about candidates. This kind of approach has become a hallmark of interactive journalism.

In addition to creating interactives, Holovaty and another staffer, Simon Willison, a programmer recruited from England, also built a Web framework, Django. The goal of Django was to give Python programmers a starting point to build Web sites and Web features that were often used by news organizations, but Django was and still is not just for news. However, the two did develop a content-management system bolstered by Django for newsrooms, called Ellington, one still used in newsrooms today.

The blog Holovaty kept at the time became a focal point for the small community of journalists like him and journalists who were interested in what online journalism could create, particularly when programming and journalism were combined. On it, he wrote about experiments in Lawrence (and elsewhere as his career continued), critiqued news Web sites about almost everything from user registration practices to the difficulty of finding someone to email on the homepage, and he helped build community through posting job ads from around the country, including at some tiny newspapers along the "Treasure Coast" of Florida. The comments created a lively community that fostered sharing of experiments and ideas—those involved would go on to have significant roles at major institutions, including *The New York Times*, *The Washington Post*, NPR, Facebook, Twitter, and The Advocate/Here Media, among other media and tech companies.

As we saw, before there was Holovaty, there were others laboring in pockets of newsrooms across the country and the world, experimenting with interactives as ways to tell new types of stories. But Holovaty became a focal point for the myth of the programmer journalist and would see it to his peak involvement in journalism and programming in 2007. Lawrence was part of the myth of the birth of this programming-journalism convergence; but it's important to give credit to others working in this area—especially those who saw the promise and importance of developing a new subfield of work. And technological developments (created, of course, by people) made a big difference, too.

## Technological Developments

Technological developments contributed significantly in enabling interactive journalism to play the role it does in newsrooms today. These innovations empowered journalists to create better and better projects, and as the technology for consuming them also improved, the contributions that interactives could bring to the news experience became clearer. Similarly, these advances are also not necessarily linear: one development does not, as a matter of course, flow into or set the conditions for the next—but the way journalists have described these changes is constructed as a holistic narrative that brings interactives from linkless pop-up windows to sophisticated, personalized, even virtual-reality-enhanced projects—and further emphasizes the special knowledge and contributions interactive journalists make to the profession. The technological developments include the increasing sophistication of the Web itself, the rise (and decline) of Flash, the importance of the rise of the "social" open-source community, and cloud computing. Some of these innovations are technical and jargon-y, but I hope, by reviewing what they have contributed, readers can acquire an appreciation for how things look today—and why interactive journalists have a special claim to esoteric knowledge, both practical and normative.

### Table Percentages and Iframes

In the days of early interactives—most Web pages were constructed of HTML (HyperText Markup Language), which was complicated for the time but would seem simple now. HTML was well understood, although it was limited. The introduction of tables allowed spreadsheet layouts to be put into Web pages, and it soon became clear that it was easy enough to get rid of the visible lines and construct column layouts. Tables enable programmers to create more visually interesting pages and facilitate the placement of captions, titles, navigation bars, sidebars, and the like. A major innovation, according to DeVigal, was the ability to play with table percentages, or have more control over the sizing of these elements, and thus it was easier to create more customized and better-looking pages. Table percentages enabled designers to do with Web pages what someone might do with a traditional print layout. As mentioned, the rise of CGI was important because it became a powerful way to experience a more dynamic Web. It would take input from a Web page and then run a program to generate a new Web page. It has limitations because it is slow—it requires recall to a server—rather than other developments (for example, asynchronous Javascript or Flash) that engage with the local computer rather than the server.

The table developments were followed by the rise of iframes, which further enabled interactives. An iframe makes it possible to embed a Web page within a Web page. Think, for instance, of an image on a page that can have its own scrollbar, or other configurations that can be changed without navigating or reloading from the hosting page: only the content of the page changes, not the entirety of the page itself. This technology meant reduced loading time, which, in an era of dial-up modems, was everything. Iframes further enhanced the ability to build interactives that offered a better user experience and featured more dynamic properties.

### Flash

Interactive journalism was taken to a new level when Adobe's Flash was invented. By the mid 2000s, Flash became integrated in newsrooms as the critical tool for making interactives. Flash has its origins in a program called

Macromedia Director, which was used to make multimedia content. Shockwave, a plugin, was used to play Director files within Web pages. Adobe bought Macromedia in 2005, and from this foundation created Flash. Thanks to Flash, it became relatively easier for people who did not know programming languages to build interactives, and the software had a short learning curve. *The New York Times* had been an early experimenter in Flash beginning in 2004, producing political interactives such as election maps.[25] By the mid-2000s, Flash, based on the ActionScript programming language, enabled easier video hosting, dynamic displays of visualizations, smoother integration of photos and audio, and was well used and well loved by many newsrooms and even tech companies (when YouTube began, it relied on Flash for its video player). Flash had great traction, in part because the Flash plugin was bundled so well with browsers, and since every browser had or could have the plugin, almost every user could access content created by Flash.

Flash also aided the transition of infographic specialists who had worked mainly in print design and brought them online, as they were able to produce their products with the same kind of visual details as print but with enhanced capabilities online. Some of these infographic specialists (Cairo among them, as well as Jon Keegan at *The Wall Street Journal*, whose team is profiled in chapter 4, and others) have emerged as thought leaders and key figures in interactive journalism. Flash played a major role in popularizing interactives because they were easier to make, so journalists could make more of them—underscoring interactives' value to the newsroom—and their quality helped make a case for their relevance as storytelling vehicles. And Flash also enabled more would-be interactive journalists to become part of the growing subfield.

However, Apple essentially killed Flash on mobile devices by not allowing it to function on the iPad and iPhone starting in 2010.[26] What had made Flash so appealing—its cross-browser integration—was no longer available. I distinctly remember in 2010 (after the iPad was first announced) when *New York Times* tech writer Nick Bilton was coming up with conspiracy theories about the demise of Adobe due to Apple's decision not to allow Flash on the device. Given the rise of mobile, this meant that if newsrooms continued to create interactives in Flash, they wouldn't work on the most popular mobile devices. Though some interactive teams were already programming outside of Flash, the forced end to Flash meant that people who knew programming languages became hot commodities in newsrooms.

If you could program an interactive in Java or Ajax rather than Flash, you were wanted. As Cairo describes, "Using Flash was so comfortable and so powerful, and you could create some very sophisticated work, not with minimum effort but with reasonable effort. Why would you care about learning about JavaScript or programming languages [when] you could just leave that to the developers? But once Flash was gone, we were in the desert and we saw we needed to embrace other technologies used by people who were not journalists." For example, in 2009 *The New York Times* was still using Flash to create sophisticated interactives. Case in point: in "How Different Groups Spend Their Day," *The Times* visualized a survey that asked thousands of Americans to recall every minute of every day.[27] The interactive looks a lot like many of the interactive data visualizations *The Times* does today, only now they have to rely on actual programming to create them. This moment—the demise of Flash—helped further solidify the importance of designating a specialized set of people in the newsroom who could create the now more widely used and increasingly sophisticated interactives that had become more and more a part of the user experience online.

### Ajax

But most of what we think of as being essential to the experience of interactives—the ability to move an object on a Web page without refreshing the page—is thanks to Ajax, a combination of technologies that eliminated the need for a "start-stop-start-stop nature of interaction on the Web," as user-experience guru Jesse James Garrett explained in a 2005 essay that popularized the name Ajax. He explained the innovation further: "Instead of loading a webpage, at the start of the session, the browser loads an Ajax engine—written in JavaScript and usually tucked away in a hidden frame. . . . The Ajax engine allows the user's interaction with the application to happen asynchronously—independent of communication with the server. So the user is never staring at a blank browser window and an hourglass icon, waiting around for the server to do something."[28] Ajax wasn't just about visual images (you can see what it does by comparing your standard Gmail to the html view). But it meant that a program like Google Maps could enable clicking and dragging of the map without a user having to wait around for a page to reload. This single improvement in the design of interactives offered not only a better user experience but also made them truly interactive, because the interactive gave a seemingly immediate response, truly browsable and searchable without complications, and generally put the experience of the interactive in the hands of the user in a way that helped to tell stories in a seamless fashion. This advance helped interactives really get the attention of the news industry in 2005. As DeVigal remembers, "Ajax made things on the page dynamic. You could suddenly start typing in the same space and it would work . . . it was mind blowing. Next thing you know, everyone started doing Ajax."

But the advances of Ajax represented a double-edged sword; now, the new realities of Web design and Web programming had suddenly made it more difficult. Java was hard to build and didn't necessarily work properly on every platform. Web design had once been about graphics and layout; it was now about programming and, as Ethan Zuckerman put it, was responsible for "turning the web design job into a highly technical, programming job in some cases."[29]

### Social Open Source

The open-source software movement has been around since the 1970s and early 1980s but perhaps got its true start when Richard Stallman founded the Free Software movement in 1984. The ethos of this movement was that if code was open, people had freedom to use this code, modify it, and share it—either after making changes or in the code's original form. The underlying spirit was that "coding in the open"[30] would encourage community, provide transparency, and let others build new and better projects on the structures of existing projects, as well as refine and fix projects, making software development faster and better. But for journalists working in newsrooms, the rise of open source didn't really make much difference until the early 2000s, when platforms were developed to host open-source code in a way that helped promote social networking.

Some of the benefits of open source for the newsroom (and elsewhere) were explained to me as critical to the widespread growth of interactives. Nathan Ashby-Kuhlman, who began his career at small Florida newspapers and now works at *The New York Times*, explained:

> Smart people were having to solve these problems over and over again. In the second half of the 2000s, social open source only started to emerge. But we were starting to do the pattern recognition and say, I see a repeatable way to save myself a heck of a lot of work, so instead of the repeated task of building a framework, I can use open source. It was a prerequisite to doing more of that type of work [interactives] at scale.[31]

Adrian Holovaty echoed this point—and actually called open source the "biggest thing" to influence interactives in journalism: "It's free, really high-quality software that does all the bookkeeping and boring stuff for you as a programmer, so you can focus on building your site, and because of that it became much much faster to develop high-quality [work].[32] Sharing code enables faster development time, exposure to new ideas, and a shared community of interested parties seeking to improve news software (or app) development more generally. Open-source repositories had been around for decades (much of what we know about the Web is built on open-source software: Linux, Apache, Perl, MySQL), but the social open-source community may have truly blossomed in the first years of this century, a time when newsrooms discovered these open-source repositories and began using them for development. Open-source repositories that allowed for a social dimension were critical, as Ashby-Kuhlman notes, for giving interactives the capacity to scale across newsrooms big and small.

Depending on whom you ask, the social open-source experience can be traced to a number of starting points. Brian Boyer of NPR argued that it began first with Source Forge in 2000 (though the principles of social open-source platforms go back decades earlier to these early open-source repositories).[33] Source Forge was the first platform that was a truly large repository (or place to host code) that allowed people to see what other people were doing in an easily navigable way and in a variety of programming languages. Google Code, in 2006, was also widely adapted by many in the news industry. And by 2007 it was clear that open source had become integrated into the social networking movement more generally. *Mashable*, for instance, wrote an article titled "Open Source Social Platforms: 10 of the Best."[34]

Now, most newsrooms use and collaborate on GitHub, an open-source repository that began in 2008 and came into its own a few years later. Almost every news organization discussed here has a profile on GitHub that hosts at least some open-source code. As Boyer noted, "Now, you're standing on the shoulders of giants," referring to the fact that the best minds creating software are sharing their work and making it possible for others to create high-quality work with similar utilities—and perhaps improve on them.

### Cloud Computing

Interactives take up space on servers, demand computing power, and may not work well with the rest of a news organization's technical infrastructure. And getting space on physical newsroom servers used to require careful negotiations with higher-ups that could slow down the development process. The rise of cloud computing reduced the price of Web servers, gave interactive journalists more computing power to work with, and helped them bypass the organizational and technical problems of their organizations.

As Holovaty explained, "If you wanted to run a site before 2005, you had to pay for a Web server. You had to physically buy a computer and put it into a server rack and pay for it. Now with cloud computing you can rent out a computer by the minute or hour, and if you get a lot of traffic, you can spin it off to extra computers on the fly. [Cloud computing] solved a lot of the technical challenges of the infrastructure."[35] So cloud computing essentially made the software-development process more flexible and more powerful. Ashby-Kuhlman added that before cloud computing, "you could either try to become best buddies with people who maintain the webservers or take over the system, which was maintenance, not journalism."[36] As such, cloud computing was just another technology that helped bring interactives to the forefront of the newsroom, as interactives could be more powerful and plentiful. Experiments could take place without having to garner hierarchical newsroom support, ultimately making interactives better.

Overall, interactive journalists were able to marshal the benefits of new technologies to support their work. Each technology helped underscore the differences in interactive development from the rest of the newsroom process—yet while these technologies helped ultimately make the news website better, it was interactive journalists who were directly making use of them to change the way that news itself looked. Using and understanding these changes and their potential separated interactive journalists as having a special claim on knowledge and a specific utility in the newsroom from other professional journalists who did not.

## A Turning Point: Adrian Holovaty and Chicago Crime Maps

Holovaty, who was working in Chicago for *The Lawrence Journal-World*, created a project called chicagocrime.org in 2005 in his spare time. The project was called the first news "mashup," as it combined two sets of data—Google Maps plus data published by the Chicago Police Department—and made it interactive. The effort cemented Holovaty's reputation and resulted in loads of press attention; consequently, he often gets recognition for being the first true hybrid—as both a programmer and a journalist.

In a blog post announcing the project, he described the site: "[It] is a freely browsable database of crimes reported in Chicago. My scripts collect data from the Chicago Police Department once every weekday. The site slices and dices crime information in a ton of different ways, complete with a wide assortment of Google Maps."[37] It takes some imagination to remember what life was like before Google Maps was widely used, but think of a world that had not yet seen what most people consider to be a truly basic function: think about what Yelp can do—how it has restaurants plotted on a Google Map, for example.

Holovaty—first with his project that put Chicago Transit maps on Google Maps, and now with this journalism effort—was the first person to show it was possible to see data plotted on top of maps through a truly dynamic experience.

He explained in the post what some of the site's unique features were:

- The *map view* lets you view crimes by a number of criteria, all updated dynamically on a Google Map via Ajax.
- *Find your district* uses the Google Maps interface to guess which police beat you're centered on.
- Every city block in Chicago has a detail page with its latest crimes and links to crimes within 1, 2, 3, 5 or 8 blocks.
- It's got RSS feeds for every block and police beat in the city.[38]

This was the most technically sophisticated yet easy to use interactive that the news industry had yet seen.

Holovaty garnered some serious recognition from the industry. He received the 2005 Batten Award for innovation in journalism (now the Knight-Batten award). He was interviewed by *Editor and Publisher*, the *American Journalism Review*, *The Online Journalism Review*, Spain's *El Pais*, and was covered in *The Chicago Tribune* and *The New York Times*.

*The New York Times* praised chicagocrime.org in its 2005 Ideas section:

The most influential mashup this year wasn't a Beatles tune remixed with hip-hop lyrics. It was an online street map of Chicago overlaid with crime statistics. ChicagoCrime.org, which was created by the journalist Adrian Holovaty, was one of the first Web sites to combine publicly available data from one site (in this case, the Chicago Police Department's online database) with a digital map supplied by another site (in this case, Google).[39]

This was big praise from *The Times*, which credited Holovaty for setting in motion the mapping of real estate, classified ads, sporting events, and movie and gas station pricing.

*The Chicago Tribune* caught up with Holovaty in 2008 after he turned chicagocrime.org into a startup called EveryBlock (which was later bought by NBC). The praise was effusive:

Holovaty [is] part programmer, part journalist. . . . [He] and his team have fashioned a site hailed in both tech and journalism circles for its multiple innovations. Although it's still fighting, like almost every other new Web destination, to find a mass audience—and is even further from finding revenue—EveryBlock, many believe, *will help define the future of journalism*.

. . . Holovaty is a sought-after speaker on the Web 2.0 conference circuit, where the people remaking the Internet gather to discuss the hows and whys of the venture. There are philosophical and personal disputes within and between the many Web communities, but most everyone seems to agree on Holovaty's merit and fundamental good-guy-ness.[40]

Holovaty was the prototype for the programmer who could also be a journalist, someone who forms the backbone of interactive news teams today. An article by Mark Glaser in *MediaShift* in 2007 was perhaps the first to emphasize the importance of hiring programmers to work on editorial teams.

> Whenever journalist-programmer extraordinaire Adrian Holovaty speaks at a conference, newspaper executives approach him to ask, "Where can we find another person like you?" Unfortunately, not a lot of people combine journalism with computer programming to create mash-ups like Holovaty's seminal side project, ChicagoCrime.org, which feeds the city's crime blotter into a searchable online database and onto Google Maps.
>
> Holovaty has repeatedly called on newspaper editors to hire programmers, and many of them are finally heeding his advice and considering ways of getting computer programmers onto their news staff and out of the trenches of tech support or doing work on web classifieds.[41]

This article profiles how even small newspapers like *The Tacoma News-Tribune* and *The Greensboro News and Record*, as well as large newspapers like *The Wall Street Journal*, have hired what they call a "news programmer." Though Holovaty had majored in both computer science and journalism, the focus of this article was on finding programmers who could come in and work in newsrooms. After all, as Glaser wrote, "As for teaching journalism students how to do computer programming, that's a long way from happening." Today we see computer programming offered in some form—if just as an introduction to how to build a Web page—in almost every journalism school in the country.

Glaser pointed out the cultural clash between programmers and journalists: pay and lack of experience in journalism versus communicating an editorial vision. And some editors worried that their teams would be disappointed that they were wasting resources on programming rather than hiring reporters, though journalists quickly came round. What was notable, though, was Glaser's insistence that programmers would come work in newsrooms even though the pay was poor. He argued that the job would appeal to them because of the creative freedom it would allow, an undercurrent that occupies many contemporary hacker journalists' motivations for leaving programming jobs behind. Holovaty explained on his blog what being a developer on a newsroom team could mean: "Sure, the money isn't as good as a straight-up tech job, and the geek cred is nonexistent. But it's worth it for the chance to be creative and to make a difference in your community. If you're a hacker, would you rather be a cog in the machine or an independent voice?"

This was perhaps the first time the idea of a *hacker* working in a newsroom was expressed: the hacker programmer coming into the newsroom to be creative and serve a greater good, a reality that is now a critical part of interactive journalism. Hackers possess different ways of thinking about journalism and doing work (such as experimenting and iterating), and in chapter 3 we'll see how hacker journalists articulate these ideas. But the underlying message from this *MediaShift* article highlights how programming was becoming something seen as essential to editorial work—and how a new trend in newsrooms was upon us.

Holovaty was a defining figure for his innovations but also because he became a legend—not necessarily because he deserved it, but because the news industry was fascinated by what he represented. He was the first high-profile programmer journalist, the first person who really got programming and journalism and treated them both as equally valuable. As Rob Curley describes, "Adrian Holovaty was a big deal. This was first journalist I ever met who could write sentences and write code, and that made him really powerful." The coverage Holovaty received and his constant presence on the news-innovation conference circuit helped spread the message that programming and journalism were complimentary, necessary, and critical to the editorial project. As such, he set the example for news organizations about the type of people they wanted to work in their newsrooms—a critical development that essentially helped spur the evolution of the subspecialty across the industry.

## Rich Gordon and the Creation of the Knight Foundation Scholarship

In the mid-2000s, the prevailing attitude seemed to be that programmers had to come into the newsroom and help with interactives, and the widespread assumption was that most journalists simply didn't have the skills to do the complicated programming required to produce interactives. Even though newsrooms were working in Flash, a tool that required less know-how with fairly admirable results, and there were staffers who were programming and had been trained as journalists, the consensus seemed to be that programmers would help bring the best of technological innovation into the newsroom.

With this in mind, Rich Gordon, a professor at Northwestern University, attempted to find a way to create an army of Adrian Holovatys: journalists who could program. In his 2006 initial application to the Knight Foundation's News Challenge Grant, he wrote:

Adrian Holovaty, now of *The Washington Post*, is widely recognized for the innovative projects (Lawrence.com, chicagocrime.org and *Washington Post* projects on congressional votes, political campaign ads, etc.) that combine his expertise in computer programming with his journalistic understanding and commitment. His understanding of technology, melded with a journalist's sensibility about what's important to people and our society, gives him the ability to find stories in data and to recognize opportunities to make data valuable to media consumers. The journalism industry needs more journalist/programmers, but there aren't many to be found. [Northwestern University's] Medill [School of Journalism] is well positioned to start turning them out.[42]

Gordon had been invested in the combination of computing and journalism since the late 1980s, when he attempted to use computer-assisted reporting techniques on a Lotus 123 spreadsheet using the one computer in the newsroom. When he learned about the Internet in the early 1990s, he began thinking about how programming might help newsrooms. But at the time, he was mocked: when he was working at *The Miami Herald* in the mid-1990s, a higher-up at Knight Ridder castigated him for hiring a developer. Gordon recalled, "He said, you don't need programmers, you just need journalism."

As a long-time advocate of developers in the newsroom, Gordon used Holovaty's stature and influence to garner enough support within the news industry to persuade newsrooms to bring in programmers. But Gordon also saw the value of giving these programmers journalism training in order to avoid cultural conflicts and to make them not only able to understand the editorial process but also able to think editorially. Northwestern's M.A. in journalism had been fashioned and marketed as a one-year program that could train anyone, without any journalism experience, from fashion designers to artists to scientists, how to be a journalist—and would train programmers how to become journalists, too. As Gordon wrote in the Knight application, "Every year our one-year master's program takes dozens of students with little or no journalism experience and turns them out ready to start working in newsrooms. . . . It is an ideal program for someone, such as a computer science major, who did not study journalism as an undergraduate."

Gordon's Knight News Challenge proposal called for money to fund nine full scholarships (three awards over three years) with a $25,000 stipend to journalists who have undergraduate degrees in computer science, with a goal to then place them in jobs and internships in the news industry. He proposed that the buzz from the program could have a wide-ranging effect on encouraging other programmers to think about journalism as a viable career option. He wrote, "Publicity about the program will also lead other young technologists to consider journalism as a possible outlet for their talents, leading to more applications—to Medill and other schools—from skilled programmers seeking a journalism degree." Gordon was awarded $639,000 for the scholarships.

These nine scholarships were eventually funded with $900,000. The winners have gone on to have an outsized role in interactive journalism: the first winners included Brian Boyer and Ryan Mark. Boyer coined the term "hacker journalist" to describe programmers who could also do journalism, and Mark headed the Chicago News Applications team (after Boyer) before leaving for *Vox*. Others have gone on to work at *The Palm Beach Post*, *The Washington Post*, and in public radio; one co-founded Narrative Science, one of the first algorithmically generated news-content creators. The program has been successful in attracting and producing hacker journalists, though, as we will see, journalists have also taught themselves how to code, and they now form the bulk of interactive journalism teams.

The scholarships helped further define this growing subspecialty. The creation of institutional funding and training suggested that there was a definable type of person who could become an interactive journalist, with a clear background and skillset. Similarly, professions have traditionally been defined in part by whether specialized education was necessary for employment in the field, and in this case, the programmers received a specialized education about journalism. The idea of a specialized education in helping to create the profession is more convincing when reversed, when journalists in journalism schools enroll in computer science programs or enroll in a blended CS/journalism program. Columbia launched an M.S. in computer science and journalism in 2011, intended for programmers with previous experience; in 2014, Columbia introduced the Lede program, a twelve-week or twenty-four-week nondegree program intended to give journalists "computational skills needed to turn data into narrative."[43] The program announcement advertised:

> Data, code and algorithms are becoming central to research and creative work, and are setting new parameters for the exercise of responsible citizenship. Columbia's Graduate School of Journalism and Department of Computer Science have together created two new post-bac certification programs that will offer hands-on training in data and data technologies, all taught in the context of journalism, the humanities and the social sciences. These programs assume no prior experience in these topics and, in fact, are explicitly aimed at students with little or no formal training in computation and data.[44]

This program began enrolling journalists who had no programming skills in basic computer science classes. Medill began training programmers in 2008, but since 2012 has been facilitating journalism students' wish to double major in computer science. Similar efforts have emerged throughout the country as journalism students either receive training in how to code as part of their core journalism curriculum or find that majoring in computer science and journalism has become easier, and more desirable. Though this sort of training does not serve as a specific entry requirement into the field, as some might think necessary to define a profession or subfield, it does signify the kind of specialization necessary and the way education helps to specialize both programmers and journalists. In many ways, Gordon popularized the idea that a journalist could learn to code and a programmer could learn journalism within an educational setting, underscoring just how distinct this subfield was from other forms of journalism.

## Key Moments at Big Papers

As interactive journalism came into its own from the mid-2000s through today, there were a couple of key moments that helped convince leading newsrooms of the potential of these projects and the importance of having people who can program on staff. Smaller newsrooms have employed programmers in one fashion or another for as long as the big ones, but the efforts of big newspapers were what got the attention of the industry. Moreover, big newspapers, for better or worse, codify and reinforce existing trends: even if they do not set them, they compound their influence. *The New York Times* and *The Washington Post* are the principal newsrooms where interactive successes have helped establish the potential of interactives, not only in their own newsrooms but also to the industry at large. Each newsroom had key moments in the 2000s that set into motion the support for the large teams that exist in their newsrooms today and further signaled the importance of interactive journalists to newsrooms at large.

*The Washington Post* had the early initiative in terms of interactive journalism. Holovaty came to *The Post* in 2005 and started a separate site designation (now defunct) called Post Remix. The site hosted the initiatives of outside developers who used *Post* data to create projects.[45] Holovaty was also responsible for pioneering political infographics that same year, when he and his team (including future prize-winning *New York Times* interactive journalist Derek Willis) created "Congress Votes," a database that let users browse every vote in Congress since 1991 in a number of ways, as Holovaty explained, "such as votes that happened after midnight, vote missers and, on a lighter note, vote totals by astrological sign."[46] Amusingly, the blog post Holovaty wrote announcing the project included a direct shout-out to a search for "the page for Barack Obama."

And in 2006, Holovaty would create "Faces of the Fallen," an interactive database that would allow users to search through a browsable database of U.S. service members who had died in Iraq and Afghanistan. He notes that the first version of the interactive was in Flash, but that he had used Django (the Python-language framework he created) to improve its look and functionality. Holovaty described the project: "The site lets you browse by age, death date, home state and city, military branch or multiple search criteria. Each soldier gets his or her own page, as does each date, American city, age, military branch, etc. There's an RSS feed for recent casualties, a feed for each state and a feed for each military branch. We've integrated Google Maps on several pages to highlight service members' hometowns."[47] The project drew attention from industry publications and mainstream press. And to provide further evidence of its effect on the industry, *The New York Times* soon followed with its own version of chronicling war casualties, "Faces of the Dead."

These projects at *The Post* that got attention (and replication) positioned the newspaper as a forerunner in interactives. With Holovaty, *The Post* was in many ways setting a precedent for the rest of the industry. An interactive team in the newsroom could produce compelling projects that were alternative yet effective ways to tell stories. The projects enhanced and created news value, and captured the attention of the news industry. For the first time, on Web sites of a big news organization working in the age of broadband, users were in control of the information they could access once they arrived at a specific piece of content. Storytelling was changing, and so were the storytellers.

At *The New York Times*, a field trip and the 2007 collapse of the I-35 bridge in Minneapolis set in motion what would become *The New York Times'* Interactive News Technologies Team. Head of the team, Aron Pilhofer, went on a trip with other key digital staff to show and tell Google about *The Times'* digital products and to see the latest from Google. The Web giant was dismissive of journalism's efforts, as even *The New York Times* didn't have much going in terms of cutting-edge digital endeavors at the time. This insult made *The Times* start thinking about how it could be more effective in a digital format. And when the Minneapolis bridge collapsed in 2007, Pilhofer and Jacob Harris, a programmer who had started working at *The Times* after leaving a financial-services firm, began thinking about how they could marshal the data about the bridge conditions. But, as Harris remembers, "We wanted to have everything up with what conditions and we couldn't do it in the time we had."[48]

For *The Times* and most other news organizations, though, presidential elections require advance preparation. And creating at least some interactives for the presidential elections could be done in advance. The small team

Pilhofer had assembled created projects for the primary and general elections with campaign information. But the most significant effort was the team's response to the release of Hillary Clinton's White House calendar. Harris remembered, "Her campaign claimed that she did all these things," but whether she had or hadn't would require going through the calendar documents. *The Times* digitized the documents and created an interactive PDF viewer (a project that would later become Document Cloud, a collaborative document-sharing platform). Now, *The Times*' reporters and editors and ordinary readers, too, could sort through Clinton's calendar and help spot inaccuracies. This project showed *The Times* how interactives could contribute to breaking-news projects and helped justify devoting resources to interactive efforts.

The 2008 election prompted the creation of other key tools, including one called Puffy, which enabled users to submit photos of the presidential inauguration and which *The Times* could moderate and then post. The effect was that inauguration coverage was augmented by hundreds of user photos capturing photo angles, crowd shots, and emotions that *The Times*' coverage team could not. Interactive journalists could also build tools, thanks to their programming skills, ones that clearly had the capacity to enhance news coverage. The case for the interactive team, however—for bringing on people with special skills and knowledge and for giving them the opportunity to contribute to big news events—was brought into sharper focus after the 2008 election.

*The Times* continued to work on interactives, but it wasn't until 2010 that it became clear that interactives were a critical part of *The Times*' claim to prestige and recognition. That year, Matt Richtel, a tech journalist, had been working on a series of stories about distracted driving, or what happens when people use their cellphones and other electronic devices behind the wheel. Key members of *The Times*' staff with programming experience built an interactive game: while navigating a computerized version of a cellphone, you were also meant to use your cursor to navigate a video-game-style street made in the image of the Nintendo game Paper Boy, with obstacles and all. It was essentially a video game built as part of the Pulitzer package, but it drove home (literally), in a way that a story alone could not, that distracted driving could get you killed.

Richtel won the Pulitzer Prize that year for national reporting. The Pulitzer committee gave a nod to these efforts, granting Richtel and *The Times* the award for "incisive work, in print and online, on the hazardous use of cell phones, computers and other devices while operating cars and trucks, stimulating widespread efforts to curb distracted driving."[49] And when Richtel gave his thank-you speech to *The Times*' staff, he acknowledged the interactive team, saying, "And, we have video game making skills. Old-world journalism is the essence of new-world journalism. The series was long form [journalism] with video, audio, and, yes, video games."[50] The interactive team had now been, in part, responsible for a Pulitzer Prize. The interactive news department had truly arrived: for better or worse, *The Times* is in a quest to win Pulitzers, and the interactive team was now recognized as a critical part of this mission. Elsewhere around the news industry, it was also clear that *The Times*' Pulitzers, which in 2010 included investigative and national reporting awards, also commended interactive and multimedia elements recognized by the Pulitzer committee as critical to the success of the reporting efforts. This kind of external validation—these prizes—are critical for securing a sense of occupational identity, and in this case, the recognition reinforced the growing sense of both importance and self-definition of interactive journalists at *The Times*.

And perhaps, in the age where traffic ultimately decides how much advertisers are willing to spend on online news sites, and as news sites are struggling to survive, one linchpin for the subfield's arrival in newsrooms was evidence between 2012 and 2014 that interactives were traffic drivers. At *The Times*, in 2012, there was "Snow Fall" to show the potential of bringing new visitors to *The Times*. As mentioned in the introduction, this included 2.9 million visits for more than 3.5 million page views (each visitor was reading more than one page). And at any one point during the story's peak, of the twenty-two thousand people looking at "Snow Fall," about seventy-five hundred of them were new visitors to *The Times*. That kind of ability to attract new visitors is critical to the site's growth. Subsequently, in 2013 and 2014, interactives were major drivers of traffic over the course of the year on *The Times* site—in fact, *The Times* produces so many interactives that members of the interactives team, graphics team, multimedia team, and others might be responsible for them ("Snow Fall" was actually technically a project of the graphics team, not the interactives news team). A quiz that tried to identify your dialect garnered the first spot on the 2013 list—it was the most viewed story of the year—even though it wasn't a story per se, but an interactive that helped you learn about regional dialect variation.[51] In 2014 eight interactives made the top-twenty list of most-visited stories.[52]

The most-visited story of 2014 on nytimes.com and the mobile site was a photography-focused interactive slideshow featuring two sisters who had been photographed forty times over the course of forty years ("Forty Portraits in Forty Years.") The Dialect Quiz came in again at third. Then in fourth, "52 Places to go in 2014"; in eighth, "Ebola Virus Q&A" (complete with a map of

TRAVEL

→ SHARE

# 52 Places to Go in 2014

Witness a city in transformation, glimpse exotic animals, explore the
past and enjoy that beach before the crowds. UPDATED September 5, 2014

"52 Places to Go in 2014," *The New York Times*

Ebola cases in the United States and in Africa, and some reassuring facts);
in tenth, "Where are the Hardest Places to Live in the U.S.?" (Clay County,
Kentucky, was number 1); in eleventh, a breakdown/explainer of a popular
video game ("10,000 League of Legends Games in 30 seconds"); in sixteenth,
"Is It Better to Rent or Buy?"; and in eighteenth, "The Ukraine Crisis in Maps."
Other top traffic drivers on other measures (such as most-shared on social
media) included "Mapping Migration in the U.S." (which tracked where
people were born versus where they moved) and "The Premiere League If

Table 2.1. "The Year's Most Visited Articles, Blogs, Multimedia and Interactives"

| 2014 Rank | Page Title | Interactive? |
|---|---|---|
| 1 | Forty Portraits in Forty Years | Yes |
| 2 | An Open Letter from Dylan Farrow | |
| 3 | "How Y'all, Youse and You Guys Talk" | Yes |
| 4 | The 52 Places to Go in 2014 | Yes |
| 5 | "Philip Seymour Hoffman, Actor of Depth, Dies at 46" | |
| 6 | What You Learn in Your 40s | |
| 7 | For the Love of Money | |
| 8 | Ebola Virus Outbreak Q&A | Yes |
| 9 | "Robin Williams, Oscar-Winning Comedian, Dies at 63" | |
| 10 | Where Are the Hardest Places to Live in the US? | Yes |
| 11 | "Watch 10,000 Leagues of Legends Games in 30 Seconds" | Yes |
| 12 | Autopsy Shows Michael Brown Was Struck at Least 6 Times | |
| 13 | The Scientific 7-Minute Workout | |
| 14 | Thanksgiving Recipes across the United States | Yes |
| 15 | Jaden and Willow Smith Exclusive Joint Interview | |
| 16 | Is It Better to Rent or Buy? | Yes |
| 17 | Suicide Bomb Trainer in Iraq Accidentally Blows Up His Class | |
| 18 | Ukraine Crisis in Maps | Yes |
| 19 | Doctor in New York City Is Sick with Ebola | |
| 20 | The Horror Before the Beheadings | |

Source: nytimes.com and m.nytimes.com, adapted from nytimes.com data.

Only English Players Counted" (an entertaining portrait of globalization in soccer). Out of twenty stories that referred traffic in a single year on the Web site and mobile site, *eight* were interactives; this means that *almost half of all the top traffic referrers to* The Times *were interactives in 2014.*

You can see a mix of entertainment-focused interactives, data-focused interactives, and some directly news-related interactives. This suggests the wide-ranging appeal of interactives. This kind of external measurement of success underscores just how important interactives were becoming to *The New York Times'* overall economic health and its future plans. Interactive journalists had the case for their work's importance made through the popularity of interactives. The reification of interactive journalists as not only a specialized subfield but also as a respected and critical part of the newsroom had truly come to fruition at *The Times*, and this effect was also being seen throughout the industry.

A few news sites have seen tremendous success with news quizzes and games. These are often dismissed as not-serious news, but they may be related to a news event, or they may provide useful information, or at the very least, they are bringing new people to the news site who may never have been there before. *Slate*, for instance, received its most traffic ever for a quiz that mocked

John Travolta's attempt to say the name of a Broadway star at the Academy Awards (called "Travoltify Your Name"). People had fun, they shared it, and they came to *Slate*. *Time* magazine's 2014 quiz about how much time people waste on Facebook got 4.7 million hits and gave *Time* its biggest traffic day ever, with 3.8 million uniques. Yes, this was not a strictly "news" interactive, as some detractors might suggest, but it contributed useful information to people, offering guidance to them about their world.[53]

Quizzes aside at *Time*, a *Digiday* story notes that a new leader of the "interactive data team" was brought on (at *Time*) in 2013, and "the stories his team have produced have been *Time.com*'s most popular for three years running."[54] As a result, *Time* has even created a separate page to house all its interactives, called "Time Labs," in order to maximize the visual exposure that the interactives can get, though for maximum impact the interactives will still appear on *Time*'s site. The justification for the new site was put in financial terms, according to *Digiday*: "Advertisers are gaining interest in how much time readers are spending on a site versus just clicks, and Time Labs also is a way for the publisher to capitalize on that interest. Buyers said more time spent can lead to a greater advertiser benefit, which in turn could help a site command higher ad rates, or at least more advertising."[55] As such, interactives are critical to newsroom survival—tied to economic success and seen as a way to marshal audience attention, throughout the news industry. And the people who build them have begun to matter more and more to the success of these news organizations. The importance of interactive journalists as a significant subfield within journalism has been enshrined by these external measures of success they now achieve and the critical role they may play in the survival of these news organizations.

## The Beginnings of Data Journalism through Computer-Assisted Reporting

In this case, it's also helpful to offer a quick history of how data journalism came into its own in today's newsroom. We can see through this historical lens how data journalism is a bit different from the overall project of interactive journalism. In the eighteenth century, tables in early American newspapers kept track of stock prices and the import and export of commodities into ports.[56] The first issue of *The Guardian* newspaper featured data charts on public education. More complicated tables emerged in the early, specialized business journals, particularly with the rise of *The Wall Street Journal* in 1889. Early box scores for sports appeared at the end of 1870s. And by 1896, maps with electoral information appeared on front pages.

C. W. Anderson argues also that some form of data journalism has been present in journalism throughout its modern history. He notes a variety of instantiations of data in journalism: from the turn away from documents to oral reports in the age of the penny press, to the turn to social science in the 1960s, to the early 2000s and the interest in building patterns through mathematical models. He argues that the survey movement of the 1900s offered new techniques for visualizing and collecting social data, which in turn inspired journalism. [57]

Computational journalism, defined broadly as the application of computer science methods to journalism (or more specifically, using algorithms, data, and knowledge from social sciences and applying them to journalism through computing technologies)[58] only emerged in the 1950s. Melisma Cox argues that the first instance of computer-assisted reporting (CAR) in the United States was in 1952, when CBS used the Remington Rand UNIVAC to predict the outcome of the U.S. presidential race between Eisenhower and Stevenson.[59] Matthew Reavy also points to innovators such as Philip Meyer, who in 1967 used an IBM 360 mainframe to analyze survey data about the Detroit riots.[60] Other early-adopter journalists began using computers in their work to analyze data.

In 1973, Meyer wrote *Precision Journalism*, advocating for the greater integration of computers, data, and social science methods in journalism practice.[61] That same year, in perhaps an early iteration of open-source ethics in journalism, *The New York Times* made public an interactive information system with data about New York City police statistics.[62] Around this time, famed *Philadelphia Inquirer* reporters Don Bartlett and James Steele, with help from Meyer, put court records into a computer for their series "Unequal Justice."[63] Possibly the most visible moment for computational journalism came in 1989 with *Atlanta Journal Constitution* reporter Bill Dedman's Pulitzer Prize–winning report on unequal housing practices and red-lining.

An anecdote from the late 1980s underscores the complexity of retrieving information from databases. Elliott Jaspin, a *Providence Journal* reporter, just wanted to do one thing: get government data and use it for stories. But the information hadn't come in paper form, unfortunately; no, in 1987, the U.S. government was storing data on nine-track tapes resembling film reels that could be read only by giant mainframe computers (a common practice for large organizations at the time). Jaspin had access to his newsroom's mainframe computer and had some success using state databases, even finding information that led to the head of a state housing agency going to jail. But many smaller newspapers did not have access to mainframes—and journalists who could access mainframes at larger newspapers were often uncomfortable using Unix and EBCDIC (used in binary file encoding). He wanted to make accessible to other journalists what was then a modern method for using databases.

Thanks to a fellowship through Gannett at Columbia University, Jaspin learned enough about nine-track tapes that he could access the data through a PC. Jaspin said he thought, "If I could write the software that would allow a reporter to read and download the data to a PC, I could mimic a mainframe for $10,000."[64] With Dan Woods, one of the journalism students who had a background in computer science, he wrote the program in nine months. But it was still too complicated for most, and special training was needed. Jaspin explained that there was still a "serious learning curve. How do you use relational databases? How do you convert files from EBCDIC to ASCII? What are variable length records and how do you download them to a PC?" So Jaspin approached the University of Missouri, and thus began the discussions about what would become NICAR. The group was a subset of the Investigative Reporters and Editors professional group and was founded in 1989 with the goal of helping journalists extract, analyze, and report on electronic information.[65]

By 1991 the second edition of Meyer's book argued that journalists interested in CAR were a separate breed of reporters who often bought their own computers in advance of newsroom technology. Journalism scholars began writing about the CAR movement around this time, and in 1996, Brant Houston identified three key aspects of technological innovation and journalism production: database reporting, spreadsheets, and online-reporting.[66] Other articles in the late 1990s and early 2000s function as scholarly discoveries of the increasing prevalence of the CAR journalist; at this point, though, computer-assisted reporting was still looking for stories through anecdotal pieces of data, rather than being able to use raw computing to find overarching patterns to process large datasets.

But CAR is only part of the data journalism equation. CAR speaks to the computational aspect, whereas the application of data journalism helps ascribe additional importance to the presentation of data and how to examine data beyond anecdotes to a more comprehensive analysis of the entirety of the data. Chapter 3 will discuss exactly how data journalists understand and depart from CAR, and how these journalists are connected to but not always a part of interactive journalism.

## From the History to the People

From Chicago and South Florida in the mid-1990s to Lawrence, Kansas, in the early part of this century, to *The New York Times'* most-viewed list of 2014, the history of news interactives has developed to the point where interactive journalism and journalists are now a regular part of newsrooms. The subfield of interactive journalism has emerged thanks in part to changes in technology, to changes in economics, and to claims to the ability to do particular kinds of work. These journalists have also been accorded cultural power in the newsroom as their work has developed at scale, grown more sophisticated, and demonstrated success online and on mobile devices. As such, they have also been able to influence news organizations with their work.

Unlike other subfields, there isn't much contest between interactive journalists and the rest of the newsroom. Certainly, there may be difficulties when interactive journalists and journalists who don't understand how software works try to collaborate. But with everyone in the newsroom wanting their story to be "snowfalled," and with news organizations investing more resources in interactive departments and interactive journalists, it becomes only more obvious what practical and abstract claims to knowledge these journalists have and what they can offer to the newsroom. Thus, we turn to who the people are who actually make up the subfield of interactive journalism.

## 3  Hacker Journalists, Programmer Journalists, and Data Journalists

Brian Boyer was casually scanning Boing Boing, the tech blog, in May 2007. The previous day, the blog had featured its usual mix of oddball news with tech info—favorite podcasts, interviews with bloggers, Mac updates, and an amusing feature on a robot that looked like a chicken, which had been taught to dance by Japanese scientists.[1] But on May 24, Boyer found a different kind of post—an announcement that would change the trajectory of his career and his life. It read:

### TURNING CODERS INTO JOURNALISTS
#### (HINT: ADD SPELLCHECK, SUBTRACT SKITTLES).

Rich Gordon of Northwestern's Medill School of Journalism says The Medill School of Journalism just won a grant that will allow Medill to offer master's degree scholarships in journalism to computer programmers. It's among $12 million in grants awarded via the Knight News Challenge.[2] The general idea is to lure talented coders, immerse them in the practice of journalism, and then turn them loose to figure out interesting ways of putting journalism together.

Boyer, who was designing medical records software for small doctors' offices, said he enjoyed the "craft of making software," but had lost interest in making software for businesses. He wanted to make something he was proud of: he wasn't, so he was looking to do something other than what he had been doing in the business world. So when he came across the Boing Boing post, as he put it, "I Googled journalism and said, shit, that's what I want to do. Literally, journalism is about enabling people to do better, to self-govern, and I said I wanted to do that . . . let's give people information and build democracy from the grassroots."[3]

Boyer became part of the inaugural Medill program, where he learned everything from how to cover crime to what libel laws were. And by 2011 he was running a full team at *The Chicago Tribune*. But his wasn't your typical newsroom reporting team. Instead, Boyer's group—*The Chicago Tribune News Apps team*—built tools for data analysis and visualization, ultimately creating software for new types of storytelling as well as for traditional text-based accounts. Programming was the starting point for their work and the beginning of their contribution to the editorial workflow.

Boyer is one of a small but distinguished group of journalists who have come to the newsroom from the programming world. He is a hacker journalist—with a past in software and now in the newsroom. He is not alone: today, as journalism contends for relevancy in the digital environment, coding skills have become increasingly important. He is joined by other former professional developers who now spend most of their time programming in the service of news. Some resist the label "journalist," but to be successful they must understand the editorial workflow, demands, needs, and expectations, communicate according to journalistic norms, and, more important, expand the professional jurisdiction over work and knowledge for journalism.

Accompanying Boyer, in newsrooms across the country—in greater numbers in large newsrooms, but also in midsize and small newsrooms[4]—are his journalism-first counterparts, those who began working in journalism or in liberal arts disciplines and have taught themselves to code. These programmer journalists think in terms of the story first, and they have a different way of thinking about interactive journalism. Adding to these ranks are data journalists, who work closely with data, often use computers to help with reporting, and may not always know how to code. These journalists descend from a legacy of computer-assisted reporting to work to manipulate data in the service of journalism—they are data specialists who may also create interactives. They, too, think about journalism differently from traditional journalists, often looking for numerical or categorical data rather than qualitative evidence. These categories as defined here may not make much sense to interactive journalists themselves; indeed, they may find such distinctions to be arbitrary or overlapping. Those I've defined as hacker journalists might call themselves programmer journalists or data journalists, and these terms get further muddied outside of the United States in practice and in academic discussion. What, then, do we make of this labeling quandary?

It is difficult for those within the field to remove themselves from day-to-day work to consider larger conceptual categories, even though they think they may be doing so. Nonetheless, the advantage of academia is that we can provide such a perspective to begin to draw outlines of the emerging field—academics have the luxury of having the distance to make distinctions and provide analysis. The empirical data here gathered from across fourteen different newsrooms around the world provide the evidence to draw these distinctions. Empirical data represents what people have actually said, and it offers a rationale directly from the words of the people who work inside these newsrooms. So these journalists essentially come to *define themselves* through how they talk about their backgrounds and perspectives, and I offer the analytical distinctions through the way they talk about who they are.

The diversity of terms and descriptors used to define practitioners can be seen as varying across the work of different scholars. Katherine Fink and C. W. Anderson make the decision in their work not to create their own definition of data journalism to begin their inquiry.[5] Australian scholars Terry Flew, Christina Spurgeon, and Anna Daniel see the origins of interactive journalism as beginning with computer scientists who augment journalism.[6] Sylvain Parasie and Eric Dagiral, who offer an ethnographic study of *The Chicago Tribune*, use the term "programmer journalists" for what I define as hacker journalists, but they conflate their study population with data-driven journalism.[7] Cindy Royal, who spent a week embedded with *The New York Times* Interactive News Team, discovered that the team's journalists had various backgrounds: some had worked in tech companies, others had worked in journalism and had journalism backgrounds, but all were united in the service of a journalistic endeavor.[8]

Others have also tried to break out interactive journalists into a specific typology. Wibke Weber and Hannes Rall define three groups of journalists working in interactive journalism: the programmer, the designer, and the statistician.[9] Astrid Gynnild contends (curiously) that data journalism is only data journalism when it deals with open-source data.[10] Mark Coddington, offering another attempt to define the field, distinguishes computer-assisted reporting from data journalism by noting that CAR is a "historical mode of quantitative journalism."[11] Even Adrian Holovaty, the first breakout interactive journalist, had difficulty with labels. He wrote a blog post arguing "who cares?" about whether his work was called data journalism or not, but then he used the phrase "journalism as programming" as a way to talk about the back end of his work. All of these definitions are so different that it's important to take a stab at finding conceptual clarity using field-based evidence derived from an analysis of the patterns through which journalists talk about who they are and how they approach their work.

But it is fundamental, now more than ever, to understand and to categorize interactive journalists. These terms are all quite popular, but used as buzzwords, there's not much consistency about what they mean. Rather than leaving "hacker journalist," "programmer journalist," and "data journalist" at the level of buzzwords, only to be discarded in a few years, the words actually have some staying power in the discourse of journalism if they can come to mean something clear and definable. Similarly, these categorizations make it apparent that such terms do matter because they have specific histories and cultural assumptions built into their practices and identities. Categorization through empirical work helps us understand what is novel, old, and the same about these groups and as they compare to traditional journalism; in turn, such sorting helps us get a more complete grasp of the phenomena at hand.

This chapter looks at the *people* behind the work and knowledge of this expansion of professional journalism. The reason to offer this perspective is that backgrounds and perspectives help us understand their approaches to work. A look at journalists' ways of thinking opens an examination of how they will offer distinct claims to abstract knowledge that will inform and expand the larger journalism profession (further explored in chapter 5). This "people" chapter helps us see clearly that there are indeed new kinds of journalists—those who work with code and those who use computational work to approach data holistically—who signal by their presence just how journalism is expanding.

## Hither Come the Hacker Journalist

Who is a hacker journalist? A PowerPoint presentation created by the Knight Foundation featured the idealized story of the hacker journalist. The hacker would fuse with the traditional journalist to become "Journalist 2.0." On one side of the slide was the programmer/hacker, wearing headphones, a black t-shirt, jeans, and "chill clothes," and was described as a "problem solver, process oriented" and a "builder." On the other side of the slide was the journalist, wearing dorky clothes—a shirt and tie under a buttoned cardigan, holding a reporter's notebook and wearing glasses. This traditional reporter had the words "Big Picture thinker, storyteller, wordsmith, contrarian, investigator" associated with him.[12]

After journalism school—or, perhaps, after experience with traditional journalism—the hacker journalist, or "Journalist 2.0," would become socialized into the newsroom, and in the middle of the slide he is shown wearing new clothes (a plaid shirt instead of the black t-shirt) and is associated with the words "translator," "info distiller," "impactor," "data visualizer" (he's holding a digital tablet now) and "pragmatist." This hacker journalist, then, would bring his way of thinking to the needs of the newsroom.[13] The slide noted that the hybrid figure was "loosely based on the life of Brian Boyer,

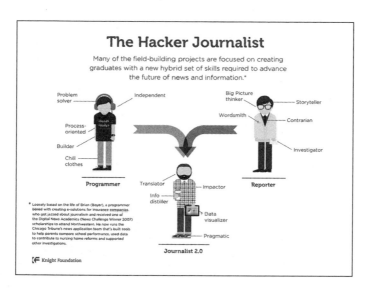

"The Hacker Journalist," *Knight Foundation*

a programmer bored with creating e-solutions for insurance companies."[14] *Hacker journalist*, then, describes those who come from a programming background and are now part of the newsroom.[15]

Boyer says he, to the best of his knowledge, coined the term hacker journalist.[16] In fact, he owns the domain hackerjournalism.net. He wrote in 2008: "If you're a hacker, you're an especially good programmer. So, what are you if you're a hacker journalist? Think about what photojournalists do—they tell stories with a camera." The hacker journalist would tell stories through code. Hacker journalism is as much a type of journalism as it is a type of person who now works in the newsroom. And this hacker journalist comes from the outside, bringing in new skills, ideas, and perceptions of how to do journalistic work.

The hacker journalist should never be conflated with anti-social hackers who have nefarious intentions—hackers who break into computers or steal passwords, who steal data from governments or news organizations, or who obtain credit card information illegally. Hacking is instead used here to mean a pro-social activity and outlook toward creating software. These programmers "hack" out of the joy of building software for the common good.

Hacking as a technical craft has a long history of innovation and creation with the goal of using code to improve society. This vision of hacking dates to the early computer culture of the 1960s at MIT—where email was developed as an early "hack"—and it continues to imbue a spirit of community, openness, participation, and experimentation. Another way to think about hacking is as a solution to a problem, taking the easiest route to get something to work. Hacking values, one of which is "do no harm," emerge from principles of the open-source software community.[17] Newsroom programmers themselves and programming in newsrooms generally are tied to this hacker culture, which is inspired by an inherent desire to use code to do good and to share this work with a wider public.

As hacker journalist Jonathan Stray of the Associated Press asked of tech experts who might become journalists, "Can you code, are you good at helping people learn about their world, and do you see how software as civic media might contribute to some sort of democratic or social good/making the world a better place?"[18] Hacker journalists, then, come from programming and can better the world through applying code in the service of journalism. They are outsiders who leave behind industry, where they have sometimes been programming for a product they consider soulless and with low creative value. Now, they have the opportunity to program in the public interest. These programmers have been more than welcomed into the news industry, as their ability to construct computational solutions and innovations has been heralded and turned into aspirational myth—as we see from the Knight slide for the promise of the Journalist 2.0. Out of all the journalists who can program, though, journalists who were programmers first are in a distinct minority.

### Why They Come

The reason programmers leave particular jobs is because they say they can't find in commercial programming anything like what they might do in a newsroom. Most of the hackers who have come to newsrooms have backgrounds in commercial IT, which they left because of the emphasis on client-side work and the limits on creative expression. The newsroom, with new challenges every day, offers hacker journalists a chance to build new projects to help illustrate social problems and issues in the public interest, which they argue would have otherwise been impossible in their old jobs. Consider what Ryan Mark, a hacker journalist who also came through Northwestern University's program, had to say: "I think there are a lot of software development shops out there who are just kind of like factories and people put in their 9-to-5 and don't really care too much about what they're working on. . . . But in media and journalism it's the total opposite. People really care about their work and really care about doing the right things."[19]

His colleague Joe Germuska noted, "I worked in interactive marketing for 10 years, mostly doing web development that wasn't very public. Toward the end, I didn't care about what I was building. The technology itself was not enough."[20] Software developers, according to Mark, Germuska, and Boyer, among others, seek to "scratch the itch" or find a solution through programming to what they saw as a problem—or just bothersome. Working in commercial software doesn't offer that chance to explore or solve problems in the same way that coming up with creative solutions for news might.

Other hackers across the world have also traded corporate jobs for the environment of public service. Tsan Yuan, a hacker journalist at the BBC, was employed in large Web site development for banks and insurance companies: "I came to a newsroom because I was interested in digital media, new media and the technical shape of news in a different way . . . being here has a huge impact."[21] In short, if you care about making a difference, leave behind the big bucks and work in journalism.

Another British journalist, Alastair Dant of *The Guardian*, talked about his work in San Francisco at a series of "soul sucking JavaScript jobs," which were a "lucrative dull enterprise."[22] While he managed to create a kids' video game in his spare time, he wanted to come to *The Guardian* because of its commitment to good journalism at a time when the business model needed help. "*The Guardian* has a great liberal voice. . . . It's doing high-quality journalism."[23] For *The Guardian* to survive, it needed to innovate online, and Dant believed he could be part of this effort.

At *Al Jazeera English*, Mohammed el-Haddad thought that he could be better integrated in world events with a job in the newsroom. Haddad was hired just after graduation. He said he came to *Al Jazeera English* at a time when the region was particularly active.[24] He told *MediaShift*: "I was very fortunate to join *Al Jazeera* in 2011 just at the time of Egypt's revolution. The energy was tremendous. I think we all had a sense of how big a moment in history that was going to be. For me, being fresh in the news business, it didn't take long to see how the combination of traditional media and technology was able to impact hundreds of millions of people in the region."[25]

Doing hacker journalism would be a way literally to change the way people were experiencing the Arab Spring and beyond. Hackers may also espouse a commitment to free speech; in fact, hackers have a reputation, at the most extreme, of freeing secret documents they believe belong to the public (like Sony's internal emails, for good or bad). In this case, though, I did not come across any hackers who were interested in coming to journalism because of their commitment to free speech. Perhaps the commitment to free speech was implicit in their larger commitment to serving the public interest.

Since journalism has the potential to harness new technical capacities, programmers have the ability to bring their unique skills together with journalism's distinct mission. The profession has created an opening for skilled individuals with knowledge of code to come in and change the way that technology is used in the editorial process; this has meant a place for hacker journalists inside the newsroom. It's also clear that their belief in public interest melds well with the larger, overarching goal of journalism itself, suggesting that these programmers do not have to change their goals or aspirations when they come to the newsroom.

### Ways of Thinking

This different background—the programmer who comes to journalism— presents an opportunity for thinking about journalism in a new way. The experience of building software and working in programming communities also means being connected to a particular set of approaches, problems, and solutions. The so-called "hacker" approach to software design permeates interactive journalism, and some of its ambassadors are these former programmers. Hacker journalists think about journalism as a site of play, exploration, and problem solving.

AP journalist Jonathan Stray has explained what it means to approach journalism with this hacking perspective on his blog. In a post titled "Journalism for Makers," he discusses the important theme of hacking in creating and improving journalism. He points to the qualities inherent in people who come from programming to journalism and how they think about their work:

> [They are] geeks who like to understand very complex systems, and tinker with them. I want to borrow from the culture of "makers," because maker culture plants a flag on this idea. It draws on the hacker tradition of technical mastery, the DIY aesthetic perfected by the punks, and the best disruptive tendencies of global counter-culture. It lives in online forums and nerdy meetups and on the dingy couches of hack spaces. This is the chaotic ecosystem that powers Silicon Valley.[26]

In Stray's understanding, hacker journalism would bring together the best of hackers and the ethos of doing it yourself to try new things, to "tinker," or make small adjustments and changes to see simply what happens, and share a different attitude that comes from an entirely different perspective. This "inquisitive passion for tinkering," as Gabriella Coleman writes,[27] is a cornerstone of hacking culture.[28] Hacker journalists come from this hacking counterculture with the goal of being disruptive, making and doing through "technical mastery."

Hacker journalists talked about how journalism was a problem that could be solved, and emphasized this rather than the story. Stijn Debrouwere, a hacker journalist working at *The Guardian* who came out of a commercial programming background, tried to explain what he saw as the kind of thinking hacker journalists provided to the newsroom—a problem-solving skillset:

> This is an absolute cliché but I do believe it's true: developers are trained to be lazy, and that's a good thing. Journalists are used to manual work: looking through that same courts database every single day to see if there's any new documents, poring through huge amounts of documents by hand, doing the same calculations over and over again, or they might simply give up stories because the challenge might seem insurmountable.
>
> You could never get a developer to do things like that: they'd write a small application so they never ever have to do the same task twice. And along the way you reap the benefits, because some of those applications can be used in very different contexts by other reporters, and other applications can be opened up and repurposed into news applications you can share with your audience. That's a really valuable attitude and skillset, I think.
>
> I also think programmers are more used to thinking in terms of *information* rather than stories. That's both a valuable asset and a shortcoming, because it means programmers spot valuable information we can share with readers, even when it looks boring or "not a story" to a reporter, *but OTOH* [on the other hand] *it also means that programmers perhaps don't have as great a feel for storytelling.*[29]

Debrouwere points out two distinct ways of thinking about journalism. First, journalism is something to be hacked; second, journalism is information. Programmers bring to journalism a focus on the "hack"—looking for the quick solution to the big problem in order to find an easy way to do things; this solution, of course, comes from code. Journalism is a process that can be made easier through programming solutions. The hacker journalist offers the mindset that if the right code and the right methods are applied, then journalism will be efficient and answer the questions posed.

Programmers also don't think of journalism as stories but as a product with component parts—"information." This suggests that to the programmer, journalism may be able to be detached from a narrative and a longer context. Instead, journalism as "information" may be moved around, disaggregated, and re-ordered. Each element a reporter uncovers for a story should be thought of like a line of code: information as building block rather than the end point of story. The information then becomes the scaffolding for other projects, which may or may not ever become stories.

Hacker journalists approach their work with a perspective not found in traditional journalism. Rarely has the word "play" come up as journalists talk about their work. But hacker journalists take the idea from the spirit of programming that they can constantly test things out. They enjoy the process of crafting new ways of doing work. They like messing around, trying to get computers to approach journalism in new ways; they experiment knowing that they may fail. Ransome Mpini, a hacker journalist at the BBC, explained the attitude this way: "It's pretty interesting. You have to have an interest in playing around with tech. There was a definition of a hacker that I liked, [which] I found [last night], that I thought was quite right—it went something like 'a passionate skill and an innovative skill.'"[30]

Hackers are experimenting and innovating. The attitude is also one that ushers in a desire for doing work as playful and fun; they look at journalism as information and journalism as a problem that can be solved. These are not ways of thinking that have normally been found in newsrooms; they come instead from the programming culture that now feeds into newsrooms as code becomes more integral in daily news work, and coders more ingrained in the life of a newsroom.

Hacker journalists also say that they will disrupt newsroom workflow. At a panel at West Virginia University, the head of *The Seattle Times'* News Apps team, Lauren Rabaino, said that she found traditional workflow restrictive: "There is this newsroom structure of project management that is an assembly line."[31] She talked about how this assembly process was not nimble enough. Instead, she pointed out how "agile" software development was simply much better. Agile is one method for software development wherein production happens in rapid cycles with key players reporting in to assess progress. This agile development brings with it the opportunity to create prototypes rapidly, for good or for bad, and can work well for both long- and short-term projects. This prototyping again speaks to the temperament for experimentation that hackers bring with them to the newsroom.

And there's simply a cool factor that hackers bring to the newsroom. Hacker journalists are the people in black t-shirts. In 2010, after winning a Pulitzer with a major interactive project, Bill Keller at *The New York Times* pointed out how the newspaper suddenly had people with tattoos and piercings working there.[32] These hacker journalists may even have a look (stereotypically imagined as having bushy beards—a problem underscoring a more complicated gender issue), and there is an outsider, rebel mentality that nonetheless tries to build on a communal project, what you might find in open-source communities. Rabaino added, "We want to empower people. We want to be the cool kid in the newsroom."[33] In this respect, some leaders of these teams hope to infuse a new kind of energy and attitude.

As a result, the attitude hackers bring to journalism is associated with a newfound approach to innovating in the newsroom. Journalists who do not come from a hacker background expressed what they saw this world of hacking as offering to news. Jon Keegan at *The Wall Street Journal* explained: "The idea of hacking and journalism comes a bit from tech hacking—it's seeing how journalism can go in new ways and it's not just solving a tech problem."[34] He suggests the term raises a key question: "Can you creatively solve the problem?"[35]

Other journalists in his newsroom also took inspiration from what they saw as the philosophy behind hacker journalism. One of Keegan's deputies, Sarah Slobin, explained: "I learned that the hacker piece is that you can figure it out yourself. . . . You have to figure out things you can't do and if you can't answer a question, *you* have to figure things out. . . . You also have a DIY mentality."[36] It inspired her, as a journalist and then programmer, as it "makes me do new things."[37] At the same time, *The Wall Street Journal* would never use the term "hacker journalism"; as a NewsCorp paper, it is especially sensitive to the word hacker because of the UK phone hacking scandal, where journalists hacked into potential sources' voicemails.

But the term still remained a source of inspiration at public radio station WNYC in lower Manhattan, about forty blocks away from *The Journal's* headquarters. Head of the Data News Team John Keefe traced the idea of hacker journalism back to the idea of openness and community. He noted, "With hacker journalism, there is a sense among the crowd that they are doing good things. That is really cool. We are sharing and building on work."[38]

In this way, the infusion of hackers into the newsroom represents this Journalism 2.0—the journalists are indeed offering a new way of approaching journalism problems. Not only is the platform different—through software—but also the process is different. Other journalists embrace this hacker mentality and draw inspiration from what hacker journalists have identified as some of the benefits they bring to the newsroom. Play, problem solving, experimentation, "making," and "doing" are all terms that embody the action behind the code-based thinking these programmers bring. And as we can see from other journalists, this kind of approach is welcome.

### Are They Journalists?

If the focus is on assembling code and writing programs, then this raises the question of whether this is journalism. Certainly, this is not traditional journalism if hacker journalists are writing scripts to generate interactives, from maps to charts to databases. Often, hacker journalists are working with more traditional journalists who will then do the work of finding stories, though hacker journalists can and do have Page One bylines. If the product is an application—and the hacker journalist isn't offering analysis—are they just programmers in the newsroom?

By self-description, many resist the label journalists. They don't see themselves writing the traditional story. Germuska says that he is not a "real" journalist, though he is proud to collaborate and get A-1 stories, which certainly makes him feel like more a part of *The Chicago Tribune* news-creation experience. Mohammad el-Haddad of *Al Jazeera English* has only recently started calling himself a journalist—when I met him in 2012, he said, "I would not call myself a journalist."[39] But after two years of speaking about interactive journalism, with continued questions about his efforts in programming and journalism, his bio now reads "data journalist." Haddad explained to me, "I have had to learn a lot about journalism." Notably, as he said, the word hacker would simply not be used at *Al Jazeera*, either to describe what he does or to talk about the kind of journalism he works on—hacker comes too close to the kind of anti-social efforts Syrian computer terrorists continually engage in to undermine *Al Jazeera English* content.[40]

Most of those I spoke with suggested that while they cared about journalism deeply, they didn't feel equipped to engage directly with the processes of daily journalistic work. Boyer told traditional NPR journalists in a meeting I observed that they were the ones in charge of the story, not him.[41] At the same time, his group was collecting the data that would populate the search fields, and he had, on his team, an expert in getting these reports. Perhaps, then, he was working as a data collector and data presenter for interactive journalism, but not for traditional radio news. In this way, he was doing journalism work, even if his output wasn't the work of traditional journalism.

In the United Kingdom, hackers on news staffs deflected the label journalist, arguing that they were much closer to developers that happened to enjoy working in a newsroom. A *Guardian* employee explained it this way: "I guess as a developer I see my contribution to the content production and the content of the story as an application of technical knowledge and web text and html to make more complete interactives to visualize something and make something interactive . . . to provide a different way to look at expert feedback—I suppose I am doing journalism but I am not a journalist by background."[42] In this respect, many of those with developer-type skills who come out of the technical world are not the traditional journalists we might expect from the newsroom.

It's still important to call hacker journalists "journalists" even if they might not consider themselves by this term. There's considerable power in using the word "journalist"—and it is an important claim: these hacker journalists must be considered critical to the future of journalism and be recognized with this symbolic power. If we fail to consider hacker journalists as journalists, we are disregarding the value of what they add to the editorial process. Their product is software, certainly, but what they do is journalism in another form. The process of creating an interactive often requires hacker journalists to dig into data, gather information, and render it ready for news consumption. This collating and collecting is a critical element of journalism. Similarly, the integration into the editorial process signals the role these hacker journalists play as journalists: without them the final output—the piece of journalism—would not be possible.

These hacker journalists have to understand journalism in order to do their work and must communicate with a news sensibility. To create interactives and work with other journalists requires news judgment, the ability to understand the needs of the larger journalistic output, and therefore underscores the integration of hacker journalists into the newsroom. They would be unable to successfully do their work if they could not communicate across journalistic endeavors, as they do. And most of these hacker journalists readily accept, respect, and wish to pursue common journalistic aims, as Germuska, Haddad, and others suggest and as indicated by their willingness to learn about journalism and their hope of working to help further journalism's larger goals. In fact, even before these hacker journalists come to the newsroom, they have an idealized sense of journalism's public-service role. Their willingness to turn away from lucrative positions elsewhere out of a desire to contribute to the large project of journalism signals their acceptance and understanding of the aims of the profession.

Thus, to move journalism forward and to think about how journalism must change, it is critical to recognize hacker journalists as fully integrated members of newsrooms. For journalists to make a claim to relevance, news organizations and the profession must claim what these hacker journalists do as journalism. This work is critical to establishing a unique entry point for journalism in the larger information ecology. Though they might not use the label "journalism," their role in the news process, while different, nonetheless requires understanding the news process. So hacker journalists are journalists, and it is important to see them as such.

Hacker journalism knowledge is critical for journalism to remain relevant—a defining pressure on the profession that helps create a subspecialty.

Hacker journalists are needed to create something new in order to help journalism change to meet the needs of the digital conditions it faces. This need for abstract knowledge is critical to expanding what journalism can do in order to respond to the sociocultural, technological, and economic pressures it faces. New ways of thinking about and doing journalism are required, and hacker journalists help push the profession forward with their influence on the profession. Their counterparts, programmer journalists, or those who started first as journalists rather than programmers, help further expand journalism as a profession.

## Programmer Journalists: The Traditional Background

Most journalists who are programmers do not come from the tech world. Instead, the majority of journalists who code have some sort of journalism background before coming to programming, either from journalism school or from working in a traditional newsroom with traditional duties. They have taught themselves to program and generally talk most about the importance of the story as central to their mission. This distinction, and the importance of identifying as a journalist first, is critical to their self-perception.

Michelle Minkoff's tale of becoming a programmer journalist illustrates the flipside of the stories told by the hacker journalists, who began in a world immersed in code. Instead, Minkoff had virtually no idea that coding or programming even existed while she was an undergraduate English major at Brandeis. In an August 2014 tweet, she noted "2008! I was graduating Brandeis & blissfully unaware of code & future."[43] While a graduate journalism student at Northwestern, Minkoff took a class that she describes as literally changing the future direction of her life. She recalled that her class, "Digital Frameworks for Reporting," taught by *New York Times* programmer journalist Derek Willis, was so transformative that "life would never be the same again from that day" she entered the classroom.[44] Her blog chronicles the steps she has taken to learn programming, from beginning efforts at learning coding languages, writing wish lists for programming journalism classes, and "thinking programmatically,"[45] to her current and public efforts at going through far more complicated experimentation with "refactoring," or improving code design, such as making it cleaner.[46]

She has gone on to have a storied career in just few years: she began as a "data developer/journo intern" on *The Los Angeles Times*' data desk, went to PBS as a data producer, and now works as at the Associated Press as an interactive producer. Interestingly, her two most recent titles don't have the word "journalist" or "reporter" in them. But Minkoff certainly sees herself every day in the process of producing journalism. To her, the titles she's given—whether she is called a programmer journalist, a data journalist, or something else—mean little to her: "I fundamentally don't care what it is called. . . . You do what your job is and you do what your job takes."[47] For her, though, unlike some of the hacker journalist types, the focus is distinctly in the service of the story, and she directly identifies as a journalist. "I am about the journalism." She added, "No one sees the code, you see the analysis."[48] The ultimate goal is to "create a story through data and apps for people . . . to easily find things to zoom in to and drill down online."

In one of her posts, she described what it meant to her to be a programmer journalist—if she had to define it: "I don't spend a percentage of my day in journalism and a percentage in programming—I spend most of my day in programming in order to practice journalism. I do other things, too: write documentation, pitch ideas, go to meetings, but always, always, always in the service of the journalism."[49]

From the case of Minkoff, we see the progression of the programmer journalist. These journalists often have no previous exposure to code—and often have backgrounds with no association with programming (they sometimes just start as liberal arts majors, like many journalists who didn't go to journalism school). A number of these programmer journalists may learn some basics in school, but they continue also to teach themselves skills, experimenting with programming to make journalism better. Minkoff's focus on the journalism suggests a different orientation from the hacker journalists—for her, the priority is always on the story, and her primary self-conception is as a journalist.

Other journalists have similar backgrounds as Minkoff's, underscoring the difference between programmer journalists and hacker journalists. They, too, suggest that they have varying perspectives in approaching the work they do—with the major difference being the emphasis on thinking about journalism as it is traditionally idealized, though they also talk about adopting new attitudes and ways of thinking from programming into their work. The programmer journalist is often looking to use computational skills to work with data they have obtained either for themselves or from fellow journalists and then to help turn such material into stories. This adds to the messiness of defining journalists as programmer journalists, as data journalism also describes what many of these journalists spend their time doing.

## Backgrounds and Perspectives

As programmer journalists talk about how they came to combine facility with code and journalism, we see a process of discovery that has developed outside the traditional technical route taken by hacker journalists who come later to journalism. Programmer journalists describe their backgrounds as either rooted in traditional journalism schools or in more humanities-based majors in college. They often tell a story of teaching themselves to code in their spare time. Many programmers are self-taught, too, and programming involves a considerable amount of new learning as languages change and improve, but these journalists are journalists before they ever become programmers.

Sisi Wei, a journalist at *ProPublica* and formerly of *The Washington Post*, told me that she had been a journalism student at Northwestern whose only introduction to programming was a quick intro to Flash programming in a journalism class, though Flash is now obsolete (yet it was helpful to her at the time). Wei took one Introduction to Programming for Non-Majors class to make sure she was learning the right things,[50] but mostly, she spent time "learning programming through extra-curriculars and summers." In her observation, it's actually a "common problem in the room" that most journalists are programmers without CS degrees and are self-taught, meaning they won't "confidently say they are developers,"[51] though she thinks this confidence issue is changing.

Emily Chow, a programmer journalist at *The Washington Post*, calls herself a "journalist-developer." She tells a story similar story to Wei's, also coming out of the Medill program, and she joined Wei for an independent study with a professional programmer journalist. "I taught myself to code," she said. "We had a one-week Flash intro. . . . I thought I might be a writer or a photographer, but people coached me."[52] These stories are compounded over and over by some of the leading figures in the interactive news world, including Aron Pilhofer, head of *The New York Times* team, who had been a computer-assisted reporter before morphing into the self-taught programmer journalist he is today.

*The New York Times*' Jeremy Bowers also shared his experience in an email: "I identify as a journalist → programmer rather than a programmer → journalist because I learned to write software ad-hoc after getting my job at a newspaper and was a political science/English major in college." This ad-hoc programming knowledge still means, though, that Bowers can spend most of his day working in code, as I observed him doing when I visited NPR.[53]

Some journalists have had a lifelong interest in programming but focused on building a career in journalism. John Keefe of WNYC "programmed for money as a kid" but became a straight-up traditional news director for the public radio station. In his spare time, however, he began thinking how interactive journalism should tell a story and tell it "really well in a way that you can't . . . easily in word or sound." He explained that he got as "good as he could get" and relied on conferences and the help of other programmer journalists in New York to show him what he didn't understand.[54] In fact, he recounted for me how he learned some programming from a few fellow New York journalists in exchange for Chinese food.

And Danny DeBelius of NPR is a programmer journalist who never imagined he'd end up working with code. He studied journalism at the University of Colorado. "I didn't have a lot of digital skills," he told me. "I think I took one electronic [journalism] class . . . maybe it was the intro to HTML." He interned at the Boulder *Daily Camera* and began the "unglamorous role of getting content on to the digital CMS" for two years until the terrible graveyard shift so burnt him out that he went to work in a guitar shop. DeBelius got hired at the *Rocky Mountain News* to design special projects, such as election coverage in 2004, and the rest of his career took off. DeBelius told me, "I think most would say I'd fall into the programmer journalist category as I do spend a significant amount of my day writing code."[55]

These programmer journalists spend much of their time working with data. We will see this focus on data and programming in chapter 4, where we will look at the workflow of interactive journalism teams. Their work involves either rendering the data ready for particular presentation or potentially crunching the data for stories. The raw material for much of their software is data, though certainly not all of it. They must know how to work with data and how to make it into a software product that has an unstructured but clear narrative. Often, programmer journalists have the goal of creating stories through interactives wherein software is the output and data is the input. At times, they may be called data journalists, and many programmer journalists might call themselves data journalists because of their intense work with data. However, I want to suggest that data journalists may be data specialists and far less focused on data visualization and interactive presentation—though they may indeed do some of this. And many programmer journalists may also fit this description as data experts. One can be both a programmer journalist and a data journalist; or one can be just a data journalist according to the separations suggested by the evidence compiled here (data journalists spend most, if not all, of their time specifically working with the actual ins and outs of data).

## Thinking about Stories

Like Michelle Minkoff, programmer journalists identify first as journalists, though their titles might range from interactive news producer to data developer to news application designer. Many programmer journalists say that they are always thinking about the story first. They have some theories on how they are different from hacker journalists who focus on development first rather than working with journalism. Nonetheless, what they bring to journalism is a distinct approach to thinking about how to create journalism.

Scott Klein described the attitude he saw as pervasive from the journalists whose background was not in programming. "Software is outside of them and journalist is inside of them. . . . There is much less magic to software development. They work primarily as journalists."[56] Within the professional tradition of journalism, the programmer journalists affiliate themselves with a tradition of working within the goals of first telling a story related to public information and then thinking about how they tell that story in code. They are journalists first, not coders. Sisi Wei, who works for Klein, added that the perception of her team was focused on being journalist as well as developer. "[You] are not just a developer. . . . You are thinking about things editorially." Still, she pointed out that the idea of being a journalist was "probably what people cared about most."

Jeremy Bowers, who was deeply invested in solving the technical problems of the NPR interactive projects when I visited the news organization, defined in an email what he sees as the different ways of thinking about approaching programming and journalism.

> There are some projects that programmers → journalists won't enjoy building because they do not represent an interesting technical challenge. Many journalism problems are not particularly interesting technologically (though of course, some are). The result is that journalists → programmers are interested in solving these "easy" problems that have high journalism value and programmers → journalists might be more interested in solving more complicated technical problems that have a lesser journalism impact.

He added:

> Many programmers → journalists I know become obsessed with not repeating themselves and thus want to build "platforms" or other broad tools. As a journalist → programmer, I have a higher tolerance for repetitive software.[57]

So for Bowers, the distinction is that hacker journalists may be more focused on the origination of new technology. They may be interested in solving new problems rather than thinking about how to work within what they have already created—and may be more focused on technical solutions rather than on the journalism output. This difference in focus might be a point of contention between hacker journalists and programmer journalists, yet it seems to be more simply a distinction rather than a point of disagreement.

Notably, it is also clear that ideals from hacking have indeed permeated the newsroom. Programmer journalists do speak about what they do in terms of hacking culture; the major difference, however, is that programmer journalists make comparisons between the programming process and traditional journalism processes, looking for links rather than positing differences between the two. These programmer journalists talk about rapid prototyping and experimentation, but they frame this kind of approach to programming in much the same way one might approach traditional journalism.

Sisi Wei argued that journalism has much to do with the programming process: "I guess things in programming go hand in hand with journalism stuff; there's almost an analog with journalism. Journalism is a lifetime of learning and new information, and with programming you have to have the willingness to try new things all the time because technology is changing so fast. . . . You are iterating and it's very similar to writing drafts and cutting things out."[58] However, she also emphasized that since technology is rapidly changing, and as the tech world introduces new products and services all the time, a programmer journalist simply has to be adaptable. As we have observed in the process of moving to online journalism in traditional newsrooms, journalists are certainly not always the most adaptable to new technological challenges.

Minkoff similarly agreed that programmer journalism seemed to be a lot like breaking-news stories. She pointed out that programming interactives fit the model of story writing used at the AP, her current site of employment.

> We have tried the agile process—and I think that is a lot about what we do in a news meeting: you get multiple iterations of news and that's especially the case at the AP. The first thing that happens is that you get a news alert and then you have a quick story—the 70-word story, and then you write through it, and sometimes that's very intense, and that's a lot like technology, like I'm going to show something but it doesn't mean it's the final product.[59]

These journalists see the importance of rapid iteration. The agile software development process focuses on quick development and on releasing beta versions before a final product. The idea that you could release a product for consumption that might not be completely error-free—at least from the programming side—seems different from the idea of putting out a fast story. In the case of the AP, that fast story can't have any errors—the quick first draft matches well with the idea of the quick first draft of an interactive, but there is more room for experimentation within building software.

These programmer journalists much more clearly identify with journalism than hacker journalists. They are journalists first and then programmers. What they say about how they approach interactive journalism puts journalism at the center of what they do—the story comes first. On the other hand, some of their identity and ways of thinking about themselves and how they do what they do are distinct from previous kinds of journalism—a focus on experimentation and a work product based in code.

For the first time ever, journalists equate the importance of knowing code with doing journalism. Programmer journalists work in both worlds in order to further the journalistic process. This provides evidence of the expansion of the profession as journalism adopts individuals with new skills. Similarly, these journalists embrace ways of thinking that are not found in traditional journalism. The focus on trying new things that require distinct adaptation has not been shown to be particularly prevalent among the majority of journalists, though they are trying. The ability to put something imperfect out for audience consumption, such as experimental beta versions, signals a departure from journalistic norms. These are commonalities, though, with their counterparts, the hacker journalists, signaling the consistency of both of these specialists within the larger occupational subgroup's development. One might think that there would be some conflict between hacker journalists and programmer journalists in their slightly different approaches to thinking about journalism work, and while workflow does vary depending on who manages a team, as we will see in chapter 4, programmer journalists and hacker journalists work side by side, well-integrated into newsroom teams.

## Data Journalists: Uncertainty in a Definition

To many people in journalism and academia, data journalism is an all-encompassing term for the type of work described here. But it's not entirely accurate. Not all interactive journalists are data journalists, and not all data journalists are interactive journalists. Data journalism can include numbers, statistics, names, categories, documents, and other kinds of information that can be coded and arranged in ways that computers can help analyze in the service of journalism. Howard's definition of data journalism (reiterated once more) brings some clarity: "the gathering, cleaning, organizing, analyzing, visualizing, and publishing data to support the creation of acts of journalism."[60] But data journalists should be broken out as a specific category, one that stands on its own. Based on the empirical data, data journalists are distinct; they are primarily working with data in the service of stories, actively trying to tell stories with data, and spend most of their time working specifically with data. Certainly, some of these data journalists may be programmer journalists or hacker journalists, who may also at times work with data, but data journalists employ data as their primary focus in their work—and many of these journalists do not see themselves primarily as working with code. In fact, some data journalists may not do any coding at all.

Rather than being associated with programming, the term data journalism has its historical origins in the American term for earlier ways of working with data in the newsroom: "computer-assisted reporting" (CAR) and its practitioners, computer-assisted reporters. Data journalism is, in fact, an evolution of CAR. Colloquially put, working with data does not an interactive journalist make; instead, for a data journalist to be included under the umbrella of interactive journalism, he or she has to be working on interactives. These terms matter, but let's be explicit: data journalists can be interactive journalists, but they aren't interactive journalists if they aren't making interactives—this should make sense. If they aren't making interactives, they're probably a lot closer to CAR journalists, discussed below. And it doesn't quite matter, in fact, whether data journalists can actually code—just as long as they're creating interactives. This seems complicated, but when you read the empirical discussion and how journalists talk about themselves, it makes sense. Thus, it's important to look at how data journalists talk about what they do and how they understand their work. Even though not all data journalism is interactive journalism, much of it can be included under this emerging subspecialty.

As Alexander Howard points out, everyone in newsrooms uses computers: all journalism is computer-assisted now. CAR might be said to represent a point in time when data was used simply in the service of the story, whereas now, the data can be a story on its own. Data journalism seems to be a better term to describe and account for the rise in data and also for the more comprehensive ways of using computation and visualization to look beyond just anecdotes to overarching systemic analysis. Data journalism brings the entirety of the data set to the public, at least as much as possible, whereas CAR journalists would likely use internal databases sharing just key details for their analysis.

As Howard and others point out, perhaps the public's first introduction to data journalism in interactive form may be coverage of WikiLeaks. *The Guardian*, *The New York Times* and *Der Spiegel* all put out searchable, interactive databases and maps, allowing users to browse through the massive amounts of war logs and, later, diplomatic correspondence. Nate Silver, statistician wunderkind, relied on his data journalism skills to accurately predict the 2008 and 2012 presidential elections. In 2012, he drew 20 percent of *The New York Times*' online traffic.[61] Other prime examples, as Terry Flew and his colleagues suggest, include the disclosures in *The Guardian* of the expenses of parliament ministers.[62] Insight into nearly everything, from the 2010 earthquake in Haiti to data about campaign contributions, can now be found at many newspapers and some broadcast and cable sites across the world.

Today, however, what some call data journalism differs from CAR reporting in seeing the end product not as a story but instead as a "productive artifact" of "information filtering."[63] As Powers explains, the computer programmer and the Web developer were long singled out as non-journalists and thought of as unrelated to editorial work; they were considered "different tribes."[64] In interactive journalism, the programmer and the journalist are brought together as one in the context of interactive journalism, moving beyond just using computers to enable journalism but using computers to actually create alternative forms of news. In data journalism, computers aid journalism, but the work may not be directed toward a visible, tangible, usable output for news consumers.

Data journalism is a contested term. Is everyone in the newsroom doing data journalism if they work with data in some way? Is there a level of sophistication? In what way is their work a legacy of computational work? Journalists I spoke with tried to articulate the differences between past practices and the way CAR still works in the newsroom—as both CAR and data journalism involve using a computer to analyze data in the service of a story. Aron Pilhofer, head of Interactive News at *The New York Times*, explained in 2011:[65]

> A lot of times, people doing CAR have skills very similar to folks that work for me [in the interactive news team]. . . . X has exactly my background as a congressional reporter and did a lot of database analysis, what we would call CAR back in the day, and is now a coder.
>
> The difference is that interactive news is primarily focused on telling stories via web applications and making th[ose] public facing, using data to construct a narrative, or creat[ing] tools.

He tried to articulate whom he saw as a data journalist within definitional constructs:

> [Who are] data journalists versus programmer journalists? In the last three years, a lot of terms have been coined. Data journalism is a loose term that back in the day meant someone who does CAR. Now the boundaries are much broader.
>
> What unites us is that we are building Web apps. CAR was fundamentally in pursuit of doing [written] stories. The Web app doesn't have an obvious lead. I don't think it matters what terms you use. You don't have to be a developer to be a data journalist under this broad definition.

Pilhofer brings out a number of critical points in this interview. First, he distinguishes interactive journalism and data journalism from the traditional forms of CAR. Interactive journalism, and today's data journalism, is focused on the Web application. While data journalism certainly has a legacy in CAR, CAR was about a traditional story; data journalists can create tools or Web apps for public-facing data.

Another key observation here is his distinction that data journalists do not have to be developers. This suggests that while data journalists are invested in a world of code, they do not actually have to be creating code. So programmer journalists may know code and may write in code, and some programmer journalists may consider themselves also working with data or even call themselves data journalists; data journalists do not necessarily have to work with code to be considered under the broader umbrella of "what unites us"—which is working to the Web application. Thus, in this rendition of the term, data journalism can indeed be different from traditional data reporting because it has this online element.

Data journalist Matt Stiles at NPR explained his perspective on CAR versus his current work: "It is different because data is working on a spreadsheet versus working on JavaScript or Python for a project. . . . It's not that different from CAR but there is an online component."[66] Stiles distinguishes current data journalism from past CAR: old spreadsheets would be Excel, whereas today's data journalists would use more sophisticated programming languages online.

Head of the News Apps team at *ProPublica*, Scott Klein, a programmer journalist who works with data, went further in his attempt to delineate the evolution of data journalism:

> CAR in the 70s or 80s meant working with computers but not in an interactive way. You would look at a data set with a class prediction [for example] and go and find and write a story about a few of your examples. The newer path is to expose entire data sets to people in a clear and honest way—[asking] how do we show it to people, with analysis and stats and clean data.[67]

Today, as Klein went on to say, manipulating data sets is in the service of the whole body of data, "instead of finding two or three examples and working hard over weeks to find anecdotes" [as you would with CAR].[68] CAR, then, was about showing just a few data points, and data journalism means making all data points available to the public, or making it possible, at least, to examine all data points in a systematic way. The efforts must be focused on *"how do we show it to people"* or rendering the data sets in a way that people can easily manipulate. The output is a news application, not a static story. In addition, old-school CAR was not interactive.

Some journalists focus explicitly on what's different about the journalism—and speak less about the interactive elements, suggesting that data journalism *does not* have to have anything to do with an online component. Instead, data journalism is an intellectual approach. Journalist Derek Willis of *The New York Times* gives this definition: "Basically, if a journalist works with tools that assist in interviewing, analyzing or conveying data for stories of any kind in any medium, then that person could be called a data journalist. I think it can be divided into roughly two camps, with some overlap: journalists who work with data for analysis, and journalists who work with data for presentation."[69] The first descriptor seems to describe much more closely the traditional CAR journalists, while the idea of data for presentation seems to more accurately describe the way I categorize data journalists here. Willis does not even speak about the idea of visualizing data in his definition.

Some journalists have attempted to work together to standardize some form of a definition. At the 2011 MozFest (a media and computing festival hosted by the Mozilla Web company), journalists from Europe and the United States came together to create the *Data Journalism Handbook*. Paul Bradshaw of Birmingham City University wrote the introduction, which attempted to tackle the fluid idea of data journalism. In it, he began with the rejection of the idea that the definition of data journalism was simply journalism done with data. He noted that twenty years ago, journalists simply thought of data as a collection of numbers "mostly gathered on a spreadsheet."[70] But at the time, he notes, "that was pretty much the only sort of data that journalists dealt with."

The difference today, Bradshaw observes, are the "new possibilities that open up when you combine the traditional 'nose for news' and ability to tell a compelling story, with the sheer scale and range of digital information now available."[71] He adds to this definition that it involves programming or software to automate gathering data, combining information, or finding connections between "hundreds of thousands of documents."[72] Data journalism, he notes, is "often told with interactives—and the data may be a source or a tool to tell stories."[73] Every example in the book he offers is an interactive. But data journalism is not *always* about interactives, according to this handbook. Despite disagreement around the definitions, the guide is significant in its own right because it signals an attempt to standardize and codify the subspecialty by creating a sense of accepted practices with the larger goals of furthering this kind of journalism.

Notably, in Europe some journalists tend to use the term "data journalism" to describe interactive journalism as a whole, not just activities associated with processing data. But depending on the organization, one could be called a developer or a data journalist and still be working on interactives either way. According to Pilhofer, an American, "Data journalism is just what they call interactive journalism over there."[74]

Yet this is not always the case. In some newsrooms, such as *Zeit Online*, data journalist Sascha Venohr explained to me that "developers" did the programming, whereas he did nothing with code and instead "worked on interactives with data," a distinction that seemed to be more and more confusing as I asked him for clarification.[75] At *The Guardian*, data journalists kept the DataBlog and worked with publicly available data, writing posts. The "developers" rendered the complicated interactives for major projects and stories such as the Olympics, yet this kind of work still required data—but these individuals were more skilled with code. The BBC mirrored *The Guardian*'s distinctions, with "developers," "designers," and "data journalists" on its News Specials team. This suggests the terms are just as confusing in Europe as they are in the United States.

Whether all programmer journalists are data journalists is a matter of degree and depends on self-perception and perceived amount of working with data. Almost all U.S. journalists I spoke with who were programmer journalists said that they might call themselves data journalists if the term were loosely applied. Many of these programmer journalists are working in what Fink and Anderson characterize as key components of data journalism: data procurement, graphic design, and statistical analysis.[76] But many are quick to point to the "the real data journalist," thus identifying the journalist procuring the data or doing statistical analysis as distinct from programmer journalists or hacker journalists.

Data journalists are *interactive journalists* when they distinguish what they do by having this additional online component. Findings here confirm that data journalism is difficult to define and comes out of a larger tradition of CAR. When there is focus on Web apps, software, and/or interactivity, data journalists are connected most directly with the larger subfield of interactive journalism.

## Not a Coder

Pilhofer helps us to understand that not all data journalists are programmer journalists, as not all of them code. Some data journalists can't code at all and instead focus their time on cleaning, sorting, and interpreting data. Others use less sophisticated tools to build interactives. They remain integral to the construction of the subfield, though. Their work still relies on additional code layered on top of an existing Web site. The code they use is often already programmed within existing software. They could not create interactives without working in this world of code.

Simon Rogers, a journalist at *The Guardian* and head of DataBlog, described himself as a data journalist. But he doesn't code and instead relies on existing libraries and templates to create visualizations for his work. His goal was to make data more easily available, searchable, and interactive for users. He told me: "After 9/11, I began collecting a lot of data sets, and I asked if I could have an open platform data blog. I was hoping to see if we could give the collected information of the paper via a data blog to give it a longer life."[77]

However, he emphasized that he was not a programmer or a coder in any way.[78] But he was using the free tools that made it possible to create the kind of interactives—primarily the free Google Fusion program, which offers a variety of options for creating interactives where the code is already complete, from charts to maps, and relies extensively on spreadsheets. Other noncoding data journalists may work with tools as simple as Microsoft Excel or Access, or tools that enable interactives like Tableau, Carto DB or Data Wrapper. Some journalists do learn the basics of code to help input data, scrape data from Web sites, adjust interactives, or become more proficient and begin on the road to programmer journalism.

These journalists don't work with sophisticated code, but they see what they do as critically integrated into a traditional reporting project. Brian Boyer called his staffer Matt Stiles the "real data journalist" on the NPR team. Stiles explained why: "I have a reporter sensibility. I am the guy with a phone on my desk. I am the one with the FOIAs. I am the reporter getting the data."[79] He noted:

> I wouldn't call myself a coder. I can write some basic code in JavaScript, Python, SQL and R, but I'm not a programmer by training or skill, like the other members of the NPR team. . . . I do make interactive graphics, but I can't be trusted to build a complex Web application. I'd need help with that.
>
> I'm also slower than a lot of "coder/journalists" at even basic code like CSS or HTML. The difference between me and (some of) them is that I got ten years of traditional news reporting experience before I started hacking a bit.[80]

Stiles brought up a number of key points in his self-assessment. He sees himself as a data journalist, and he does define interactive graphics as part of his daily work. But he doesn't do any sophisticated coding, though he knows at least some code. He sees himself as having and using traditional journalism skills to do his work.

Other journalists agreed but noted some differences in their expertise. Mona Chalabi, a data journalist who works on *The Guardian*'s Reality Check blog and renders her work in Google Fusion for visualizations, explained what she does this way: "As a data journalist I suppose for me the way that I explain it to other people is that I work with numbers—that's what concerns me."[81] She said that she visualizes the data to help make it easier for people to engage with the data, though not all of her work is always interactive or always visualized.

Each year at the NICAR conference, data journalists can learn more code—the conference program now has a serious programming component intended to help data journalists become more proficient with using code to both analyze and present stories. For instance, the 2014 schedule included a workshop that promised:

> Give us four hours and your laptop, and we'll send you into NICAR with a fully-functioning data-crunching machine and the knowledge to use it.
> One of the biggest hurdles to learning programming is the often-bewildering process of setting up your computer.

Promised setups included the following programming potential add-ons:

> Participants will walk away with a fully functioning dev machine (on their personal laptop) that includes: VirtualBox, Ubuntu/Xubuntu, csvkit, Python, Git, Django, SQLite, MySQL, PostgreSQL, PostGIS, PANDAS, Ilene, virtualenv/virtualenvwrapper, QuantumGIS, Node.js, NPM, Ruby, Rails, RVM, Bower, Grunt, Fabric, Yeoman, CIR news app template.[82]

Other sessions included: NewsCamp, getting started with data viz, a mapping mini boot camp that promised: "ArcGIS, QGIS, PostGIS, TileMill, GDAL, GeoDjango and probably a few more acronyms for good measure"; A PyCar mini boot camp, which advertised: "[We] teach journalists basic programming concepts using the Python language."[83]

Thus, we can see that there are no bright lines between programmer journalists and data journalists, though programmer journalists do spend time fluent in code and journalism. Data journalists identify as working closely with the analysis of data, and see themselves as concerned with the presentation of this data for the public. And when they express what they do, we see how they associate data journalism within the umbrella of interactive journalism. Not all data journalism is interactive journalism, and not all data journalists are interactive journalists. However, this close association with programmer journalists as well as the story output and goals of interactive journalism signals the importance of including this subgroup in the larger understanding of interactive journalism.

Data journalists have the closest legacy to traditional journalism. Computer-assisted reporters have been part of journalism since the 1960s. Their work with data has been included in many award-winning stories, and concurrent with the rise of graphics, in graphical representations as well. Data journalists work with categorical, numeric, and document-based data across all vectors of social life, rather than on relying on qualitative accounts for journalism. The emergence of this subgroup of reporters signals an expansion of the profession as journalists have needed new skills to account for more sophisticated data. Increased computing power has given these data journalists the tools to not only process more data but also to work in an interactive environment—without knowing more code.

## Rounding Up Definitions and People

The goal of this chapter was to help elucidate the types of people who do the work of interactive journalism. To understand the formation of the subspecialty of interactive journalism, it's important to understand the backgrounds and self-perceptions of the actors involved in carving out this new element of journalism. We find three key groups: hacker journalists, programmer journalists, and data journalists. These categories work more as Venn diagrams than they do necessarily independent categories. In some cases, backgrounds are similar; in other cases, ways of approaching journalism are similar.

Hacker journalists come to newsrooms from programming backgrounds. They often work primarily in a coding capacity, though some do share A-1 bylines and work with data analysis. They may not identify as journalists but are called journalists here because they must know how to communicate in a newsroom workflow, build products for acts of journalism, and are integrated into editorial workflow.

Programmer journalists are as fluent in code as they are in journalism, but they started with no background in coding and identify first as journalists. They speak primarily about their focus on the story, often work with data (though their manipulation of data may not be as sophisticated as that of data journalists, who spend more time with data), and their output is primarily interactives that serve stories on their own and complement traditional news stories.

Data journalists may sometimes be grouped under the programmer journalism category but also may be journalists who are not fluent in code. These are the kin of the old-school computer-assisted reporters, who relied on computers to produce a few key insights for stories. Now, data journalists work to reveal far more data and often use computer programs in the service of interactives. Their focus on an online component ties them into the larger subfield of interactive journalism, though not all data journalists will be interactive journalists. And it should be noted that at some large news organizations, like *The New York Times*, the graphics desk works on interactives, too, and some of these visual journalists know incredible amounts about data *and* code (including "Snow Fall"), and some visual journalists argue that they specialize in data visualization but cannot program, even if they do a little, like Alberto Cairo, interviewed in this book.

It is helpful to have conceptual categories because they map how journalists talk about themselves. Self-perception gives us insight into how journalists ultimately see their jurisdiction over work. These divisions help us understand similarities and differences in ways of thinking, which ultimately helps us determine how these backgrounds contribute to the development of abstract knowledge that expands the profession. There are particular aspects, such as the various ways journalists came to programming, that do suggest some natural divisions of how they describe their own backgrounds and approaches. Similarly, these distinctions help show how the subspecialty is negotiating definitions as it develops internal cohesion. When it comes to working together, differences among these smaller subsets of interactive journalism complement and enhance the functionality of the product and process.

Some journalists reading these descriptions are likely to resist these lines I have drawn, however faint or permeable some of the divisions may seem to be. Journalists may likely want to claim that they have all of the qualities that I see as actually distinct among these groups. What hacker journalist doesn't want to say that they think about the story? Programmer journalists and data journalists of course want to claim that they are deeply inspired by programming perspectives, and indeed they are. But there are differences, and these differences, while perhaps of degree, do reveal themselves in the data.

It matters to include hacker journalists in the discussion of "Who is a journalist?" because hacker journalists need to be recognized as included in the larger development of the subfield. Their role is integral to creating the work product of interactives. It's important to recognize programmer journalists because it underscores how journalists are now learning different skills and approaches beyond what any journalists ever before have considered journalistic work. And the discussion of data journalism reveals how dealing with data in the newsroom has evolved and how this is integrated into the larger subfield.

The rise of the subspecialty of interactive journalism becomes clearer as we define these different actors within this new form of journalism. We see different ways that external pressures may influence each group. Recall that journalism is challenged not only by economic pressures but also by advances across the development of a more sophisticated and engaging Web, which underscores the importance of making the journalism profession expand and adapt.

There is little contest that emerges between professions. Programming claims no jurisdiction on this public-service enterprise to provide individuals with knowledge about their communities. Rather, journalists take skills and thinking from programming and apply this without any sort of evidence of internal professional tension. This signals a departure from traditional notions of the development of professions, where there is latent contest between different ways of thinking. It may well be that interactive journalists are accepted into the newsroom with little resistance because they are viewed as so critical to change and the future of journalism. Newsrooms appear open to these changes, even if they suggest at times a somewhat different approach to news work. And internally, journalists within traditional journalism are not approaching these coding projects and data interactives asking to do them or hoping to take over these roles; rather, the backgrounds distinguish these individuals as having skills and perspectives no one else can claim. Similarly, an acceptance of the dominant norms of professional journalism across these new kinds of journalists may help integration—their work in the service of a story, a public-service orientation and aspiration to work, and the belief in traditional journalistic practices, even if the output is an interactive.

We see how journalism is expanding its professional domain as journalists take up code. These journalists help the profession make a claim to relevance. Never before have journalists—editorial members of the newsroom—taken up code in these larger numbers and in this significant a way to the extent that it is literally changing the form of journalistic work. This development makes hacking relevant within the newsroom and makes journalism more adaptable to the demands of the digital environment. But it is important to see what, exactly, these journalists do inside newsrooms to create this kind of new journalism. To this end, we look at how journalists work and how they explain what they do.

# 4 Inside the Interactive Journalism Newsroom

Just fourteen miles outside Washington, D.C., lies one of the most dangerous regularly paddled whitewater rapids in the United States. Great Falls of the Potomac River, a series of complicated drops, waterfalls, and swirling whitewater hydraulics, is one of the steepest waterfalls on any river on the East Coast. The hazardous drops of Great Falls include The Spout, a drop of eighteen to twenty feet alone; Charlie's Hole, which can swallow and recirculate an entire kayak; and Subway, a sixteen- to eighteen-foot rush of water with a cave at the bottom that has taken the lives of two expert kayakers. Great Falls, a class 5 rapid, can only be successfully run by the most expert kayakers. If an onlooker were to fall in, it would mean almost certain death.

In the two miles below Great Falls along the Potomac lies a series of other charging rapids with water that on normal days can have whirlpools larger than a kayak and waves that stand five feet tall. The rough waters appear calm from the edges of the stunning Mather Gorge. And in the D.C. summer heat, visitors to the popular Great Falls National Park find the water especially enticing. Despite the posted signs warning people not to swim, people still do, often with grave consequences.

In the summer of 2013, four visitors were claimed by the river: a woman who came to the park from China, a recent high school graduate, a soldier with a promising career, and a respected kayaker who simply got unlucky, trapped in what experts call the most dangerous place on the towering falls. Countless others who jumped into the seemingly placid waters had to be rescued—by kayakers and the local firefighting rescue crew.

*The Washington Post* diligently chronicled these dangers. But it wasn't enough to warn people. Something more, journalists decided, needed to be done. So the graphics team at *The Post* went to work, using their wide set of skills to put together a compelling interactive designed to tell the story of the river's dangers in a way that words on a page simply could not: the mission was to give the reader a sense of the river's power in order to prevent other needless deaths and dangerous accidents.

In the past, the graphics team could have put together a static graphic—a drawing of the river with labels to show the rapids, or perhaps some sort of chart of the water's depth. But the graphics team of 2013 wasn't the graphics team of old. Instead, interactive journalists were on staff, and the talents of this new team composition showed in the final product.

In "The Perils at Great Falls," the reader is greeted with a stunning experience. The river is animated, showing the current clearly moving in the water. Conical shapes hover gently above, with a click revealing more information about key river features. A static graphic within the page invites the reader to look at still more information. A clear, brief story brings an explanatory element to the experience. The combination of text and the user-directed engagement with the interactive elements offers a visitor to the page the chance to meander over the presentation. A solid week of constant, rapid-fire coding, reporting, and skillful engagement with programs like Adobe After Effects, a software used by gaming companies, brought this to life. As programmer journalist Emily Chow put it, "We have always done the explanatory double truck, but we can improve the entire experience on the web in a way that works."[1]

In newsrooms across the country and the world, work like *The Post*'s "The Perils at Great Falls"[2] is now a regular part of news production. Many newsrooms are adding interactive journalists to their staffs if they can, though outlets are finding their own rhythms and processes for working with these new types of journalists. Those newsrooms with dedicated interactive staff are particularly lucky, for these news organizations can devote resources to developing a consistent stream of interactives. At *Al Jazeera English* in Doha, one interactive journalist stands ready to teach fellow journalists how to work with interactives. In Washington, D.C., a team of seven sits together on the perimeter of the brand new NPR newsroom, speaking in what at times seems to be an unintelligible babble of technology terms. At *The New York Times*, interactive journalists balance the immediate deadline with longer stories. At *The Guardian*, data journalists work with basic tools to create daily stories. A look at two Associated Press bureaus, New York and Washington, shows that the experience of interactive journalists couldn't be more different—with N.Y. focused on the daily deadline and D.C. focused on the long, investigative story.

The perils at Great Falls

From thundering falls to placid-looking shallows, deadly hazards lurk in water all along the Potomac River Gorge. Read related article.

Click on the markers to see the dynamics of the river.

THE RIVER CAN KILL — STAY OUT. That blunt warning greets visitors at Great Falls Park because subtlety hasn't deterred people from illegally wading, swimming and diving into this treacherous slice of the Potomac.

Since 2001, 27 people have died in river accidents in the area, including three since June. Few wore life jackets.

The death toll is low in the raging falls, because the danger is obvious and few people venture there. More often, the river's victims are people who came to hike, fish or swim and who disappeared after entering tame-looking water downstream.

The geology is complex, but in a nutshell, 200 million years of the river's flow barely eroded some of the bedrock. Waves of sediment from melting glaciers in western Pennsylvania exposed the same kinds of jagged cracks, outcroppings and rocks under the water as you see above it.

Water rushing through this obstacle course creates rolling underwater currents in even the calmest-looking places.

"People think, 'If this place was dangerous, they wouldn't let me be down here,'" said Lawrence Mullin, a member of the white-water rescue team from Fairfax County.

But people do get hurt in the park, and more than half the injuries that occur in the river are fatal, according to a 2011 study by the National Park Service.

This graphic looks at three types of areas, but most of the hazards listed can occur anywhere in the roughly 15-mile Potomac River Gorge, according to the scientists, kayakers, police and National Park Service officials who lent their expertise to this project.

FASTER THAN IT LOOKS

Narrower stretches such as this near the Rocky Islands may appear easy to cross, but currents quickly capture swimmers, waders and people who slip and fall into the water.

"The Perils at Great Falls," *The Washington Post*

Through an in-depth look based on these seven field sites, the chapter is intended to offer a thick description of how interactive journalists work. We learn about the time pressures these journalists face, how they interact with other members of the newsroom, and the work product they produce. One point of contrast is whether interactive journalists are producing daily or more project-oriented work. Another differentiation is whether interactive journalists generate their own standalone work or instead pair their efforts with other editorial initiatives.

The forms of interactives produced vary across the newsrooms explored here. Many of the interactives I discuss are data-driven but vary in the ways the data are acquired and the sophistication of the analysis—some could not exist without careful searching and requests for federal documents, others exist only because of public databases, and still others come from data journalists generate on their own. But there are also other kinds of interactives, discussed here and elsewhere, ones that are focused on different ways of storytelling that are not explicitly geared to be data-driven; for instance, "The Perils at Great Falls" is more focused on visual storytelling than data presentation.

This exploration of how people work and what they do gives insight into professionalism. Sociologist Andrew Abbott looks at jurisdiction over work—what a profession actually *does*—to understand the claim to expertise it offers. In each vignette of a newsroom, we can see how interactive journalists establish their domain over the kind of work that it aims to offer. What is less clear from these daily examples caught up in the everyday motion of news are more complex considerations, such as the kind of normative implications for the work that these journalists do—the abstract knowledge they bring to journalism. But before taking a step back to explore knowledge, it is important to consider what, exactly, interactive journalism means in the context of everyday work.

This field-based research has been gathered between 2011 and 2015, and much has changed. Digital technology moves quickly, and the profession can change and adapt quickly as well (though culture change is often slow). What you see portrayed here reflects one particular snapshot for each of these media organizations and is not intended to be a definitive account of how they work at the moment you are reading this book. That said, these ethnographic details from the field are nonetheless valuable because they illustrate broader trends that are invoked by interactive journalism and its relationship to the larger profession. The specifics may change, but the overarching temporal, organizational, and structural arrangements of work described in this chapter are indicative of patterns and processes worth unpacking for larger trends about how programming is changing journalism.

## *Al Jazeera English*: A Small Staff for a Coordinated Effort

In summer 2012, I journeyed to Doha for two weeks to explore the *Al Jazeera English* newsroom's use of interactives. At the time, *Al Jazeera English* was the only portion of the *Al Jazeera* empire that was producing English-language news. Its broadcast could be seen only in a limited number of markets: D.C., New York, and Burlington, Vermont. Even post–Arab Spring, *AJE* had yet to find a spot on the cable TV lineup and faced some latent resistance from big-time cable providers.[3]

The push for interactives at *AJE* was motivated by two key factors: audience and editorial vision. The Web site at the time represented one of the few ways the United States could get *AJE* content; each month there were eight million visitors to the site, with more than 50 percent coming from the United States. And due to *AJE*'s quirks, livestreaming was available but clips from prerecorded shows were not available in the United States. This meant that online journalism was even more critical to *AJE*'s news efforts. From an editorial perspective, *AJE* was simply covering areas that most people were not paying attention to—and the news organization often had access to citizen journalism content no one else had. Interactives offered *AJE* a prime opportunity to fulfill its mission of being the "voice of the voiceless" and the "voice of the global south."[4] Interactives could help bring a picture of these far-flung places that often were not covered by Western news in any great depth.

Given some of the complicated interactives I had seen online—maps of conflict zones with layers of photos, sounds, and videos, election guides, and user-generated content efforts—I expected a robust team. Instead, when I visited, I found just one full-time interactive journalist, Mohammed el-Haddad (Haddad), busily putting together a steady stream of interactives. He wasn't entirely alone, though, as he had his fellow traditionally text-based journalists to help him. On a day-to-day basis, Haddad had a seamless interaction with his reporters, who were learning on the fly to help put together these interactives.

Haddad sat in the middle of the online reporters and online op-ed editor on the second floor of the newsroom. There were no cubicles, just low manila tables with computers on them, though some journalists worked on laptops. The online-focused newsroom was upstairs, a staircase away from the big production desk for the network, and a short walk from a vantage point that overlooked the set, where anchors rotated on and off. Other online text-based journalists, though, sat in the middle of this television production area, and these journalists were charged with maintaining a quick pace of content to the Web site. Journalists rotated off this crushing minute-by-minute cycle, meaning that most online journalists were engaged with longer-term stories as well. It also meant that these journalists all knew Haddad.

Haddad's background was as a computer scientist. He told me, "My skills are mostly technical. I don't always know what the journalism side is, but I'm learning more and more."[5] His dad, though, had trained as a journalist, so Haddad came to *AJE* interested in how his skills from programming could be used in journalism.

During my newsroom visit, Haddad's main focus was on putting together an interactive about the European Union's fiscal situation. It was the height of the European debt crisis, with the world unsure about what kinds of loans Greece would need or whether there might be a bailout. I watched Haddad work closely with journalist Sam Bollier to help explain the debt crisis through an interactive.

Haddad often began his day looking at Visual.ly to get an idea of the best designs of good static infographics. He told me, "These are really nice, so you can get some good ideas," though "most of these are flat."[6] He critiqued a few with me, and complimented a few others. He told me that many of his projects weren't successful: a Yemen map he had put together had only garnered five thousand hits, but he shrugged and said, "You have to do the small stuff before you do the big stuff."[7] Haddad looked across the Web for inspiration to make sure his interactives kept improving. This search for inspiration from other news organizations and the industry adds further evidence that those in the subspecialty are coalescing around a common knowledge base, as we will see in chapter 5.

After working for the morning, Haddad regularly attended the 11 A.M. Web news meeting and was often given direction about the latest project. During one of the meetings I observed, the main online editor, Will Thorne, after talking about the difficulty of trying to parse what was happening to the Greek debt crisis, directed a question at Haddad: "Haddad, how is that Euro interactive? Let's give this a long run. We want that up—there's a lot of chatter about Greece and the European Union and whether there will be a loan or a bailout and whether it is going to help."[8] Haddad's mission, then, was to make an interactive that would make it easier for readers to understand the Greek debt through non-traditional storytelling.

Just a day earlier, on June 10, 2012, Bollier had begun working on the interactive with Haddad. Bollier was a text-focused online journalist who spent most of his time covering Europe and America. He was gearing up not only to add data to the interactive but also to help put it together. "This is my first time ever," Bollier told me, explaining he had never worked with the Google Fusion program.

His first step would be to find government Web sites and figure out debt stats. Then he wanted to find something emblematic of the country to use as a photo. But he also had design challenges, as was made clear by his back and forth with Haddad. He shouted, for instance, "Can you help me make the circles around Belgium and France look less concentric?" Bollier frowned as some of the labels for his graphs were appearing in the wrong places or upside down.

The next day, with more progress made, Haddad and Bollier began discussing the visual elements. For instance, Bollier asked whether a button should lead to a Google map of the Fiat headquarters in Italy, but Haddad offered a design perspective—that this would be ugly and unrelated. Bollier continued to work on the interactive while Haddad tested it on the iPad to see if it was "okay and not ugly." Meanwhile, in our conversations, Haddad was relatively unimpressed about the progress Bollier had been making, noting, "Everyone works off Google Docs; it's not a big deal to transition to Google Fusion."

Over the course of the afternoon, Haddad and Bollier were in constant conversation. To make the interactive more interesting, Haddad asked Bollier to look for *AJE* video packages from each country. Haddad tried to find the appropriate YouTube embed codes. Haddad looked up in the afternoon from his work to explain to me that the work on this project wasn't going to be a one-off. "The big challenge [with interactives] is building them in a way that they are still relevant and updatable." Haddad continued looking over the interactive and then told Bollier, "France looks empty."

Bollier came over from a few desks away for a quick update later in the afternoon. He confessed that he was struggling with a factual issue: just how much Spain's debt problem was adding to the bailout. And he had trouble finding images for each country. He sighed and asked, "Should we just use chocolate for Austria?" to which another journalist added, "that's the best try for the beginning."

Bollier remained hard at work for the rest of the day—after writing a quick story, he got back to the interactive around 6 P.M. "Moldova just doesn't have compelling data." Then he began to worry about whether people would understand the interactive. He conferred again with Haddad, who explained: "A lot of people who look at interactives don't know what to do. We need to have the instructions in big text." Haddad added, "Or we should make them really bold," and suggested Bollier write out three forms of directions for the reader. Together, they went through chart by chart as Haddad adjusted the slight mistakes that Bollier had made with Google Fusion. Haddad complimented Bollier: "Ireland is really good." And after a long two days, they finally got to the point where they could proof the entire interactive together, clicking through as many options and pathways as possible.[9]

This two-day vignette underscores the close collaboration between the interactive journalist and the rest of the editorial process. Haddad was integrated into the editorial workflow. He attended regular meetings with the

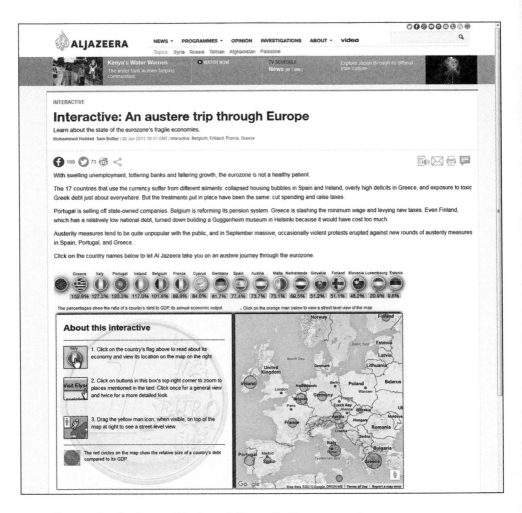

"Interactive: An Austere Trip through Europe," *Al Jazeera*

Web news team to find out the day's priorities and heard about what news would be covered and how. He was conversant in *AJE*'s daily journalism imperatives and even received directions from these meetings.

We can also see how closely the interactive journalist worked with the more traditional journalist on a project. Haddad had the vision for the design and the programming needs for the story. Though he left Bollier to find the information, Haddad played an important role in helping the editorial vision of this Eurozone interactive become more clear so users could freely navigate between countries to learn about debt. Haddad had to communicate like a journalist to understand the news sensibility that his colleagues wanted from this project.

What's particularly interesting about this example is the ready acceptance by the more traditional journalist to actually think about doing interactive journalism himself. His willingness to experiment with Google Fusion in order to make an interactive is simply seen as an extension of the journalism obligations for the day—not an added or unnecessary aspect of daily work. Bollier embraced Haddad as a guide in the process. This welcoming of interactive journalism suggests the importance of interactives within *AJE*.

I found other examples of close collaborations between text-focused journalists and Haddad in efforts to construct compelling interactives. The fighting that began in Syria in 2011 was receiving little coverage in the American press, but *AJE* was offering multiple updates each day. One journalist, Basma Atassi, was from Homs, the third-largest city in Syria and one of the sites at the center of the struggle. She had sources that were able to give her information that no other outlets were getting. With sound and video, she thought it was important to translate this into an output that she felt was more tangible than a story alone.

One Atassi-Haddad project was a timeline of unrest in Syria. Atassi explained, "I had my vision: at first I put together a Word document and I drew it out. Haddad told me what was technically possible."[10] Atassi said that she compiled views of Syrians in each of the provinces, "both pro and con views," and added, "there were so many pictures." Haddad built the interactive, she explained, while she did the reporting. They worked together to transform the material into an editorial project. From her perspective, the timeline had done well—"It's gotten 400 tweets, so there are good views for it." In this case, Atassi came with an idea and did the reporting, and through close collaboration with Haddad, the two turned this into a working interactive project.[11]

Atassi talked about another interactive she had created for the first anniversary of the "massacre in Homs." She had video and audio material: mobile phone pictures and sound from the day. She wanted to create a multimedia experience with a map and a timeline. She said: "We wanted to show what happened that day to have people imagine how much trouble activists are going through. For everyone from Homs, this was the most important day in their lives." Atassi wanted this interactive to be one that people could come back to over and over again. This could be a historic piece for people to reference, not just a news story but a testament to the ongoing struggle.[12] She explained how she put together an audio slide show with content from five witnesses. She had pictures from citizen journalists as well. But she couldn't integrate them into the interactive; instead, "Haddad put in the pictures."

Haddad also created the timeline with the key moments of the day as it unfolded across the city, based on Atassi's instructions. Again, the reporter and the interactive journalist worked together to build an interactive for a story beyond a linear, textual presentation. Haddad had to have the news judgment in order to communicate with Atassi, and Atassi had to be ready and willing to listen to Haddad in order to learn how her material could be best marshaled to provide the experience she wanted to offer. The Haddad-Atassi partnership resulted in two interactives replete with maps, timelines, photos—and one with sound and video.

On this small staff, we can see a direct, frequent communication flow between the reporter working on the project and the interactive specialist. The journalists may do more independent work to help the interactive along the way. With these examples, we can see how these interactions take place: Bollier was doing the reporting, finding the images, assembling the data, and even doing the initial interactive steps. Atassi found the images, talked to her sources, found video, sketched out timelines, and then collaborated with Haddad to put together the final vision for the interactives. We see on a micro level the partnership between the technical aspects and the content in the newsroom that led to the final interactives. And we see just how integrated the interactive journalist is within the daily news cycle. Moreover, we can see clearly how Haddad works as a journalist: he must be able to think about projects from an editorial perspective and understand how to communicate news components into an interactive. He has a news sensibility, although he is a programmer first.

The way the journalists spoke about Haddad adds to his credibility as a journalist and online team member. Dar Jamal, an online journalist, explained to me: "[Haddad] makes himself available to me. Basically I tell him I need a spotlight map and he gets a general idea. Haddad is an exceptional guy and whatever he gives me as a journalist . . . it is really cool. He'll make an interactive map and that map is journalism. He really adds a whole new dimension to what we are doing."[13] Atassi explained her perspective on Haddad's contributions: "What I like [about Haddad] is that he understands journalism. This guy understands Syria, and he understands journalism work."[14]

The interactives discussed here were considered an important part of the storytelling process. The Eurozone map was envisioned as a way to provide readers with clarity about the European debt crisis; it was seen as an interactive that could get regularly updated as more information became available. Syria interactives were intended to bring to light details that few Western news outlets were paying attention to. The interactives could highlight unique material that only *AJE* was able to obtain—the citizen journalism that it has been known for garnering from the Middle East.[15] The interactives *AJE* creates are less focused on a daily deadline, though they are tied into the news cycle; there is no immediate pressure, but the team is focused on getting the interactive done in order to be timely and responsive to news events.

*AJE's* interactive staff is lean, yet with the close collaboration among the staff, it became clear just how it was possible for the news organization to produce so many interactives. *AJE*, an outpost of Western-style journalism in the desert, may have adapted to distance from a ready supply of skilled programmers willing to work in Doha. But this adaptation may be an advantage; interactive journalism is fully integrated into the workflow, to the point that traditional text-focused journalists are now charged with thinking up interactives and even creating them. This work is facilitated by a tight editorial relationship with a journalist who was a programmer first. *AJE* was initially online-only for the United States (until the creation of *Al Jazeera America*), and in this sense, interactives have become even more important, as interactives have flourished in Doha. The *AJE* case study is helpful because it shows how a single interactive journalist can make a difference in a newsroom, how an interactive journalist can work in a cooperative and collaborative process with more traditional journalists to create interactives, and how interactive journalists can be fully integrated into a newsroom's workflow.

## NPR News Apps: Run Like a Tech Team

The shiny new NPR building is located just past Washington, D.C.'s Union Station. The glass and steel building gleams of ambition for a digital future and the prominence of public radio. NPR News Apps team helps fulfill this aspiration. These new interactive journalists sound like a technical team as they work, but they also are in close collaboration with other news teams at NPR to create projects. And though it seems that their focus is mostly to serve as a translator from editorial vision to software product, these journalists are collecting and preparing data.

The morning I visited on July 30, 2013, I met News Apps head Brian Boyer at the lobby security area, deeply recessed into the back of the wide room. He took me up to the third floor of the newsroom; the light-filled workspace has a mixed green-gray carpet, low-walled cubes, and is open and clean. There is a huge media board in the center of the room tuned to a variety of TV stations, Web sites, and online metrics trackers. The news team is in the center, with shows radiating off to the side; away, by the windows, sits the team of seven on news apps.

Boyer works at a stand-up desk with two monitors; most on his staff have two monitors, if not three. His staff begins the morning by talking with each other about code that hasn't worked quite right and who is going to fix what. They use the phrase "the ticket is open" and remark that "quite a lot of the tickets have been closed" from the previous week. These "tickets" are electronic tasks opened on GitHub, a site used as a repository for both open-source code and as a way to organize and host software development projects. Other newsrooms also use GitHub, but Boyer's team has the flair of the software-development shoptalk. This is cultivated by Boyer, whose background, as we now know, is in software development rather than journalism.

Jeremy Bowers, team member, showed me his screen. There was a long list of tickets that were open, closed, or in progress, many of which ask for bug fixes to various programming issues. Bowers started talking about his weekend's work. He said something to this effect: "I've been trying to run a migration of Django 1.5 to post GIS but you have to go to 1.45 to run the site. There's something with PostGIS to Postgres, but there's probably some combo that will work—you've got to shell the thing to place it into service." He then added, "It was one command failing. It was in my tags for the index. There was nothing wrong, every time I read the index, but it was critical for the migration."

Bowers was a political science major who discovered programming later. Yet he is quite comfortable talking in what could seem like babble. His hacker journalist boss chipped in: "Now that we know the issues, we can figure out how to ship the new PostGIS to Postgres"—or something to that effect.

The banter continued with other members of the team while Boyer got ready to host the morning scrum. The scrum may just be another fancy word for a meeting, but it comes out of a software development management technique called "agile," mentioned earlier. Through a series of scrums, "sprints" (or iterative pushes to finish projects), retrospective meetings, and other techniques pulled from this management technique, Boyer has brought the software development process into the newsroom. "I don't know if all newsrooms do it, some do, but I definitely like it when you can bring a technology term into the newsroom," he told me.[16]

The scrum at NPR functions as a meeting for the team to discuss what was achieved the previous workday and what will be achieved on that day. Boyer asked the team, "What did you do yesterday? What will you do today? What [obstacle] stands in the way?" The conversation was light; some members of the team talked about their weekends before settling into the tasks they had completed that Friday (closing tickets, assembling a better search bar for a new project, finishing updates and edits to text, and the like). The "today" goals differed slightly, and the built-in focus on completion and movement gave a sense of progress. "I closed all my tickets, and I have none outstanding,"

Bowers told the group. The focus on the small tasks is intended to keep team members accountable to each other and focused on daily progress, according to the mantra of the agile/scrum software development approach.

The focus on technical solutions to larger journalism problems continued with another morning meeting, where Boyer's team met with investigative reporters working on a project about accessible playgrounds: all new or renovated playgrounds as of 2013 have to be built for children with special needs according to federal guidelines. A reporter had some initial data and asked the team to create an online component.[17] The goal in mind was to create a searchable database with maps for parents to find accessible playgrounds where they lived. Ideally, the maps would say what features would be available. And as a best hope, this would be a nationwide database.

As team member Danny DeBelius explained to me: "This playground is part of an investigative project which will make it more clear which playgrounds are ADA compliant and which ones are more inclusive. [This will help you] if you have a blind child or a child with autism. We are not experts, but we are going to report on the state of affairs. There is no national database . . . there is no one source to smash this together for all the parks. Some states are more forthcoming." In an upstairs room, the team met with journalists working on the project and a senior digital strategy editor to talk about where the site stood as far as technical production. The meeting was also intended to offer the journalists a chance to respond with suggestions based on their reporting and their sense of the story. Boyer had a laptop hooked up to a projector/screen to show the team's work.

Boyer started updating the investigations team on the progress. He had regrouped the search, and so he showed them from a technical perspective what the page would look like on a desktop. He then showed some of the categories he hoped would be available for each playground: a name, a map, a picture, a description of features, and an official description of the playground. The investigations team chimed in and promised to find some more information about what features were going to be available at each playground—smooth-surface ramps, swings, accessibility features, and the like. The News Apps team said it would try to translate this information into shorthand—perhaps via logos that could be searchable.

Boyer provided the investigative team with a memo containing a list of completed/uncompleted items, in the following language:

# What we did
- Regrouped the search boxes
- Fixes to the search map

- Stick a search pin, highlight the result
- Fixes to the search accuracy
- Style search results page for desktop, including dropping descriptions
- Moving map on desktop updates the search
- Rearranged the home page header and sections
- Mocked up a data download UI (the download links don't work yet)
- Re-geocoded a bunch of playgrounds
- Driving directions open native apps in iOS, android
- Fixes to the location editor
- Rearranged the features on add playground
- Playgrounds can now exist without a name
- Styled thank you messages for add/edit
- Gave it a name

# What we didn't do
- Did not complete homepage primer——need more photos. Probably need to edit the copy down
- Still struggling with user—submitted photos with our comments provider, may not be solvable. Not done styling at desktop size

# Issues
- Need to sort out how we pitch this to stations and if/how they might present it on their websites

# What's next
- Desktop styling
- Station pitch
- In-house UX testing
- Homepage copy
- Sort out the name, get a custom URL?

None of these items on the list had anything to do with traditional journalism. There was no discussion of storytelling in this memo. All of the tasks listed were focused on building the application, through creating better navigation systems, creating a presentation platform for the home page, thinking about promotion, or solving problems with the data entry.

After handing out the memo, Boyer talked through other investigations team issues, such as difficulty mapping on the mobile phone, trying to figure out whether people would even know the name of the park they were going to, and bad addresses from the data. Boyer said, "They [the data] don't always give great addresses. Maybe the solution is latitude by longitude. There may be a vague address to the street in D.C . . ."

Bowers piped in with something I didn't understand: "Was the [X] reverse geocoded?"—or something to that effect.

Boyer apologized, "Sorry we're talking technical stuff." He added, "The latitude to longitude we can use from Google's API but it can produce bad addresses, and the addresses can take you to the wrong direction, so we need the street level." Bowers responded, "Maybe we do reverse latitude and longitude." A woman from investigations asked, "So the address—there is the address they have sent us, the latitude and longitude, and the entrance to the park? . . . There's the playground name versus the people's name for it . . . some people won't know the name of the playground." Boyer said the image of the playground would be a key feature.

The News Apps team acknowledged that the data was thin. Matt Stiles, the journalist on the News Apps team who had been in charge of collecting much of the data, had put in calls to municipalities around the country, scoured the Web, worked with an activist who collects the data, and put together a preliminary list. Some cities were offering much better data—New York City's playgrounds were easy to find online, and San Diego had just sent a list of twenty accessible playgrounds. In a quest for speed, Stiles and the rest of the team weren't looking to place public-records requests.

Despite this thin data, the team proclaimed they were ready to go with the project. Boyer explained how the users will be able to edit data: the names of the playgrounds, the features offered, and even add new playgrounds—in part because the audience knows the playgrounds better. Boyer suggested listeners from member stations may help edit playgrounds in their own communities, and that NPR's audience was "ideal" for this kind of data collection.

With a few more updates, news team said they would begin thinking about the headlines, while the news apps team agreed to start thinking about the URL—asking for suggestions about how to pick a name and register it to NPR. They then started talking about a target launch date.

Investigations said, "We will deadline edit and ATC [All Things Considered] will respond to the script. Both stories are written . . ."

Boyer said, "Let's launch at the end of this week."

The Investigations editor added, "We'll know at 2 o'clock if I love it."

In a meeting right after this one, Boyer confessed to his team, "I don't think we will have 'Playground' ready by the end of the week."

This next meeting was the iteration meeting. During this meeting, I heard about the past week's tasks and the goals for the week ahead—the successes, the complaints, and the failures. The focus was on user design issues, technical problems, programming concerns, technical promotion concerns, and the team debates on the status of various tickets—whether to open new ones, close existing ones, and beyond. Stiles, who says he has the "sensibilities of a real journalist," explained that what is done on the News Apps team is rendered in "JavaScript or Python for project manipulation to make the project work."

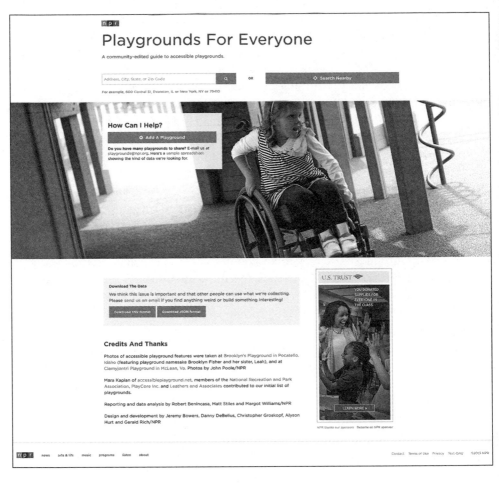

"Playgrounds for Everyone," *NPR*.

This brief portrait of an inside look at the NPR News Apps team gives some insights into how the team works and what it aims to do. This project shows a different side of a team than *AJE*. On this team, we see a greater focus on product development. The journalists view their primary output as a working app. They speak in technical terms and operate much like a software team might, perhaps because of Boyer's background. We do not hear much focus on the story. Nonetheless, this team is looking for data to help create the app. Members of the team have sought out data from various cities about the accessible playgrounds. The journalists have considered what data they need and users might need, and have thought about how to arrange and sort this data. In addition to focusing on the project output, they are also working as journalists in cleaning, sorting, and gathering data to get "Playground" on its way.

We see also a tight integration with the investigations team. There is a state-of-the-project meeting with the team where the investigations team gets an update on the project and has a chance to contribute. The News Apps team offers the investigations team a state-of-the app update to help the investigations team figure out when it is appropriate to run the radio story. Boyer explained what he saw as the purpose of this kind of app creation: "Our work aligns and promotes within the newsroom . . . vs. coming up with our own shit." The integration of the investigations team into the project suggests how each team may provide back and forth into the overarching goal of the news app. We see how each team plays to its strengths when News Apps says it will think of a URL and the investigations team says it will think of headlines. However, we see also how the News Apps team can speak in a technical language that the investigations team does not understand—signaling the special skills and knowledge these interactive journalists bring to new kinds of projects, but also underscoring just how distinct these journalists are from traditional journalists.

One aspect that seems particularly akin to the hacker journalism perspective is that the team is ready to unveil the project before it is done. The team does not feel it has a complete set of data, and there are some kinks in the platform, but they would rather release the project in the form it is in than wait until it is perfect. This willingness to experiment is distinct from the traditional investigations team, which is going to edit and perfect the story before it airs. The beta-version approach reflects the programming ethic that these interactive journalists share but traditional journalists do not.

We can also get a sense of the timeline that these journalists have when it comes to working on interactives. The project is not tied to a specific deadline; instead, Boyer's team can afford to concentrate on this single major project. This is in part what Boyer calls a "luxury" of working in public radio, where his team is given the time to focus on one project. The project is not an investigation in the traditional sense, but a public-facing project intended to help people find accessible playgrounds. Boyer later explained that this was a typical public-radio-inspired project, one that would help orient people to their neighborhoods. The idea that users would also contribute content for the interactive was novel as well; this suggested another form of public-radio inspiration where a loyal user base was seen as potentially contributing quality content for the common good. Thus, in the context of this playground project, we see many signs of just how News Apps fits into

NPR, from editorial integration to work focus to product aspirations, and we find that News Apps is distinct from traditional journalism but nonetheless works according to editorial mandates and sensibilities. NPR is a useful case study because it shows not only the impact of how a hacker journalist at the helm influences the workflow and the culture of the team, but also how a technically-minded team works with the support of the newsroom, though at times, there may be some translation difficulties.

## *The Wall Street Journal*: Data and Patterns

Jon Keegan and his team of interactive journalists at *The Wall Street Journal* sit on the main floor of the newsroom. The newsroom itself has an open floor plan, and the center is occupied by a giant hub with two sets of media walls hanging off the ceiling. But Keegan's team is off to the side, out of view from this giant circle and the main set of reporters and editors. This does not mean, as we will see, that they are out of sight and out of mind. When I visited, Keegan's team was the only team that had an analytics screen showing Web metrics of interactive projects; throughout the entire main floor of *The Wall Street Journal*, there were no other metrics boards. This focus on traffic suggests just how much the pressure for the success of interactives online may have felt to the journalists.

On September 4, 2013, journalists were sitting at desks, most with three screens in front of them, most tuned to a coding project.[18] During my visit, I learned about the inner workings of what *The Journal* called the "interactive graphics team," though the group later changed its name to "News Apps." This team focused its attention on visualizing data, both for other journalists in the newsroom and for its own standalone interactives. The journalists were integrated into the editorial workflow but able to work on independent projects and spent most of their time on off-deadline work.

These journalists, mostly programmer journalists, focused their attention on preparing data for analysis—usually relying on visualization to do their work. Keegan worked to "free" records from unwieldy PDFs in order to spot patterns, with a focus on data cleaning to mine the data to look for stories. But sometimes the data might not have a pattern at all.

As one journalist explained: "We find and look for the patterns in the data just like the Page One editor might do for thinking about story production. One thing we know is that the data might not have a pattern. With a data set we can visualize things, and we can pick the data that we can try to access ... but we may not find a story." This suggests that data analysis begins with discovery rather than a hypothesis. What's different from past data practices is that the team is focused on visualizing this data to begin the investigation.

Keegan explained the visualization process: "Every data set is so different. It depends on the size and the scale of the data. Sometimes when we visualize the data, it can become the thesis of the story." He added, "We don't know unless we visualize it."

In this way, the interactive graphics team at *The Journal* is absolutely crucial to figuring out the larger story—if there is one at all. Often, this means working in tandem with reporters who have obtained vast amounts of data that may be too large to sort through easily. Creating searchable databases, cleaning the data, and visualizing the data means that the interactive team plays a critical role in uncovering stories that might not otherwise be told—or at least stories that would be far more difficult to tease out.

At *The Journal*, the data can come from any number of directions: from another more traditional text reporter, from a mutual effort to acquire the data with this traditional reporter, or from the team seeking out the data themselves. They emphasized that there was still no set way or workflow where their work originates. But they agreed that collaboration was key.

The interactive team was particularly proud of a project called "Jet Tracker." Two reporters, Tom McGinty and Mark Maremount, more traditional CAR reporters, were trying to use private-jet records to track corporate movements. The thesis was that one might be able to figure out costs associated with this travel, highlight possible malfeasance, pinpoint key trade conversations or pre-merger meetings, for example, by taking a look at these flight records.[19] After a four-year battle, McGinty and Maremount were able to get the registration requests for takeoff and landing for private jets, but they were given only the "tail" numbers of the aircraft, not the owners. So they initiated a second request, asking for the owners' names.

In the end, the interactive graphics team helped to sort and clean the data. They also created a visual map for "Jet Tracker," where readers could pinpoint company movements and see flight patterns. By making this data searchable and visual, these reporters were able to find rich insights in the data that would have been far more difficult to find in the mass of data, and they were able to give readers the chance to explore this data on their own. Jet Tracker yielded rich insights, from Steve Jobs's cancer treatment trips to how Liberty Mutual had held a variety of meetings before particular mergers. The tracker continues to provide rich insights for stories.

In other cases, the projects emerged directly from the interactive graphics team. One particular interactive that yielded great success was a cellphone bill

"Jet Tracker Database," *The Wall Street Journal*

calculator. While the Jet Tracker led to discrete stories for the newspaper, this bill calculator stood alone. Keegan explained, "Well, one of the best [interactives] was just a calculator we did on mobile phone plan prices. There was some major data crunching and people could play with it. It's not something newspapers would have in the past used to do in traditional journalism."

A few important points emerge from Keegan's comment—as well as from the creation of this calculator. First, not all interactives have to do with stories. In fact, interactives can stand on their own and can be just as helpful and public-facing without an accompanying story. The interactive should be seen as an information provider in and of itself. Second, the interactive journalism team need not be solely a service desk, waiting to assist the rest of the newspaper. Instead, interactive journalists, at least those at *The Journal*, can generate their own successful projects.

Keegan contended that interactives open up new terrain for a newsroom. The projects can go beyond traditional storytelling because they explore areas that newsrooms would not typically engage—at least not *The Wall Street Journal*. In his view, it would be fairly unlikely for *The Journal's* traditional reporters to provide this detailed accounting of how, according to rate plans, individuals might fare. At least at *The Journal*, this kind of consumer finance journalism is not prevalent across the newspaper. But the interactive team took on this topic and went into great depth with this calculator, well beyond the usual kinds of stories *The Journal* might tell. Interactives, then, add to a larger conversation about news and public information that may not have been found through news articles before.

Keegan's team underscores some key themes we are discussing across interactive journalism. First, we can see the way his team integrates with the other aspects of editorial news flow. First, they work to assemble data, clean it, and prepare it for visualization. They rely on coding to help them with this process; this case is an illustration of how programmer journalists work with data within their every day workflow. What's distinct about this data analysis is that they work to make it easily visualized and interactive so that they can spot patterns—or not—within what they have collected. At *The Journal*, we see two different processes for editorial workflow. And we see, from what they produce, how they approach dealing with data, how they make it both public-facing and helpful to the journalists, using code to visualize it and make it easy to interpret by others.

The interactive journalists aid other journalists by offering these analysis skills to help journalists like McGinty and Maremount find data points for traditional stories. But interactive journalists at *The Journal* also work on their own projects that they have created outside the traditional story-creation process, ones that function as standalone interactives. This suggests a certain amount of independence from the newsroom's overarching priorities and underscores how interactive journalists may provide a significant and unique contribution to editorial offerings.

The process and pacing for these projects is mostly removed from daily journalism, according to these journalists. The examples they offered as representative of their work were oriented by specific editorial goals unrelated to the day-to-day demands of the newsroom. This left them time to fully explore the data for other long-term stories and may be why they were able to build interactives like the cellphone calculator that had no direct tie-in to the daily news cycle. Thus, we can see the projects, the editorial integration, pacing, and process from this visit with Keegan and his staff, which helps us better understand how a team can work off deadline pressure and be connected directly to editorial workflow while also exploring projects on its own account.

## *The New York Times*: Integration into the News Cycle

Unlike many of the newsrooms I visited, the interactive news team at *The New York Times* was in a tizzy. On September 13, 2013, the team was hard at work prepping interactives to respond to the news cycle. First up, an interactive graphic on Syria, which they hoped would illustrate, through a map, the conflict between the rebels and the Syrian government. One journalist, Ben Koski, formerly of Microsoft, was busily working on a project for Fashion Week that had to be ready to go almost immediately. He was staring at lines and lines of code running down his screen, checking to see if there were any possible errors on the back end of the interactive. Other members of the team were busy working on an interactive for the upcoming New York mayoral election.

This is certainly *not* to say that *The Times* does not work on long-term projects, but the quick-response interactive is also part of the team's DNA. *The Times* team thought about its role as critically engaged with the news needs of the newspaper rather than as a standalone source of news products. I also found that without much prompting, those at *The Times* quickly articulated what they brought to the newspaper's offerings. Notably, *The Times* is a good reminder that interactives are more than just data: they are playable, clickable, and/or immersive experiences that do not always relate back to a database structure. *The Times'* interactive team serves all parts of the newsroom, from arts to culture to politics to sports, and the graphics team also chips in with many sophisticated interactives of its own.

In September 2013, the interactive news team was a formidable force in the newsroom, responsible for creating a wide variety of projects. There were the charts and graphs similar to those seen across many other newsrooms. Then there were interactive slideshows, such as one from Fashion Week, inviting users to send in photos;[20] there were others featuring dining guides, Oscar ballots, interactives on how successful (or not) NFL teams were in picking the best players in the draft;[21] other interactives produced by the newsroom included an interactive (which had a 3D effect) to show how pitcher Mariano Rivera dominates batters,[22] and, of course, storytelling efforts like "Snow Fall." *The Times'* Interactive News Team included about twenty people, and Aron Pilhofer, head of the team, had support to add staff even during troubled times at the paper. He hired hacker journalists, programmer journalists, and data journalists to round out his team, giving depth to the group's offerings.

After my visit, *The Times* cooked up a simple interactive that showed the prowess of the team and its ability to contribute to the overall goals of the newsroom. "How Yous, Youse, and Y'all Talk,"[23] a quiz created by Cambridge linguistics professor Bert Vaux, could pinpoint where people were from—to

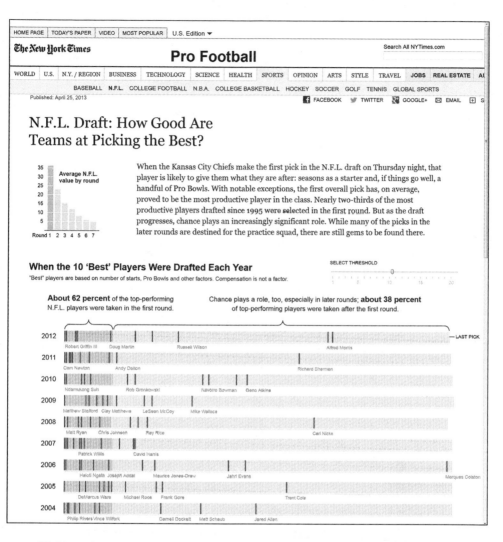

"N.F.L. Draft: How Good Are Teams at Picking the Best?" *The New York Times*

the level of their hometowns—and was scarily accurate. Introduced in the last eleven days of 2013, it was nonetheless *The New York Times'* highest traffic-getter for the entire year. As Robinson Meyer of *The Atlantic* put it: "Think about that. A news app, a piece of software about the news made by in-house developers, generated more clicks than any article."[24] With traffic essential to survival, at least according to so many in the news industry, this kind of interactive makes the case for the team at *The Times* quite well.

Published: December 21, 2013

FACEBOOK    TWITTER    GOOGLE+    EMAIL    SHARE

# How Y'all, Youse and You Guys Talk

What does the way you speak say about where you're from?
Answer all the questions below to see your personal dialect map.

QUESTION 1 OF 25

How would you address a group of two or more
people?

- you all
- yous / youse
- you lot
- you guys
- you 'uns
- yinz
- you
- other
- y'all

Next ▶

"How Y'all, Youse and You Guys Talk," *The New York Times*

When I visited, it was clear just how essential the team was to the core mission of *Times* journalism. Pilhofer spoke of the importance of being ready to help meet the needs of the newsroom's short- and long-term projects: "The newspaper is a daily miracle for a reason. It is harder to do long-term planning as a rule." To cope with the crush, the team has built a variety of tools that can be repurposed and updated, but there are always new tweaks, always new content, and this must be done on a quick turnaround. Eric Buth, a programmer journalist on the team, explained the flexibility required: "We can [make new products] fast. We can chase the speed. We can do small and long things." Journalist Mark Lavallee, the deputy on the desk, offered a recent example. As the crisis in Syria had expanded day by day, the staff worked closely with the foreign desk. The evolving relationship led to quick turnaround interactives. "We put together a map with something about all four directions Obama could go and it was ready—we can prove that we can deliver."

Interestingly, Pilhofer asserted that his team had been unable to have many standalone successes, suggesting the importance at *The Times* of being integrated into larger newsroom goals. Unlike Keegan's team at *The Journal*, Pilhofer's few standalone projects had "bombed." He gave the example of one particular interactive, an NFL Playbook. "It was thoroughly researched. It was about all the playoff teams and had experts and extensive reporting and videos of 3D animations. You could see the plays unfold in different perspectives: quarterbacks, wide receivers. . . ." And then he shrugged his shoulders, noting that it had only garnered a few thousand page views. "The journalism needs to inform the destination. You have to be going with the grain of the newsroom."

But this integration in the newsroom also means that interactives may get lost online rather than having special attention as major projects. In my book, *Making News at The New York Times,* I explained how an interactive that took three months was on the home page for a few hours. The crush of more and more content on the Web site buries interactives as more fresh work comes on to the home page and section pages throughout the day. Being part of the news cycle and attached to stories means that interactives become hard to find—even if they are these long projects. Ben Koski shared these thoughts with a colleague and me: "If something has been gone for two days you can't search for it—I saw it in the morning with the dining interactive . . ." and then, he added, that the item had essentially vanished. However, Pilhofer contended that this was simply what happened to any news story and wasn't peculiar to interactive journalism: it's just the news cycle.

For more in-depth feature stories, the interactive team works closely with individual reporters and editors on a regular basis. The team often sees drafts of stories before deciding whether it is worth creating an interactive; in some ways, the team has been a victim of its own success. Pilhofer explained, "Inevitably if we do something successful . . . people request it . . . it's hard because everyone says 'I want that.'" The fact that the team actually sees these drafts and that there is demand for these projects by other editorial members provides further evidence of their integration into the news cycle.

Like *The Journal, The Times* builds calculators, tools, and databases that work in the service of stories—tools that provide a more granular and systematic examination than a manual examination of such data might offer. *The Times* has also moved into creating particular internal tools for searching through data across different datasets. In this way, *The Times* is able to expand beyond one story to aid in reporting over time.

Elections are a key area for *The Times*. Journalist Chase Davis explained that one of his new, long-term projects was geared at clearing up some difficulties with searching for campaign-finance data—an effort which would not focus on one particular story but would instead be a database that could serve a multitude of potential needs for politics reporters. His project reflects the prowess of *The New York Times*' interactive desk. The team is up to date, experimenting with some of the techniques being explored in academic computer science departments. Davis explained a new project: "Right now, I am looking at applying machine learning to political stuff. We were presented with campaign-finance data, but there is no concept of donor contribution on an individual level. You might have Joe Smith listed in ten different ways. So we are using machine learning to roll up contributors into a canonical donor database to see how they behave over time."

This tool could prove tremendously helpful from an inward-facing perspective as journalists at *The Times* look for patterns and discrepancies within the data. More significant is that once *The Times* can figure out how to use machine learning, a skill being developed by some of the most ambitious in Silicon Valley, it can begin to use the technology across other data sets.

*The Times*' integration with editorial workflow goes far beyond many other newsrooms. We can see evidence of this intense engagement with the larger news cycle in a number of ways. First, the interactive news team works on daily breaking-news projects, suggesting that interactives are envisioned as an important part of telling stories on a daily basis. These interactives are simply what *The Times* editorial staff as a whole thinks about when there is a major breaking story or an event that needs to be explained. The interactive news team even goes as far as to read drafts of stories when crafting long-term projects, suggesting just how much other journalists work with this team to create an interactive that compliments and enhances the text-based story. The fact that *The Times* team turns away interactive projects suggests just how, with regard to a larger editorial buy-in, these projects are important. The difficulty of creating standalone interactives further suggests just how much *The Times* team relies on a close collaboration with other editorial stories to enhance and broaden its reach. And even the fact that the team's stories get cycled out as quickly as other stories suggests that other editorial staff, for better or worse, simply regard interactives as just another element of *Times* content.

*The Times* interactive team has also been tremendously adept in showing its importance to the overall success of *The Times* online. The team's projects have been able to drive massive traffic to the site, including users who have not come to *The Times* before. This success indicates just how important interactives can be to enhancing the relevance of a news site. A measure of this success is due to the fact that *Times* interactives are not just data interactives. There are quizzes, fun interactives about Fashion Week, and other interactives about sports and entertainment, many with the ability to change the way we think of stories being told online. But the enjoyment people may derive from a simple quiz or a gripping interactive story featuring videos, animation, graphs, maps, and photos may be part of why this team has been so good at doing what it does. The case of *The Times* is important because it shows an interactives team at scale: it helps us see how an interactives team can work under both deadline and non-deadline pressure, produce a vast array of interactives, and become fully integrated into the editorial workflow.

## *The Guardian:* Daily, Simple Data

A brief vignette from *The Guardian* helps illustrate some of the practices of data journalists. Simon Rogers, head data journalist at *The Guardian*, spoke to me in between crunching on a daily deadline. Sitting on the lower of *The Guardian*'s two floors devoted to news, he was in the middle of the newsroom and surrounded by other reporters and editors. On November 2, 2011, lying on a table he shared with members of his team was a well-thumbed copy of *Precision Journalism* by Philip Meyer, the bible of CAR journalists.

The government had just released some records about recycling rates in different municipalities across England.[25] Rogers was helping to prepare a map to accompany this data[26]—using a spreadsheet through Google Fusion to easily create geo-data for the piece. He was moving swiftly, under pressure to help a reporter working on a story. The reporter came over twice in an hour to chat about the data—what he had found and what Rogers had unearthed. Rogers offered an overview, and the reporter said he was "looking for some highlights." Rogers explained the role of the reporter: "Sometimes on a story they'll get an expert who comments, and that's useful to me for the data visualization." This back-and-forth with the text-focused reporter suggests the close integration of the data journalist into the larger daily news cycle. Rogers is generally focused on deadline work. He explained to me, "What works best quickly is a swift data analysis . . . we don't have the resources of *The New York Times* or *ProPublica*, but we can [still] do it quickly . . . it can be immediate."

Lisa Evans, his colleague, gave an example of the kind of work that required fast-paced attention but was simply too big to do in a day. In 2011,

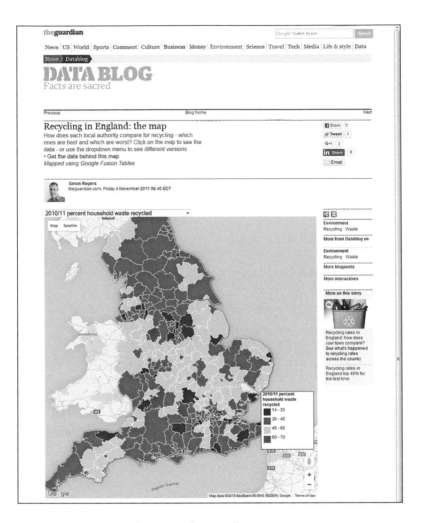

"Recycling in England: The Map," *The Guardian*

riots had gripped London and other parts of England. *The Guardian* gathered
people's observations about where the riots took place and then put this information on a map. The next task was to comb through the court registers
to see where the rioters lived with respect to where the riots occurred. These
court registers of the arrests had thirteen hundred names and addresses of
people in the riots.

The data was difficult to put into easily usable form—these were poor PDFs
that could not easily be mechanically transferred to spreadsheets. But with
Google Fusion tables, Evans pointed out how she could move quickly, once

the data was usable. "We can make a quick map and see whether poverty was an issue in the riots; we tested that with Google Fusion, and instead of doing it in one week, we could do it within days." While the legwork required to get the data was difficult, Evans nonetheless posted the data as soon as she could, noting there was a great demand to know exactly who participated in the riots and where the damage occurred. "With the riots, people really wanted to know what was happening with where [the rioters] lived."

Rogers also created *The Guardian*'s DataBlog in 2009. DataBlog produces content originating directly from his team. The data is often, but not always, interactive. The goal of the DataBlog is to provide regular, if not daily, data journalism updates. The mission of Rogers's team is spelled out in the "About" section of DataBlog: "Everyday we work with datasets from around the world. We have had to check this data and make sure it's the best we can get, from the most credible sources. Rather than uploading spreadsheets onto our server, for now we are using Google Docs. This means we can update the facts easily and quickly, which makes sure you get the latest stats, as we get them." Thus, the focus of this data journalism team is on getting data out as quickly as possible to as many people as possible. And while *The Guardian*'s DataBlog is a standalone effort, it becomes nonetheless ingrained in the daily online news offerings of *The Guardian*.

Rogers's work builds on a tradition of data journalism and computer-assisted reporting, though Rogers doesn't like the CAR term. "We all use computers," he says, also noting that CAR is an American term. Journalist Lisa Evans distinguished her work from CAR: "We just do descriptive statistics. We are not software engineers with math degrees." Thus, CAR takes on a separate focus for these data journalists.

Chapter 3 noted how data journalists may not necessarily be sophisticated programmers and often use ready-made tools to help them create interactives. We see with Rogers and Davis their reliance on the suite of Google tools; the use of these tools is even reflected in the introduction to the DataBlog itself. As Rogers explained, "I'm not a programmer. I was a news editor."[27] Instead, there is a separate interactives team at *The Guardian* that works on long-term immersive interactives that require more sophisticated coding. These data journalists are focused on the data rather than the programming.[28]

From a snapshot of a visit to *The Guardian*, a few key themes emerge. First, *The Guardian* is busy working on a daily deadline. Even long projects are cued to breaking news events, and the journalists try to get them out as fast as possible. The team is integrated into the daily workflow of the rest of the newsroom when data accompanies other stories being written in the newsroom. On the other hand, the DataBlog operates as a standalone unit of *The Guardian* with the unique offerings of the data journalism team. Still, this blog is fully integrated into *The Guardian*'s daily journalism Web content.

The projects the team works on are data intensive. The team cleans and sorts data, rendering it into visualizations to enrich the public's understanding of news events. Their focus is not, however, on sophisticated interactives. Instead, the team focuses on interpreting the data rather than building out interactives that require coding knowledge. In this, we see further evidence of data journalists knowing how to work with programs that use code, but not necessarily being coders themselves. Overall, at *The Guardian*, we can see how the data journalism team has made itself a critical part of the journalism workflow and output defining *The Guardian*'s efforts online. This is just a brief snapshot of *The Guardian* from one of the earliest points of research for this book, but it is nonetheless valuable because it shows how data journalism can be used to create interactives for daily deadline pressures, and underscores that coding knowledge is not always necessary for interactive journalism.

## The Associated Press: New York and Washington, D.C.—A Tale of Two Cities

The AP's New York bureau is located in one of the still-ungentrified areas of Hell's Kitchen, on Tenth Avenue and Thirty-Third Street past Penn Station. There's almost nothing in the way of creature comforts around the building—only one restaurant—and everything else seems to be towering gray buildings with undefined purposes. The AP itself is housed in a huge concrete building, which it shares with an NYC public broadcasting station, Channel 13.

Interactive technology editor Jonathan Stray met me in the lobby on September 26, 2012, and led me to the main floor of the AP.[29] More than one thousand journalists work in New York—and at the front of the newsroom I noticed how front pages from across the country with AP stories were mounted on thick foamboard (most in small, regional newspapers). Along the walls are feeds from AP TV. In October 2011, there was no sign of any mobile devices showing AP content, and nothing showed AP's social media presence, something Stray maligned. As we walked through a grey-carpeted newsroom so massive that the windows are lost from view when you stand in the middle, Stray pointed out that AP now gets a good bit of money from its TV broadcast segments in addition to the text stories it sells to newspapers.

Stray, a bit of a New York fashionista (who took Seth C. Lewis and me out to lunch wearing a fur-lined coat), introduced us to his small team of AP interactive designers. On Stray's team were a variety of specialists: data journalists, more design-oriented journalists, and hardcore programmers like himself who have gradually become immersed in news. Stray is well known in the journalism blogosphere for his incredibly articulate posts on everything from financial journalism to the impossibility of building algorithms for information that do not embody editorial judgments.[30]

Inside his own newsroom, though, at the AP, Stray maligned the constant deadline pressure his team faced for interactives. Across AP, a giant organization with more than thirty-four hundred employees, there were about thirty interactive employees scattered across the world and in the United States—a small staff to fill the giant needs of member organizations. Each day, Stray and his small team of six contributed to some of the dozen, sometimes even *dozens,* of interactives that might be needed to fulfill the needs of AP newspapers (though they used preexisting templates). While the team does indeed pitch its own ideas for projects, their work was mostly "routine illustrations of the top stories of the day . . . as agreed on in the morning."[31] These could include anything from maps of the latest natural disaster to election polls to timelines for developing stories. The turnover was fast and furious, with little time to do anything truly inventive.

In that context, Stray's team had little support from the newsroom. As he explained to us, he had no idea how his interactives were used. There was literally no control over which interactives the team had created that the AP members decided to run. These interactives were meant to be output for anyone, generalizable content to please these newspapers and broadcast Web sites.

It was as if the AP interactive team didn't exist at all in this sprawling environment. If his AP interactive team got credit, it was only when it was able to make a big splash on a member news site. Luckily, though, for Stray, he was at work on a project more ambitious: building a tool for data visualization sponsored by the Knight Foundation. Otherwise, he'd be caught in a crush of what he suggested was a meaningless routine to feed an endless supply of clickable daily interactives.

This intersection between the rest of the AP and the interactives team was perhaps the least effective collaboration I had seen. The interactives team was in pure service to the larger editorial offerings, unable to offer any kind of perspective, advice, or insight. The constant churn for more content made it difficult to do any sustained projects, and the inability to track where the projects ended up gave the journalists even less ownership over their work. On the other hand, this presence in the routine at least suggests that interactives were now felt to be a required part of the daily journalism output, even if interactive journalists had little say in what they created.

Yet just a hop down the eastern corridor at the AP in D.C., I found an entirely different interactive journalism workflow. I visited journalists Michelle Minkoff, Jack Gillum, and Kevin Vineys on July 23, 2013. The two years between my visit to New York might have changed the tenor of how interactive journalists worked at the AP, though it's hard for me to tell. What I was able to observe was the stark difference in their integration into the workflow of the D.C. bureau in 2013 from how interactives in 2011 were part of the AP's daily workflow.

In D.C., interactive journalists had their desks right to the back of the politics editor, thick in the middle of the newsroom. Minkoff, the respected programmer journalist profiled in chapter 3, offered some thoughts about the integration. "We were [located] near video and multimedia and we used to be by TV, but . . . we wanted to . . . have seats in the newsroom, and I am across from the politics editor," and then with a laugh, added, "It's nothing glamorous." I looked behind her, and the politics editor's office was quite literally right behind Minkoff's desk. These journalists were in the mix, at least from a physical standpoint.

Minkoff, Vineys, and Gillum were also removed from much of the daily deadline pressure that Stray said permeated the NYC bureau. Minkoff and Vineys explained how their work generally focused on big investigations and long-term projects. They brought together their skills, investigating the data for journalism patterns and then creating interactives. Vineys, Minkoff, and Gillum all saw themselves as journalists first, programmers second. In this way, they found what they did with the data and the interactives they created as a crucial means of telling a story, and they spoke far less about their work in technical terms. Not all of their efforts were even geared for the public.

For instance, reporter Matt Apuzzo had been at work on a story about steroids in college sports. The successful investigation used not just interviews with players, coaches, experts, and court records for steroid sales, but involved searching player guides and media kits to gather the weights of players throughout their time on college teams.[32] Gillum helped gather this data, and, more important, put together these sixty-one thousand records of college football players over the previous decade for year-over-year weight gains. From this, the team could establish that the steroid problem was still a major issue in the NCAA.[33] Gillum, who said he knew "just enough programming to be dangerous," had focused on creating a long-term interactive that was an internal-facing database. His focus was not on the end user but on the reporter, and he was exempt from the daily workflow of journalism.

Minkoff, who created a number of forward-facing interactives for the public, also talked about being off daily deadline. "We do more long-term work to support breaking news, but breaking news is so vital to what we do. The daily and long-term come together, so there has to be a smart approach." This translates into creating projects like census and election maps and databases that can be used and repurposed and updated for breaking news. When there was breaking news, like the NSA surveillance issues regarding personal data, the team might add developments day by day but create a longer story out of the interactive.

There was a discernible difference between the New York team under the daily gun and the D.C. team given more time. In New York, interactives seemed to be created for the sake of interactives. We don't get a good sense of whether this workflow actually helps make stories stronger, or if it is just a strategy for building clicks on member news organizations' Web sites. In this way, the interactive team is working detached from the actual process of editorial workflow—and it's worth questioning whether the process adds anything to the journalism at all.

In D.C. in 2013, however, we see a more deliberate approach to thinking about interactives. Not every effort has to be forward facing; some tools and databases may be only for a reporter to use. In D.C., this is just as important as giving ordinary people a chance to explore data—the focus is not on simply rendering data available for the sake of making it available but on thinking critically about whom it will best serve. In the case of the Apuzzo story, the team made an internal database. In the context of a census database, it makes sense to keep these interactives public facing, but they similarly serve as a tool for journalists internally as well. Long-term projects are oriented to informing daily stories. The stories in D.C. are strongly data driven—programmer journalists in D.C. are comfortable working with data and are using code to facilitate storytelling.

In just two cities at one organization, we see the diversity of possible work with interactive news. In New York, we see almost no integration with the larger editorial communication process, whereas in D.C., journalists work closely with other text-based journalists in the newsroom—symbolically, they are seated right in the center of the politics desk. We see two different patterns for doing work—in New York, the daily crush; in D.C., longform stories that inform breaking news. But one fact is clear: the AP is paying attention to making interactives part of its journalism offerings.

## Assessing Difference and Similarities

Why is it that these teams work the way that they do? What kinds of similarities and differences do these interactive journalism teams have, and how might we begin to create some sort of analytical framework for interactive journalists beyond just this sample set? Looking across these case studies, it becomes clear that there are three major differences among the teams: the people, the process, and the integration. By people, I mean the makeup of the teams—hacker journalists, programmer journalists, data journalists. By process, I mean how slow or fast the news cycle is for the team. And by integration, I mean whether the team is either *service*, needing a larger editorial participation for input into interactives, or *independent*, able to generate its own interactives without relying on other journalists outside the department for help.

I've tried to understand whether it makes much difference for a team if it is led by a hacker journalist, a programmer journalist, or a data journalist. It does seem that backgrounds do matter, at least a bit. For instance, at *Al Jazeera English*, Haddad is given the special status of technical expert because of his programming expertise—he has an otherness—yet he is welcomed because he is so able to think about how to approach journalism questions. As the sole programmer at *AJE*, his former hacker status carries significant gravitas. At NPR, the team's strategy and even typical days might well have been lifted from scenes at a tech company. Brian Boyer, the hacker journalist leading the team, explained to me that he didn't mind running his team like a software team: "I think it's good to bring in the tech mentality . . . newspaper teams don't know how to make software: it's not a diss, but we know how to make software."[34] And so his team is run a lot like a software development team, and they talk like a software team focused on a product rather than a

Table 4.1. Assessing the Similarities and Differences between Interactives Teams

| News Organization | People | Process | Integration |
|---|---|---|---|
| Al Jazeera English | Hacker journalist | Slow | Service/cooperative |
| National Public Radio (NPR) | Hacker journalist head, programmer journalists, data journalists | Slow | Service |
| The Wall Street Journal | Programmer journalists | Fast | Independent/Service |
| The Guardian | Data journalists | Slow | Independent/Service |
| The New York Times | Programmer journalist head, data journalists, hacker journalists | Slow/Fast | Service |
| Associated Press (New York) | Hacker journalists head, hacker journalists/ programmer journalists | Fast | Service |
| Associated Press (D.C.) | Programmer journalist head, programmer journalists | Slow/Fast | Service |

story when they engage with other staff at NPR. But this software approach still has a journalism mentality, aided in part by the background of Boyer's team: a data journalist and programmer journalists, who worked together on "Playground," a data-focused project helping the community learn more about accessible parks.

The Wall Street Journal has a team of primarily programmer journalists and one or two computer scientists now working together, and I would need more time with them to assess whether this kind of leadership has made a difference in their work. What emerges most clearly, though, is that the composition of this team may influence how focused The Journal is on the ultimate story.

And at The Guardian, Simon Rogers, the data journalist, was a traditional journalist focused on doing traditional journalism work wherein the story—the daily story—is what comes first. At The New York Times, what's most overwhelming is not who leads the team but just how many people are on the team; it's a mélange of those with backgrounds in software, those with backgrounds in journalism who have taught themselves how to program, and hard-core data journalists. There are just so many people on staff that The Times seems to be able simply to do every kind of project. At the AP, we may see a divergence in the teams, perhaps because of the people on the team: Stray, in New York, is a hacker journalist frustrated by his lack of integration into the workflow; in D.C., an examination two years later showed a team of programmer journalists who felt integrated into the workflow of the newsroom and invested in major projects.

Notably, in the daily workflow of each team, the melding of backgrounds did not appear as daily conversation. Each team worked together, capitalizing on strengths to build interactives. At AJE, we saw how the hacker journalist worked together with a staff that couldn't program. At The Times, there were those with backgrounds in technology and those with backgrounds in journalism, but it was unclear what difference this made in the daily news-production process. At NPR, we saw a melding of hacker journalists, a team of a data journalist and other programmer journalists whom Boyer led as a software team, less concerned with the story as a whole—but the team was nonetheless gathering data for the story. We can see within this subspecialty how different backgrounds can work together in a unified way to help create projects that benefit the newsroom as a whole, further evidence of interactive journalism's coherence as it presents a distinct contribution to journalism.

It would probably be far too reductive to lay claim regarding how a team works based solely on the backgrounds of the people working on them. Moreover, to study organizational composition, it would likely require months, not days, to learn about how these teams interrelate. It seems to me that there are a variety of other factors beyond just backgrounds that need to be taken into account to help explain why teams work the way they do.

Another possible influence on how teams work is process—which in turn influences integration: in other words, is the newsroom moving slowly or quickly? Is the team on an immediate deadline or a long-term deadline that it can control? *AJE* operates on a slow timeline, but Haddad's is a service desk, so he needs other journalists to help him figure out what to work on, and then he responds to their requests. On the other hand, he has a unique cooperative relationship with his staff because they also come to work with him. This may be in part because Haddad is one person rather than a large team, perhaps making it easier for him to bring interactive journalism into the daily news workflow.

At NPR, the speed is also quite slow, which allows plenty of time for the service relationship to reach its full potential; the interactive team can have as many meetings as necessary with other editorial members to make sure the product has the right news vision. This works to integrate the team into the news-making process. Stray at the AP finds himself so disturbed by the fast pace of the N.Y. interactive process that he feels he has little control over what actually happens: it is the ultimate service position. On the other hand, the slow-moving D.C. bureau, which does adapt its work to breaking news, has enough lead time to work on more substantial projects. This lead time doesn't mean that they are working independently but rather that they have more time to work with others.

Then there are *The Guardian* and *The Wall Street Journal*, both of which can also be independent actors. *The Guardian* is motivated by the fast pace it hopes to maintain on its blog to put out daily data updates for the public. This is a unique, specific product coming from the data desk, though the team still works on bigger *Guardian* daily and long-term stories. Acceleration works in favor of independence in this newsroom. The opposite is true at *The Journal*, where a slow news cycle of long-term projects increases independence; journalists can craft either standalone projects of their own creation or work with other *WSJ* journalists to help them do their work. Yet standalone projects are welcome.

Perhaps most interesting is that a place as formidable as *The New York Times* has chosen to be a service desk because of past failures. Independent projects didn't work. Instead, projects that were integrated, ones that came out of other editorial initiatives, were more successful. The speed didn't seem to matter here; *The Times* is so big that it works at every speed—slow and fast—though the day I visited it was moving mostly on a fast, daily deadline.

Other signs of the interactive team's close integration may be the attitude that interactives are just as forgettable as a daily news story, erased from prominence on the Web site over the course of the daily churn. This sense that the interactive team is very much caught up in the day's work may aid communication efforts. But pace alone, while incredibly important, is not enough to explain why the teams work the way they do. Other factors, such as overarching relationships and felt newsroom needs, the success of past projects, and the skills of journalists to do independent work, as well as intangibles, influence the process and outcome.

Integration in the news process is also related to some very physical factors—such as the location of teams within the newsroom. The AP's D.C. team is directly in the mix of the rest of the bureau, with Minkoff sitting right next to the politics editor's office. *The Guardian*, working on the daily deadline, is also integrated into the middle of the rest of the newsroom. Perhaps the teams at *The Journal* and NPR have a bit more autonomy with their schedules because they sit far away from the center of the newsroom. Haddad sits directly with the online team. However, physical proximity does not account entirely for close integration; *The Times* desk has its own space set in the back of the second floor of the newsroom, away from many reporters. Yet the team is still very much involved in daily workflow; physical integration may not matter as much at a huge organization like *The Times*, where there are so many people that few are really close to those whom they work with each day. Again, proximity may be only a partial explanation.

One difference among these teams is their business model. NPR, *The Guardian*, and *Al Jazeera English* are newsrooms where finances are nonprofit or at least benevolent (NPR is a public-service news outlet, *The Guardian* is administered by a nonprofit trust, and *Al Jazeera* is heavily subsidized by the supremely wealthy emir of Qatar). The rest of the newsrooms examined here are publicly owned and operated for profit. Yet it does not seem that the financial models actually make much difference in the integration and the pace that the interactive teams maintain.

Significant here is how many of these interactive teams approach their work as beta versions—not-quite-finished presentations of news content. Traditional journalism processes focus on a final finished product. One might expect some tension affecting integration because of this experimental approach, but there's little evidence that these trial projects in their unfinished states cause much chagrin. This may be because there is a latitude of acceptance of experimentation from these teams, who are seen as innovators.

In fact, one might expect to see far more conflict in the integration process. Only at the AP in New York do we see significant feelings of resentment, harbored perhaps because creating interactives there is done in a way that is divorced from any kind of input from the team. This strikes me as an organizational-culture issue, where the interactive team is not actually given respect for its work. But generally, there is significant respect accorded to the interactive teams because of what they add to the news product, perhaps because interactives are seen as increasingly critical to the online journalism experience. And interactive teams still are united in the goal of ultimately creating a product to serve the further journalism mission, one that works with larger newsroom aspirations and projects, therefore not clashing with the dominant norms of the newsroom.

For future work, looking at the influence of background, process, and integration together may help provide a more complete portrait of the many moving parts involved in the routines of not just interactive journalism but for occupational subgroups within a newsroom and beyond. The contingencies of each context underscore how different each of these settings are, which makes it even more interesting to think how the subfield nonetheless has such uniformity in what it produces and the contributions it offers. And while many of these routines are highly predictable in the end, it still gives us pause to question just how idiosyncrasies contribute to news—a larger question than I cannot answer now, but worthy of future consideration.

## Translation Issues

There's a rumor I've heard about a *New York Times* hacker journalist who asked to be invited to an editorial brownbag lunch series and, when he was declined, promptly quit working for the newspaper. He was, in his mind, a journalist, and the fact that *The Times* didn't recognize him as such was a serious problem—after all, he was on the team winning Pulitzers for them. And while there is no established conflict between the *idea* of interactive journalists working in the newsroom—and they do have the gravitas within the newsroom to command respect and admiration—there are, nonetheless, communication issues and misunderstandings of the emerging occupational identity of interactive journalists. These issues have less to do with journalists failing to integrate interactives into their daily work; as we have seen, journalists at *The Times*, for example, ask to be "Snowfalled," and the demand for interactives placed on most interactive journalists outpaces their ability to actually complete all of them (the idea of "cherry-picking projects"). Instead, the problem lies in the translation between more traditionally narrative-focused journalists and interactive journalists, as there is not always an understanding of the potential of their collaboration and their limitations.

Because interactive journalists are closely embedded in a technology world, there is the potential for difficulty in communicating expectations with those who are unfamiliar with what interactives can bring. Speaking in software terms, as Boyer did in the meeting with the investigative team at NPR, served to underscore differences in a meeting where journalists were working together. Putting out early prototypes that may be imperfect, as journalists at *ProPublica* did with their Dollars for Docs database, challenges journalists' expectations for perfection before publication.

The programming world doesn't always make sense to the newsroom. Ryan Mark, a hacker journalist trained at Northwestern University after working in commercial programming, described some of the communication challenges at *The Chicago Tribune*:

> I think the biggest challenge has been the lack of understanding about what we do. To a lot of people, it seems like we're magicians to a certain extent, where we just make a computer do things. It's difficult to communicate how long things will take. . . . there's lots of moving pieces in software development. There's lots of software. There's multiple layers of it and you can run into strange problems that you've never seen before and have to take time to deal with.
>
> And trying to communicate what it is we do on a day-to-day basis as people pass by and make comments like "you sit there with your headphones all day I have no idea what you're doing." It's like I sit there with a bunch of open windows with a bunch of colored words in them, and people just have no concept of what it is we're doing.[35]

Michelle Minkoff explained a potential difficulty in trying to get people to see beyond just "flashy things." She asked for advice on her blog: "Show me the best way to present these ideas to traditional editors at news organizations. How do we convey that this isn't just a flashy tool, not a distraction from journalism itself, but instead a way to extend our craft?"[36]

Interactive journalists, precisely because they can make software that enhances story presentation and adds engaging value to news, do sometimes seem like they are incorporating an element into the story that offers the best of the Web. But it is also journalism, not just a fancy trick that involves magical computer language. And sometimes, interactive journalism is viewed at the fancy-trick level rather than being recognized for the alternative ways of storytelling it offers.

In other respects, some hacker journalists lack familiarity with basic newsroom practices. Some have never even been inside newsrooms and are not well versed in the norms and culture of journalism institutions. Jonathan Stray of the AP explained the problem facing hacker journalists: "Coders from outside do not have as well developed a sense of journalism. They have no experience in newsroom. There's an almost stereotypical, relatively simple idea of the newsroom."[37] Programmers have experience in big for-profit companies, where they can earn high salaries but where there are few opportunities for creative experimentation. Programmers are also acculturated with an acceptance of "hacking," experimenting, and simply playing around, which does not always translate well into a news organization seeking perfection before publication.

These translation issues mean that interactive journalism and interactive journalists, despite their tremendous potential and welcomed efforts, nonetheless face some challenges in bringing new energy to the newsroom. Getting past translation problems will be critical: the interactive journalists will be better able to think about problems in creative ways while communicating with journalists who understand the potential and capacities of interactive journalists. As long as interactive journalists continue to work well with newsrooms, as most of the cases within the book detail, and needs are successfully articulated and met, there's a bright future ahead for interactive journalism.

## Professionalism through Work

These portraits of seven newsrooms—*Al Jazeera English*, NPR, *The Wall Street Journal*, *The New York Times*, *The Guardian*, and the AP (N.Y. and D.C.)—highlight the kind of work that gets done by interactive journalists and the way that they interact with the rest of the newsroom. This chapter helps elucidate further how this subspecialty is developing within the context of traditional journalism. We can see the kind of jurisdiction over work that interactive journalism has apart from the rest of the newsroom.

Abbott argues that jurisdiction over work can be seen through tasks that can be objectively defined. In this chapter, we see how interactive journalists make a specific claim over "certain kinds of work"[38] within the workplace—interactives. In these examples, we see how interactive journalists negotiate their abilities to offer new kinds of content to the newsroom. The "actual divisions of labor are established through negotiation and custom"[39] as interactive journalists define their relationships, from their timelines to working with other journalists. And the boundary of the profession has changed to incorporate this subgroup with its new ability to do these tasks; journalism expands to include interactive journalists, in some newsrooms almost seamlessly.

Various forms of work emerge in each newsroom. Each newsroom specializes in particular types of interactives, which may speak to the expertise of the journalists present or the socialized demands of each newsroom. More research could be done to tease out why these differences emerge. Nonetheless, these newsrooms are all linked together by the desire to create explanatory forms of journalism through software. The form departs from the traditional narrative structure and speaks to the original definition proposed of interactive journalism *as a visual presentation of storytelling through code for multilayered, tactile user control.*

In the case of *AJE* we find journalists working to put together first a map-based interactive built on a simple programming platform as well as on other more sophisticated interactives that further engage sound and visual material compiled by reporters. At NPR we find a team trying to create a map-based database for users to locate playgrounds in their towns. The *Journal*'s examples included a visualized, interactive database and a clickable calculator. At *The Times*, entire interactive stories, multimedia-based interactives, and data-combing efforts underscore the variety and capacity of this massive team. *The Times* worked not only with big dumps of data but also with pictures and sound (such as for the Fashion Week interactive or Dining interactives). Inside *The Guardian*, daily data efforts included charts, maps, and simple, clean data released to the public. And at the AP, both in New York and in Washington, a variety of interactives were built to illuminate data—from quick daily items to internal investigative pieces built for journalists to help them do their own work. Across all of this, we see a focus on new ways of telling stories, though the goals of each interactive may be slightly different.

Subspecialties show their strength when they can make a claim to external and internal measurements of success. Within each newsroom, journalists have a sense that their interactives need to succeed online: this is measured by traffic. The clearest example of journalists watching traffic is at *The Journal*, where the interactive team is the only team with a screen mounted on the wall to showcase real-time analytics. At *The Times*, the successful dialect quiz at the end of the year garnered considerable attention even from outside the newsroom, validating interactives as a traffic driver. Other newsrooms kept an eye on tweets and shares. Getting what is perceived as "good" traffic helps justify the continued need for interactives to help bolster the online presence of these news organizations.

Internal measurements of success might be considered the demand for interactives within the newsroom. As we can see across these newsrooms, there is considerable demand for interactives, and in some cases interactives are considered a must for regular daily online journalism. This is a sign of the subspecialty's success. There are failures, too, though, like *AJE*'s Yemen map and *The Times*' NFL Playbook. These failures are seen as experiments from which important lessons arose; in the case of *The Times*, the NFL Playbook was a sign that standalone interactives at the newspaper were not likely to garner traffic. But the overall claim to success through internal and external measurements showcases the rise of this subspecialty within the context of the profession.

More generally, subspecialties emerge out of internal and external pressures on the profession to change; similarly, journalism must also change to show its relevance. To review, external pressures are perhaps most clearly expressed by the need to respond to the demands of an increasingly interactive Web; not only is it faster, but it's better at engaging with immediate user demands for something that is truly immersive beyond a textual environment. This means journalism has to offer content beyond what it has traditionally produced and serve readers in new ways. The rise of increasingly larger data sets and simply more kinds of data creates an imperative for journalists to respond. Journalists' work must incorporate this new data in order to continue to be an authoritative voice for public interest. Internal pressures are overwhelmingly those associated with financial survival—just how journalism can continue to be profitable—and that means keeping readers online. But there are also internal demands of the journalism itself—the daily pressure to produce something new and the need to find continual content—a need more significant than ever before in the online environment. Interactive journalism helps respond to that need by providing more new content in a Web-relevant, dynamic fashion for the news production cycle.

We can see evidence of the subspecialty's importance to journalism as it helps the profession respond to these pressures. In part, we can see this by the increasing standardization and integration of the work of interactive journalists. At the AP in New York, the staff felt it was imperative to produce daily interactives for stories without having much say over what stories would even deserve them. At *The New York Times*, the newspaper has enough staff in the interactive news team actually to make interactives a regular part of daily news culture. With every major news event or feature, the assumption is that an interactive will accompany a story as an additional but almost required aspect of the story presentation. And at *The Guardian*, there is a felt demand that the DataBlog should put out daily doses of data for a public hungry to explore the vast outpouring of new content available for analysis. Thus, there emerges a daily imperative for interactive journalism, solidifying its importance in the newsroom.

The imperative emerges in another way—the perceived need to do something different to create a distinctive online offering. *AJE* journalists think that interactives are now critical to understanding complicated news stories like the Euro crisis and the war in Syria. NPR's audience is perceived as hungry for this kind of more specific content beyond simply the investigative story. *The Wall Street Journal* feels a need to wrestle with more complicated data in order to do critical reporting. The team also feels a need to offer something different to readers with a calculator for cellphone pricing, a tool that exists outside of what *The Journal* would traditionally ever offer. Thus, we can see interactive journalists as critical to filling the need to produce distinctive content through they work they do.

Finally, there is a tale of dominance as well as independence from traditional journalism that provides further evidence of the subspecialty's growth. Each newsroom has a different way of interacting with the norms of the dominant newsroom workflow: in some cases, there is a daily conversation about work, in other cases there is a focus on long term projects, and in some newsrooms there is little conversation at all. In some instances, the subspecialty produces content that stands as distinct from traditional newsroom efforts. Overall, there is a give and take between the norms of the dominant newsroom practice and what interactive journalism offers as its contribution to journalism. Yet we can see that interactive journalism remains distinct because what it offers is indeed unique from anything that has come before—a new form of journalism that provides a fresh context for experiencing content online. In the next chapter, we will see how interactive journalists, with the different ways of thinking they bring to their work, enable new forms of abstract knowledge, both for journalists and for the public.

# 5   Interactives and Journalism's Systems of Knowledge

*ProPublica*'s Dollars for Docs underscores the promise of interactive journalism: an in-depth, immersive database that allows users to search through more than $4 billion worth of Big Pharma disclosures showing which doctors the companies paid for talks, research, and consulting.[1] The interactive enables the user to put in his or her own query—the prompt provocatively offering, "Has Your Health Professional Received Drug Company Money?" When I searched for my own doctor, I realized that he had been paid $35,000 for talks at GlaxoSmithKline—which prompted me to ask why (the answer: to present research). The interactive isn't a traditional text story: its design visually walks the reader through tables to click on and explore, offering *tactile, user-directed, multilayered control for the purpose of news and information.* Beneath the surface, the project also underscores the different skills and ways of thinking that interactive journalists bring to journalism, expanding the profession.

This chapter focuses on how interactive journalism contributes new kinds of knowledge to journalism, expanding the work product and ultimately the profession. There are a number of ways to think about how professions come to have a special claim over knowledge that establishes their expertise. Andrew Abbott offers two types of professional knowledge that are useful here: practical knowledge and abstract knowledge. He argues that there are a variety of steps for an occupation to becoming a profession, and one of them is the acquisition of professional/practical knowledge. This is practical knowledge that directly serves a client—in other words, specific skills that solve problems and, in turn, provide some form of product—in this case, to news consumers. Abbott notes, "Professional knowledge enables the defense of a profession's jurisdiction."[2] The subspecialty has a distinct claim to professional/practical knowledge as interactive journalists know code. Others in the newsroom cannot make interactives because they don't have these skills.

The interactive also showcases the ways interactive journalists are bringing new forms of abstract knowledge to traditional news work. Abbott explains how abstract knowledge helps "refine" the "problems and tasks" of a profession.[3] This abstract knowledge is bound up in the system of professions and offers a distinct contribution to how work is understood and ultimately produced. The abstract knowledge emerges from a historical and social context and is applied to particular cases, rather than an "abstraction relative to some supposed absolute standard."[4] As Abbott contends, one of the "central tasks for professionalization [lies] in the construction of a knowledge basis for an occupation."[5] As Wilson Lowrey notes, subgroups control a work area's knowledge base to gain legitimacy and control over work and helps the subgroup foster subgroup cohesion.[6] In this case, we may think of journalism's abstract knowledge as journalism norms, the understanding of how to generate news work—what Silvio Waisbord sees as the special ability of journalists to see the world *as* news.[7]

The subspecialty of interactive journalism, then, changes the tasks of journalism and contributes new forms of abstract knowledge as it refines the profession's work—in the form of different ways of thinking, though perhaps not quite as new norms. This is important because without abstract knowledge, the subgroup (and professions more generally) would be unable to conceptually redefine and reposition the profession. And as we have found here, there is little conflict between the subgroup of interactive journalists and traditional journalists, as some might have expected;[8] one reason may be that interactive journalists are indeed viewed as heroes to the newsroom. Even though they accept dominant norms of the newsroom about how to do journalistic work, interactive journalists are still able to challenge and expand notions of how journalists think about traditional news work.[9] The combination of both old and new ways of thinking nonetheless coalesces into one coherent news product.[10]

The Dollars for Docs interactive brings together the five different ways interactive journalism adds new kinds of abstract knowledge to doing news work: build-it journalism, near/far journalism, openness, see-it-for-yourself journalism, and a focus on reorienting a nut-graf. Dollars for Docs is an example of an outward-facing tool that enables users to search for information about their doctors. It is a software application layered on top of the existing Web architecture. This focus on building tools and applications for journalism products is what I call "*build-it*" journalism, where journalism is understood as making a product. The interactive gives the user the chance to search for personally relevant information, as I did about my doctor, and to see national trends, like the fact that Florida doctors receive more than $338 million in pharma payouts. This is the *"near/far"* approach to thinking about journalism, where the personal—the actual specific personal details of a user—and the public are incorporated in one experience.

Others have observed this feature of Dollars for Docs. Chris Anderson, Emily Bell, and Clay Shirky write:

> Dollars for Docs was not just a new report. It was a new kind of reporting. Though much of the data used were publicly available, they had not been centralized or standardized in a form that could make them useful. . . . In addition, it has been able to make its database as local as any news story can ever get: individual users can type the name of their doctor into the database and get a customized report. The harvesting and organizing of publicly available data thus became a platform for national, local and personal reporting.[11]

The near/far approach, then, is a "new kind of reporting."

In addition, the Dollars for Docs project embodies *"openness"* or a way to approach news work as a process visible to the public. Interactive journalists wrote about their struggles in creating the project on the "Nerds" blog, which offers not-so "secrets for data journalists and newsroom developers."[12] Similarly, the fact that users can look for information on their own and explore at their own pace, testing out hypotheses and searching for information, underlies a *"see-it-for-yourself"* approach to thinking about a journalism experience. This see-it-for-yourself experience of content is embedded in the experience of the Web but has not been a way that journalists have thought about creating news. Interactive journalism challenges but ultimately accepts the dominant way of thinking about journalism: as *a coherent narrative*. While the narrative of the interactive is self-directed, the narrative is also clear: your doctors, and the nation's doctors, are taking in enormous amounts of money from drug companies.[13] The connection to the larger journalistic project of narrative storytelling, albeit in a different way, is critical for establishing these interactives as firmly grounded within the practice of journalism. These approaches to journalism do not begin to address on a conceptual level how journalists approach ethical, epistemological, and normative questions of this kind of work;[14] my findings here instead focus on how interactive journalists create journalism in a way that is distinct from past practices and, through this, ground themselves not only as having professional jurisdiction as a subprofession but also as contributing new knowledge to the profession—new ways of thinking about news work.

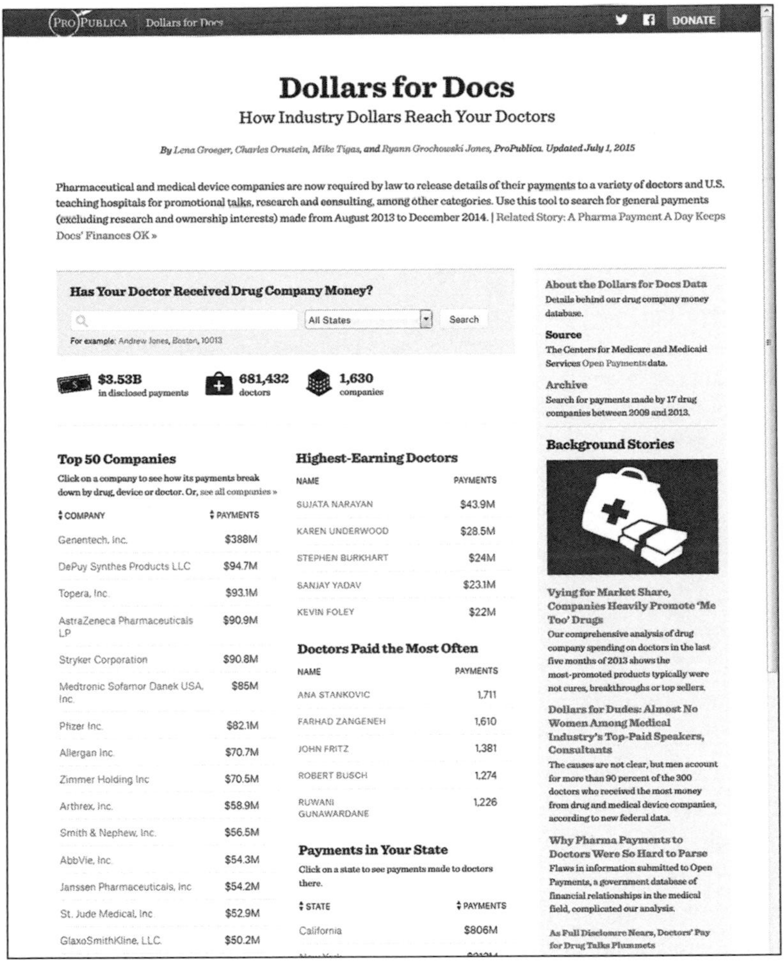


"Dollars for Docs: How Industry Dollars Reach Your Doctors," *ProPublica*

Interactive journalists, emboldened with new kinds of skills, bring knowledge from the programming world and combine this with news work to change the way that news gets created, rendering different ways of thinking about doing journalism. This practical and abstract knowledge challenges and expands the profession, which lays special claim over the ability to offer this kind of experience to users. And without the coding skills, this project would have never happened. This chapter begins with an analysis of the different kinds of skills required to be an interactive journalist. It then focuses on the kind of abstract knowledge interactive journalists bring to traditional journalism, expressed here in ways of thinking about and doing work. These new understandings broaden what it means to do journalism.

## Skills

A comparison of traditional journalism job postings and interactive journalism job postings reveals the difference in what newsrooms are looking for when it comes to the kinds of skills that each brings to the newsroom. These differences showcase the unique skills interactive journalists now bring to the profession. To underscore this juxtaposition, consider the following traditional journalism jobs and job descriptions, like this one for a reporter at *The Wall Street Journal*:

REPORTER-NY[15]

Job Requirements: *The Wall Street Journal*'s Law Bureau is seeking an aggressive and independent journalist to cover legal issues across the U.S. The person will be expected to break news and spearhead coverage of important cases, especially those arising in the New York area, but also those commanding attention in other jurisdictions around the country. The person also will need to produce thoughtful enterprise work on major issues like terrorism, cybercrime and nationwide trends in law enforcement.

The beat has been central to *The Journal*'s coverage of everything from the prosecution of Osama bin Laden's son-in-law and hacking groups such as Anonymous to investigations into the virtual currency bit coin and online marketplaces like Silk Road. It is a regular source of stories for the front page and other section fronts. The ideal candidate will have a proven ability to develop deep sources, the versatility to quickly master an array of subjects, and the temperament to work closely with other reporters and bureaus across the organization. He/she will be a self-starter with a curious, inquisitive mind and at least three years of reporting experience in daily journalism.

Key skills required of this potential hire are almost exclusively related to what he or she can do as a reporter. "The ideal candidate will have a proven ability to develop deep sources" and the ability to "produce thoughtful enterprise work" as well as be "expected to break news." Moreover, the beat generates a regular supply of front-page news—the ad doesn't even discuss the Web.

Other editorial jobs suggest the same kind of focus on journalism as it always has been for at least the past fifty years. Even those newsrooms asking for digital chops still put forward what we can consider traditional journalism skills. Consider the quirky alt-weekly job ad from *The Stranger*, based in Seattle:

We're looking for a widely curious, energetic news junkie who wants to report on the fastest growing large city in America™ for Seattle's only newspaper™. Must have a black belt in time management and be ready to write, as they say, "in any medium now existing or hereafter developed." But especially: for our beloved blog and print editions.

If you believe that solid reporting still has a place in this godforsaken world, if you are more interested in document digging than dogma, and if you have a voice that makes itself heard, we want to hear from you! (Also, if you know what our publisher means by "Get me someone who's ready to cut cookies in the church parking lot!" please get in touch ASAP.) Send a short cover letter, your best and most honest résumé, and a few examples of your most compelling work to: newsjob@thestranger.com. No calls. Seriously. (Save that for your reporting.)

This "news junkie" will be ready to write in any medium but will be focused on "solid reporting" and have a "voice." This journalist will also be a solid document digger, suggesting that *The Stranger* wants an investigative reporter. Notice how document diggers are associated, though, not with data journalism but with traditional work. The ad is for a good-old-reporting job, with the ad explicitly saying, "If you believe that solid reporting still has a place in this god-forsaken world."

Of course, if you were to look at ads for photographers and videographers, you would find a different set of skills than just reporting and editing credentials. These specifications showcase how these groups are also subspecialties within the profession. But the job ads for interactive journalists are different from the kinds of ads that have historically appeared in news, as photographers, videographers, designers, and other specialists have long been a part of news. Thus, take a look at some of the job ads seeking programmer journalists, hacker journalists, and data journalists; they often specify a different set of skills related to programming and other ways of approaching journalism work. Consider this job ad for *The Chicago Tribune* News Apps team:[16]

We're hiring: Code in the public interest, make your mother proud
Requirements
- A passion for the news
- Serious programming skills
- An understanding of the inner workings of the web
- Attention to detail and love for making things
- A genuine and friendly disposition

We're in need of a great hacker. Someone passionate for learning programming languages, using the best tools for the job, and in general, getting things done.

We're generalists, and we expect you to be as well. On any given day you might implement a responsive web design w/ HTML5 + CSS3, explore a dataset with a reporter looking over your shoulder, or help make the servers swift.

Bonus points if you've got skills in . . .

- Data science
- Information design
- User experience / usability
- Maintaining high-performance web sites
- Graphic design

Allow me a moment to persuade you.

The newsroom is a crucible. We work on tight schedules with hard deadlines. While this may seem stressful, it's got a serious upside. Every couple of weeks we can learn from our mistakes and refine our technologies. It's a fast-moving, volatile development environment that will make you a better programmer.

Also, it's a damned good time.

There is a call for the skills demanded for interactives: a user-experience specialist who understands the inner workings of the Web. The ad isn't the typical reporting ad. Instead, it's for a hacker, someone who knows his or her way around the Web, who can program, who can build, who can design, and who knows languages like HTML5 + CSS3, which are essential to responsive Web design. Notably, in this job ad there's no requirement for a candidate to have actually been a journalist before.

*The New York Daily News* sent out a similar job ad on the NICAR email listserv:

Job description: Data journalist[17]

*The New York Daily News* is seeking a data and programming whiz with a background in journalism to join our growing interactive team. This position would primarily involve data analysis, web scraping, building internal news apps and mobile-responsive interactive data visualizations, filing Freedom of Information requests and reporting. You'd be working with teams of journalists, designers, developers and multimedia producers to create dynamic print and web packages that pop. Your work would be a mix of local and national projects; self-generated ideas and collaborations with other reporters; long-term investigations, breaking news enterprise and searchable databases . . .

Desired skills:

- Ability to work collaboratively and congenially with multiple editorial departments.
- Ability to perform advanced data analysis using programs such as MySQL, Caspio, NaviCat, PostgreSQL, Google Refine and Tableau.
- Programming skills in JavaScript and PHP, Python or Ruby.

- Ability to visualize data using tools such as D3, Highcharts, Google Fusion, QGis, ArcGIS, MapBox, Leaflet and CartoDB.
- Proven track record winning Freedom of Information battles, strong news judgment that enables you to find a great story in a sea of numbers, and the ability to report it out.
- Participation in the open-source community and maintaining a GitHub repository a plus.
- Willingness to participate in training journalists on data skills to foster a culture of obtaining and analyzing data across the newsroom.
- Ongoing commitment to building new skills, which will be fostered by attendance at trainings and conferences.

This job ad asks for everything to the point that some practitioners might even find it laughable, but it illustrates the demand for skills needed in the newsroom. Wanted is a hacker/programmer journalist with serious data journalism chops. *The New York Daily News* hopes for someone who can work with the pre-built tools like Google Fusion, CartoDB, and Tableau, which require no programming. But there's also a heavy list of programming requirements: D3, PostgreSQL, PHP, Python, Ruby, and JavaScript—not to mention the responsibility of creating a GitHub repository, where open-source code can be housed. *The Daily News* is also trying to hire someone who can create interactives *and* report, even filing Freedom of Information Act (FOIA) requests. The ad is seeking "a data and programming whiz."

These job ads underscore the kind of practical knowledge that interactive journalism requires. Notably, they are quite different from traditional reporting job ads, which focus on the ability to write and gather information according to standard journalism protocol. Instead, interactive journalism job ads emphasize the need to have specialized knowledge, particularly in code. There are aspects of traditional journalism in these job ads, such as the importance of using data to help create news stories, but there is also a focus on programming skills. As Abbott predicted, one of the key signs to establishing specific domain over work is the acquisition of skills, which interactive journalists clearly have apart from traditional journalists. But there's also a level of abstract knowledge they bring to journalism that further expands the profession. This abstract knowledge offers a different way of thinking about journalism that not only establishes the distinctiveness of their subfield but also helps expand the profession as a whole.

## Build-It Journalism

Many newsrooms call their interactive teams "News Apps": *ProPublica*, NPR, *The Chicago Tribune*, *The Texas Tribune*, *The Seattle Times*, among others. *The Wall Street Journal* changed its team name from Interactive Graphics to News Apps. Why? When the term was invented at *ProPublica*, Scott Klein and Brian Boyer thought that the type of journalism ought to be called "News Applications" in honor of applied news, like applied math or computer science. These fields have a strong connection to industry, thinking about creating products for people to use.

News Apps is a good metaphor to describe one of the ways interactive journalists think differently about journalism. They build journalism, and this approach to enabling new forms of news I call "build-it journalism," a focus on using code to create tools that improve the products and process of news. Build-it journalism also connotes the creation of new layers of technology on the basic content management system for Web, mobile or tablet: the software application built on top of this framework. Journalism is approached as an endeavor that can be constructed. Building for the *process* of journalism means thinking about how to create tools that make it easier to conduct journalistic work. Building for the *product* of journalism means building applications that help tell stories through software.

Build-it journalism comes from a larger tradition of thinking about technology—what is often referred to as "making" or maker culture. Those who talk about maker culture explain how making is central to human culture. As Dale Dougherty explains, "All of us are makers. We're born makers. We have this ability to make things, to grasp things with our hands."[18]

There is a strong connection between this idea of making and hacking. In the early days of the internet, when the technology was less established, programmers and hobbyists would work to build not only better programs but better hardware to enable communication across the new platform.[19] Stuart Brand's *Whole Earth Catalog* encouraged experimentation with the burgeoning world of the Web.[20] Later, Tim O'Reilly, the software-publishing guru and thinker, would launch *MAKE*, a magazine devoted to the experimentation of building technology.[21]

Other major thinkers in the software and entrepreneurship work have further connected the ideas of hacking and making. Paul Graham, founder of Y-Combinator and a legendary hacker himself, describes hacking as a craft akin to painting because of this focus on making: "Hacking and painting have a lot in common. In fact, of all the different types of people I've known, hackers and painters are among the most alike. What hackers and painters have in common is that they're both makers. Along with composers, architects, and writers, what hackers and painters are trying to do is make good things."[22] Hackers are working as makers to build and improve on what they see—and in journalism, this making means building tools and software for news. It is, to use the term I've coined, an ethos of build-it journalism.

### Talking about Building

Interactive journalists don't talk about writing or shooting photographs or tape; instead, many talk about "building." Many of these journalists detail how they work to make their projects, and we can see how much the idea of building comes into the descriptions of what they do. This building recalls the idea of *making*, whereby hackers work through *doing*. In the blogs many of these journalists keep to describe how they have gone about projects, they repeatedly use the term "build" to describe their activities. One example is *The Chicago Tribune*'s News Apps blog:

> 3/7/2014[23]
> So, you started **building** charts with D3 and quickly realized there are certain behaviors you want all of your charts to have
> 2/17/2014[24]
> A few months ago, we **built** a reusable JavaScript app to provide an interface to a quirky events API. Internal stakeholders needed standalone, searchable event listings, embeddable calendar and upcoming events widgets, and integration with Google calendar, Facebook, and desktop calendar software . . .
> The vision was to **build** a simple list of events with a search box at the top and calendar next to the event list.

The focus on explaining code that is in the blog helps demonstrate just how much is going into the process of refining existing code for new purposes. This building effort was project based; it was designed to help construct an outward-facing chart to help tell the story of journalism.

*The New York Times*' Open Blog uses a similar language:

> Here at *The Times*, we use a functional automation framework we've **built** in Python. On top of the framework, we use the nose unit-testing framework for test discovery and execution. Our framework **builds** in lots of automatic logging (service requests and responses, actions taken in forms on web pages, database queries, etc.) using Python's logging module.[25]

We can hear the language of frameworks being built upon. This is that concept of layering upon an existing interface new code to create an application that was not present before. This is an example of a process project, a software application that is intended to make gathering data easier—refining the way journalism gets done.

## Tool Building

The focus on building tools to improve both the process and product of journalism output is perhaps one of the clearest signs that interactive journalists are thinking about doing news work in new ways. Their tools enable journalistic work and are foundations to construct and help create journalism. Interactive journalists think not just about the story but also about making it easier to do journalism. Using code to help create editorial work on this scale is now more part of journalism than ever before.

A tool can be used over and over again. In fact, these tools reach their full potential when people without any programming knowledge can use them easily. Most often, these tools are made to harness data to make it easier for data journalists and other journalists as well to understand what they are looking at. The ability to make these tools comes out of the advances in programming and computing now possible, and while some tools have existed in proto-forms before, the tools available today offer new ways to visualize, gather, and analyze data.

Tools can be inward-facing or outward-facing, and by this I mean that some tools are intended to help journalists, while other tools are intended to help people. But most of the tools that journalists tend to talk about at conferences and with each other are the tools to help journalists do journalism. These tools are often open source and intended for use and repurposing in other news-gathering efforts. Taking a look at a few of them reveals insight into the philosophical approach taken by interactive journalists as they use programming to solve larger journalistic problems, and reveals a hope to make analysis easier across newsrooms.

One process-focused tool is Overview. Jonathan Stray, in partnership with the AP and the Knight Foundation, began a quest in fall 2010 to visualize vast amounts of data through computer programming. His talk before the 2014 Groundbreaking Journalism Conference in Berlin explained the origins and hopes for the tool.[26] He began his work with WikiLeaks data—noting to the conference that the 250,000 diplomatic-cables dump would have likely taken three years to read in its entirety. Most journalists were using computers to search for specific terms that they imagined might lead to interesting stories or were using programs to visualize dates. But they were missing one key aspect: looking at every word in the documents.

Stray's innovation was to look at the text contained within the documents to spot the stories that were not being found through the text searches—ones that were based on hunches journalists already had. Through the actual text searches of the documents, Stray's program could visualize the relationships of documents among each other, showing similar patterns of data together.

With his initial reporting, he was able to see some obvious trends—such as violence from the civil war in Iraq. This, as he acknowledged, was something journalists already knew. What they hadn't realized was the extent of incidents around tanker trucks, uncovered through the visualization. Visualizing the full text of every document enabled the journalists to find what they didn't know to look for.

The tool wasn't usable at first, but through continued refinement it has become a bona fide project that some journalists across the country may use—and are starting to do so. It is, as Stray contends, a "repeatable technique"—a tool. The project overview homepage describes some of these efforts.[27] Completed projects have included a *Newsday* effort to show police misconduct through documents, including seven thousand pages of transcripts and seventeen hundred proposed state laws. This project was a 2013 Pulitzer finalist. A St. Louis Public Radio journalist used Overview to analyze Missouri death-penalty documents to see whether the state was using a controversial lethal injection drug. He found that it was, despite claims to the contrary.[28]

This process-focused tool helps make it easier for journalists to do their work, simplifying the task of going through vast amounts of data. It solves a particular problem of too many documents with stories that might be missed. Right now, the project is under continual refinement as Stray looks for funds to continue his work. The tool is a significant move forward in an aim to think about how to best use resources at a time when there are simply fewer people and less money to allow for investigative reporting.

Other tools are also geared toward organizing data. Panda, A Newsroom Data Appliance (or PANDA) is a project started by Boyer, Germuska, and others in 2011. Also funded by Knight, PANDA aims to help newsrooms search through the data they have already collected. The program provides a searchable database that aggregates all available data, from water safety records to police records to campaign donations. It is, in essence, a "newsroom data library."[29] In its ideal form, it's a tool any reporter in the newsroom could use by performing a Google-style search across any of the databases the newsroom has. Take, for example, one of the scenarios given by the PANDA project: someone is in a car crash—a simple PANDA search would then reveal every single database containing that person's name. This can help enrich deadline reporting with context that would otherwise be impossible to find.

More significant, the idea of a newsroom-wide data library would solve the problem of journalists stashing data on their hard drives. The PANDA Project began at *The Chicago Tribune*, where these interactive journalists realized that journalists had maxed out on an old data system. The previous system was well loved but did not allow anyone in the newsroom to contribute data. It was also difficult to maintain and could not include the breadth and depth of information *The Tribune* needed. So journalists simply weren't uploading or updating new information to central repositories kept by the newsroom. This new system would be a data repository that could keep millions of rows of data.[30]

PANDA could enable a journalist with an elementary one-step process simply to upload the data he or she found. The data would then be cleaned and rendered easily searchable within the PANDA interface. So every time a reporter got a new database through the PANDA Web browser, the deed would be done. As Boyer explained, "A spreadsheet stuck on your hard drive is a sad spreadsheet." The PANDA Project has now been recognized as an important innovation for investigative journalism. It is currently sustained by the Investigative Reporters and Editors organization. And it has bolstered its claims for what it can do since its initial presentation, with perhaps one essential point at this rocky time in traditional journalism—aiding institutional memory. When journalists leave newsrooms, it's possible that their data will leave with them, unless it can be shared with the newsroom. PANDA project offers the solution. And an email alert has been added to let people know when there are new findings for a particular favorite search.

The PANDA Project again demonstrates the potential viability of tools used in the service of journalism. This is a process-focused tool that aims to help the journalistic workflow and solve problems related to newsgathering. Installing PANDA takes some know-how, but using it (once it is made part of the newsroom) is easy for any journalist who simply knows how to search, thus facilitating news work. This application is an example of build-it journalism; it has been created through code to enhance journalism efforts as an additional layer upon existing journalism presentation. And it adds one more aspect to build-it journalism through the potential to apply the application's use across newsroom projects and across other newsrooms.

So far, I have written about internal tools that serve journalists. But a number of tools are also public-facing. One of these product-oriented tools is DocumentCloud, a project begun by three journalists at *The New York Times* and *ProPublica*, which seeks to solve a common problem with documents—the fact that they are difficult to search, annotate, and share. Notes kept by co-creator Scott Klein from the first meeting offered this thought:

"This project will fight the 'dark web' nature of source documents on the Web, in which documents are difficult to find and often disappear when a news organization is done telling a particular story."[31]

DocumentCloud can be used with any kind of document that Microsoft Office can read—searchable or not. In its most common application, DocumentCloud puts ordinary pdf documents through an OCR process so that they can be easily searched for key terms. The tool enables journalists to build timelines around key dates. Documents can easily be embedded on a news site for easy reading by the public. And perhaps most significant is that the tool gives journalists *and* the public the ability to annotate documents posted on the Web.

Annotation is a key feature for a number of reasons. First, journalists can call attention to essential facts that they might have highlighted in a story or to facts that did not make it into the narrative but might also be important to alert readers to. But the annotation feature also helps gather information—readers can annotate the documents too, providing journalists with another set of eyes. Large stacks of documents now have the potential to be crowd sourced among a wide audience. The ability to make it easy to host documents online opens up a new means for users to learn about the stories at hand and potentially contribute to reporting efforts. This function not only allows for user exploration to help readers reach their own conclusions about the stories, but it can also enable partnerships. Each annotation has its own URL, meaning that each comment can be tracked and is traceable for a journalist to go through and examine. Co-founder Aron Pilhofer has contended that this is a standard tool across many newsrooms and as of 2012 had hosted more than four million pages of documents.[32] This is a tool that offers a product that displays journalistic output—documents that have been gathered from reporting—in an easy-to-read format.

An extensive partner network supports this inward/outward tool. *The New York Times, The Las Vegas Sun, The New Yorker, The Los Angeles Times, The Chicago Tribune*, and a host of other newsrooms are sponsors of the project. With initial Knight funding, the project is now sustained by IRE through a team of hacker journalists and programmer journalists. This tool makes a key contribution because it is pre-built, usable, and easy to implement across a variety of stories in multiple contexts.

In Chicago, the News Apps team has built a number of actual tools, including front-end applications the user can see, and back-end tools other developers can use. One forward-facing news app they created in 2013 was Chicago Shooting Victims.[33] The app tracks "when and where people are shot in Chicago." Interactive journalist Andy Boyle explained the process

"Chicago Shooting Victims," *The Chicago Tribune*

in an extensive entry on the News Apps blog. Since Chicago police record each shooting as a single shooting, regardless of the number of victims, the number of actual victims might therefore be higher—which is where *The Tribune*'s reporting adds subtext. *Tribune* reporters were using a spreadsheet to track the details, and the News Apps team built a map and an updating list that feeds into this single destination. The map includes clickable buttons showing each event, and shading reflects the frequency of these shootings. But creating the map required building from pieces of code.

This interactive helps users see all of the shootings in Chicago. It is a tool for those who wish to drill down into what is happening in their community. This outward-facing application is an app built on top of the existing *Tribune* platform to provide a software experience of a story.

### Build-It Journalism in Sum

Build-it journalism is an extension of the kind of "making" seen in hacker culture. Journalists are making projects by playing with technology to solve problems. They are using their creativity to build on to or create from scratch new kinds of applications and tools using code. How these journalists talk about building suggests that there is a new way of thinking about journalism: as an endeavor that can be improved through the creation of tools and applications that make journalism better through software. The inclusion of tools as journalistic output is new. These tools help contribute to the process of journalism (making it easier to do journalism) and to the product of journalism (outward-facing applications that the public can see). Journalism, then, can be in the form of a tool.

The lingo inherent in conversations about build-it journalism is not how traditional journalists speak about their work. There is little discussion of actual journalism goals; instead, the focus is on the creation of the product. Yet build-it journalism is a fundamental aspect of thinking about news and is directly related to the creation of products and processes that make news better. The overall goal is the creation of something that contributes to journalism, and the product is journalism itself. The importation of programmer ways of talking about making news software is still ultimately in the service of news.

Build-it journalism is important to the future of news. The academic community has suggested that tool-building can be a solution to the woes of journalism today. Sarah Cohen, James Hamilton, and Fred Turner identified a number of difficulties in data journalism that computational work might indeed solve. Matching two data sets can be incredibly difficult, particularly because many of these data sets contain errors.[34] Compiling data from handwritten notes, multiple sources, and different kinds of material from audio to visual data is another challenge. Information extraction can be especially difficult given this varied presentation of data, as well as the size of datasets. Grouping documents is another way tools can be helpful.[35] And we can see also, as with DocumentCloud, the beginnings of newsrooms working collaboratively to solve problems and make journalism more efficient. As a whole, build-it journalism directly recalls fundamental ideas bound up in hacker culture—applied to journalism. Embedded in this work is the desire to make something. These "tools" are the expression of build-it journalism, which is one way interactive journalists make a contribution to new kinds of abstract knowledge that augments the profession.

## Near/Far

Interactive journalism makes it possible to think about news as it applies to both the reader and wider public concerns. This is the "near" and "far" view of looking at journalism, often incorporated at once in many forms of interactives. The "near" view gives users a chance to zoom in and see exactly how a topic appears to affect them: they can choose data points or specify particular areas of interest that are unique to them, and then they can see the results. But there's also a "far" view—the interactive contains a much larger story about how this particular issue is affecting everyone included by the data. Two different narrative entry points tell the story in an organized way that offers both experience and social context; near and far. The practice of telling stories from the near and the far gives the capacity for stories to resonate across a broader social landscape and into the user's own backyard.[36]

Two examples illustrate this near and far view. WNYC, New York City's premiere public radio station, nestled in SoHo in light, lofty quarters, drew attention to a citywide quality-of-life problem: the new Citi Bike bike-share program's many outages. This had real consequences on the transportation decisions that people in New York were making every day. And at *ProPublica*, located just a few subway stops away near Wall Street, interactive journalists had created a database to show how social problems such as education inequality could be conveyed to a wide audience on a national level and on an individual level as well. Together, these groups found ways to use different types of interactives to create the same effect: giving people the chance to explore data with a near view and a far view of one story.

WNYC's John Keefe, senior editor for data news and journalism technology, explained that much of what he does is bring together the "macro" and "micro." The Citi Bike interactive shows such an interplay at work. In May 2013, bikes sponsored by Citibank (but managed by the city) became part of the city's transportation environment. The bike-share program was by most measures a popular success, with a problem: there were outages at many of the stations. This had real consequences: If the docking stations didn't work, users relying on the bikes to go to work might be late, or might have to figure out an alternate route, and those seeking to return a bike could find themselves similarly out of luck—with the worst possible consequence of paying a fine for failing to deposit a bike or even be accused of stealing the bike.

So what could WNYC do? At the time, WNYC had a fairly new interactives team, whose Twitter bio self-described as "Practicing data-driven journalism, making it visual, and showing our work." Keefe and his team began thinking about how to use data to tell the story of what was going on with Citi Bikes. Keefe soon found that the software application program interface (API) for the bikes was available from the city: "You could go to a station and find how many bikes were there . . . it was taking the data in every two minutes."[37]

This wasn't a problem that presented a serious challenge to the safety and well being of New Yorkers, but it was, indeed, a quality-of-life problem that deserved a look. And as Keefe noted, "The data set was interesting, we heard anecdotal complaints, and we said let's look at the data." And significantly, the data could tell one of the most helpful things: just how many bikes were available. This was a terrific help to any New Yorker needing to know something basic: was there a bike to use, and was there a place to dock the bike? The app was helping to take the guesswork out of the Citi Bike experience. If you needed to find a bike to use and one station was down, you could go to the next. Or if one station had no bikes and you needed to find one, a station nearby could supply you with one. But there was a trick with the publicly available data—the Citi Bike data wouldn't tell if the station itself was down—only if the station was unchanged for more than three hours. Keefe suggested that with three hours unchanged, "we can reasonably infer that no one is using it or they are broken." Keefe and his team were making that call, and putting it on a publicly accessible, easy-to-read map. This was the *near* view. This was the data a person needed to know to get along with his or her daily life: Was the bike dock working? Were there enough bikes? Was there a place to dock the next bike?[38]

But this was also about a city program, and there was a need to keep the city accountable too. Hence, the far view. The team was able to determine that about 10 percent of the docking stations were dormant for three or more hours, though the city would not admit to the stations being broken. As Keefe told me in a follow-up email: "We decided to track stations that saw no action—basically static number of bikes or spaces—during the daytime hours, and flag those with lengthy dormant times." Initially, the city simply wasn't talking, but the anecdotal sources and shoe-leather reporting filled in the gaps. The far view began to emerge. The state of the city's Citi Bikes could easily be seen in one clear, clickable map.

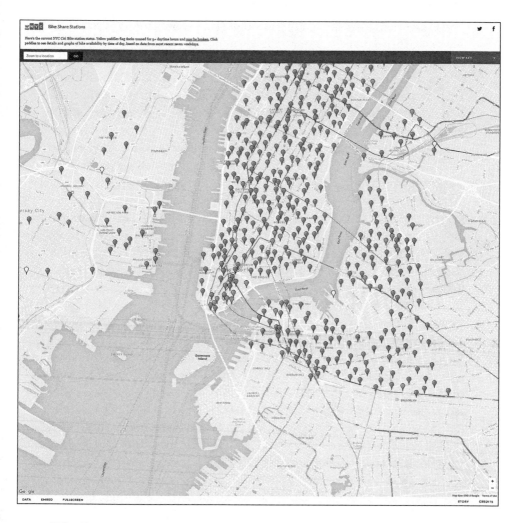

"Bike Share Stations," WNYC

Keefe explained that WNYC broadcast stories about the docking stations as they "kept watch." He said, "Outages dropped within weeks [after the story]." He added in an email to me, "After that story, the number of dormant stations started to drop—and our reporting found Citi Bike was working through some technical glitches at the stations."[39] The team at WNYC helped bring some clarity to a problem ordinary New Yorkers were having—but WNYC was also keeping the city accountable. With this near and far view, Keefe said he was showing the "macro to the micro."[40]

An important aspect emerges from this discussion that points back to a key capacity of data-driven storytelling. In the past, journalists could write narrative articles with an anecdotal lead of a sympathetic figure. They might write a sweeping story about a complicated problem facing all New Yorkers. This constantly updating data could help bring light to both—what the story couldn't say, the data driving the story could. But the story emerged out of the data, and the data personalized through interactive journalism helped reinforce the importance of the story. Through interactive journalism, people could see what was happening in the "near"—what was happening close to them. They could also begin to draw larger conclusions about the state of Citi Bike, going beyond just adding to a chorus of complaints on Twitter to the @CitibikeNYC account and to Citi Bike's Facebook page. The traditional journalism could ask questions about *why* these problems were occurring, and the data was able to offer hard evidence about the scale—the *far* view. To this end, the data was both personally and publicly accountable, thanks to the creation of a software application.

At *ProPublica*, with its offices down on Wall Street, Scott Klein's News Apps team also works on projects that showcase the near/far capacities of interactive journalism. It's an approach that can be found in many of *ProPublica*'s stories, which are data intensive and often offer many opportunities for individuals to connect with data that appears relevant to them through interactive experiences. At the same time, *ProPublica* has also cast a wider net, writing a story and providing the context for the phenomenon under investigation through a far view—what the issue at hand means to all of us.

One project, "The Opportunity Gap," helps illustrate this near and far view.[41] This interactive offers insights into public-school performance across fifty states and the District of Columbia using vast amounts of publicly available data. The dataset encompasses about three-quarters of all public-school students in the country. A publicly minded reader is invited to compare how his or her state compares. Users can easily compare states against each other across a variety of metrics: the ability to provide advanced placement classes, advanced science classes, or sports participation through a searchable tool used for entering addresses. With your school's name you can have instant access to statistics, from the number of students receiving free lunch to the students in gifted-and-talented programs, as well as the racial demographics of a student population.

The information they had about these schools was "quite little," Klein explained. "We knew just that the rich and the poor ones were different. But with data we could personalize for people, you could find out new details.

Before, unless you had gone to the schools, you would have no examples of other schools."[42] And these schools can be compared against each other; I can easily compare Walt Whitman High School in Bethesda, Maryland, to Vivian T. Thomas Medical Arts Academy, a high school in Baltimore. I can see that Whitman only has 2 percent of students on school lunch, while Thomas has 81 percent; 57 percent at Whitman take one AP course, compared with about 6 percent at Thomas. Indeed, there is a window through which to see this opportunity gap, side by side.

Klein added that they had "this big data set, and you could find your school and anchor your understanding; you could know if there was free lunch and if there were AP tests. You could remember your high school or your kid's high school and know and look and compare poor and wealthy [schools] with meaningful information and your own experience." While that's sobering for anyone living in a town with good public schools, it's also possible to compare against the neighboring public schools, in which competitive parents just outside D.C. should find that area high schools in the wealthy Southern Montgomery County area of Maryland are, indeed, as advertised. Perhaps, of course, this was an unintended consequence. Regardless of what the data is used for, it illustrates both near and far; you can see how your state is performing, and you can see how you are performing. Those looking to gain insight into a social problem—the public, education advocacy groups, and the like—can take advantage of this usable, actionable data to get a far view.

"It is broad and deep, it affects you personally," Klein said. "It goes from general to specific, it is a far view and there is a search box list, there is a national map for a broad view before the zoom and the worst/best, and there is a context point of all of this. You can do the dig and find the familiar and . . . then find something that ties to the national." The "broad and deep"—the "personal to the national" that Klein talks about—is exactly how interactive journalists contribute to bringing the near/far view to journalism.

One of the greatest differences here from traditional journalism is the ability to get the personalized snapshot *and* the large picture in one place. With traditional journalism, the attempt to create a relatable voice could be offered through a feature story, anecdote, or a quote. But the ability to search for personal experience specific to the individual is a unique result of this new *near* data capacity enabled through interactive journalism. Traditional journalism has done a good job offering the far, giving with words and images a perspective of a larger story at hand, but it does less well at tying this far into the near. Interactives bring near and far together through the ability to marshal information into a sortable, searchable, and user-directed form.

## Openness

Interactive journalists embrace openness in news work; this is a different way of thinking about journalism that comes out of hacker culture. These journalists take their cues about how to act as programmers from the open-source community. Their approach to journalism involves showing and sharing work with other newsrooms and the public, unmasking the process of creating journalism. Interactive journalists share their struggles and their triumphs through blogs and the contributions of code through the online open-source repository GitHub. In the past, newsrooms have not opened up the process of doing news work to the public and have only recently begun to ask the public to share in the newsgathering process. The radical approach to devising a collaborative environment for creating journalism work suggests how these journalists come with a distinct set of norms that they contribute to traditional journalism.

Much of the pro-social hacker culture is imbued with an ethic of sharing, in particular sharing code. As Coleman writes, "Hackers are frequently committed to an ethical version of information."[43] Hackers "open source" their code—make it available for anyone to use, change, or expand. Eric Raymond's *The Cathedral and the Bazaar*, a foundational work about open-source culture, underscores this key point: that open source offers the opportunity for a community to create a product.[44] Open source may be "characterized by a non-market, non-contractual transfer of knowledge among actors, sharing relevant information with a non-definite set of other actors without any immediate recompense. Actors share their ideas with the clear purpose of contributing to a joint development."[45]

Others help elucidate the implications for this culture relative to sharing code. As Tim Jordan argues in a journal article about hacking and power, the key characteristic of open source is "total access to source code, both to view it and change it . . . the ability to fundamentally understand how a programme works and to intervene into the programme, changing how it works."[46] The consequence of this openness is a commitment to "show your work"[47] or allow people to see how you are building your software projects.

This culture is different from traditional journalism; code and process is radically shared in a way that the guts of creating a story never would be. Scholar Axel Bruns explains the difference between open source and journalism this way: "Open source has the ethos of open participation and communal evaluation,"[48] which, as he argues, are two things that traditional journalism does not offer. Open source is a cultural orientation, which is found when hacking intersects with journalism, as Seth C. Lewis and I have found in our own examination.[49] It becomes an ethos of collective intelligence and community engagement around the desire to solve common problems. Interactive journalism becomes the conduit for this new expression of sharing across newsrooms seeking to solve the problems of creating new ways of doing journalistic work through software.

John Keefe, who had been a traditional news director in WNYC's newsroom, contrasted traditional journalism and interactive journalism. "It is not journalistic to be sharing things, but we share source [code], we don't share angles. In journalism there is this idea of secrecy, and of course competition between us remains really high, but there is this culture of open source, and we are sharing and building on our work."[50] Other journalists who have come from a traditional background have elucidated another aspect of the idea of openness. Within the context of programming for news, beyond just keeping the project secret from competitors, the interactive journalists are going one step further, exposing the backbone of how a story is made through code, something that would simply never happen in an equivalent way, say, to sharing a reporter's notebook.

Aron Pilhofer, head of *The New York Times* interactive news team and a former congressional reporter, explains why open source practices are not practical for traditional journalists: "In a newsroom context it is not always or even [actually] possible to do things in this open way. There are naive sorts of ideas out there about completely open investigations and publishing your notes and reporter's notebook. It is a competitive business, and the expectation that you are going to tip off sources or competition is kind of crazy."[51] In this case, what the journalists are sharing is *code*, not story arc, narrative, or angles for reporting; in collaborating on backbones, it may be easier to cooperate on adaptable code to multiple situations for stories told through code rather than specific stories told through words. Nonetheless, we might still think of journalists as competing to make the best interactives so as to outshine each other and garner a distracted audience to their sites, yet this attitude does not appear to be manifest in the style of collaboration observed.

### Expressions of Openness through Journalistic Work

Interactive journalists embody and express their commitment to openness in two key ways: first, through their contributions on the GitHub repositories and their use of open source code; second, through the blogs they use to chronicle their projects. Each of these activities signals a close integration with the underlying commitment to sharing code and "showing work" present in hacker culture.

GitHub bills itself, according to its Web site, as the "world's largest open source community" where programmers can share their projects "with the world." On GitHub, programmers can post their code so that anyone may see it and contribute to it, or view others' code, which may be helpful to adding on to the projects they've built. GitHub serves as a "repository" where programmers can save and host their code, which helps facilitate project management. As programmers develop their work, others can see their progress, not just in final form but *all along the way*.

While not all newsrooms are able to open source all of their code, every single newsroom I visited nonetheless had a GitHub page. *Al Jazeera English* is in a region deeply suspicious of open-source development, in part due to security concerns, but even *AJE* has a GitHub page. The BBC, which is tremendously protective of its branding, moved from being resistant to open source to developing some projects on GitHub, according to Andrew Leimdorfer, head of the BBC News Specials team.[52] Now, even smaller newspapers like *The Miami Herald* have a GitHub page, even though there was only one hacker journalist in their newsroom in 2013.

Journalists use and learn from open source in their coding. Alastair Dant of *The Guardian* explained, "Our entire tool set is open. We use loads of open tools on GitHub."[53] *The Times'* Chase Davis agreed: "I learn from reading other code because of open source. . . . It makes us better; it makes us more efficient to rely on that."[54] GitHub, as an open sharing platform, allows interactive journalists (and the public) to see the backbone of what's underneath these journalists' efforts. The news work, albeit written in code, is unmasked.

Many interactive journalism teams are keeping blogs that showcase their work and detail their approaches to various interactives or general issues with code. These blogs signal the depth of commitment to openness and collaboration. Two of the most radical blogs are from the teams at *The Chicago Tribune* and *The New York Times*. *The Tribune's* News Apps blog entry from March 7, 2014, offers a solution to a common problem—creating a chart in the programming D3 language but wanting reusable code for all charts to share the same feature. The blog offers the following introductory language, with the instructions of how to do this:

> Here's how you can use it.
> **Simple bar chart**
> Just an example of a simple bar chart. If you're not familiar with the code below, you'll want to check out Michael Bostock's "Let's make a bar chart."

Then, later in the entry, a series of code is posted for readers so they may enhance their charts with reusable code.

*The Chicago Tribune's* team has historically been headed by those who have come from traditional programming backgrounds, resulting in a strong hacker journalism influence and a direct connection to the open-source community. But newsrooms also led by programmer journalists have these blogs and embrace open source: from *ProPublica's* News Nerds or *The Washington Post's* chronicle of its interactives on a Tumblr to WNYC's Data News blog, NPR's News Apps blog, or *The New York Times'* efforts.

*The New York Times,* led by programmer journalist Pilhofer, keeps a blog that it specifically calls "Open" with the tagline "All the news that's fit to print(f)" (a coding joke). This "Open" blog does something similar to *The Chicago Tribune* blog. In a March 25, 2014, entry called "The Triumphs and Challenges of Logging in PHP (and Really Most Languages Probably)," the post attempts to help programmers look at underlying problems with their sites. In this blog, more code is offered to the public, as the blog post explains:

To build our implementation, we began with our desired log-line format: %datetime% %serverName% %uniqueId% %debugLevelName% |[%codeInfo%] %message%

The entirety of the underlying nytimes.com site is not presented, but the guts to solving the problem are offered to anyone who might have a similar problem. The post also explains that the team made the decision to prioritize an open-source library—just another confirmation of the movement within journalism programming efforts of the embrace of open-source logic and practice. These teams are led by both programmer journalists and hacker journalists, signaling the overarching commitment interactive journalists have culturally to openness. These teams are offering a way to share their findings, challenges, and projects with others—and the world. This is simply not found with traditional journalism practice on any kind of regular basis. These blogs provide key insights in an accessible and open manner to a wider community in the spirit of open source.

## Challenges

Open source itself is not always possible in a newsroom. While these journalists are relying on open-source libraries, they work within the framework of a copyrighted story context and a framework that may indeed offer insight into proprietary investigations or content. Some newsrooms are resistant to allowing the teams to open source. And from another perspective, open source is difficult for these small teams, which are working not just to develop software but are creating programs to serve a demanding schedule of news-production goals. As Brian Boyer explained to me, there are simply parts of NPR software that cannot be open-sourced—"our photos, our logos, our words." Still, NPR tries to open source as much as possible: "What we might do is copyright something to NPR so no one can rip it up, but with NPR [and] open source licensing there is a public educational benefit." Jon Keegan, head of *The Wall Street Journal*'s interactive news team, would like to open source much of his work, but *The Journal* is resistant to the idea. His assessment: "We use it [open source] so much, we would like to give back," but at this point, company policy prohibits.

Cultural resistance is one barrier, but to truly contribute back to open source, it's important to provide guidance for how to use the code. This can involve extensive documentation that explains how to implement each step of a script, for example. As Boyer notes, "It's true that it makes a lot of work: you have to document [the work]," which means providing instructions about how to implement the code, a task that would add to existing newsroom duties. Nonetheless, as we can see from those who talk about the commitment to giving back to the community, open sourcing as much as possible remains a goal.

Initially, it may seem that sharing code is distinct from sharing stories and separate from true collaboration, which would be sharing content. But code is not divorced from journalism content. Without this code, the news product would be difficult to create—code is journalistic production. The code cannot be disaggregated from the journalism because without the code there would be no news app. So sharing code is indeed a way of collaborating on journalism products; the code may be the structure rather than the specifics of that news product, but it cannot be disentangled from how journalism is created. Code sharing demonstrates a different way of thinking about journalism as collaborative work being done in the open.

As a whole, openness and open source have been primary ways of thinking that imbue the practice of interactive journalism, distinct from what we see in traditional journalism. Interactive journalists are bringing a new kind of abstract knowledge—thinking about journalism as open—to the idea of news work. The process of journalism is revealed to the world. In fact, these teams go so far as to offer step-by-step guidance for project management so others might learn from their successes and failures. In a time of uncertainty, newsrooms hoping to best each other with a better product and lure audiences could keep this work secret, but this doesn't happen. Instead, inspired by the open-source culture of programming and development, and a reciprocal sharing across newsrooms, we see an openness of practice and process emerging in journalism.

## See-It-for-Yourself Journalism

Yochai Benkler, the internet theorist, described a fundamental property that distinguishes the Web from any other kind of information technology that has come before: you can "see it for yourself." The Web allows users to discover information, as they are able to search and find information on their own. He explains in chapter 7 of *The Wealth of Networks*:[55]

> On the Web, linking to original materials and references is considered a core characteristic of communication. The culture is oriented toward "see for yourself." Confidence in an observation comes from a combination of the reputation of the speaker as it has emerged over time, reading underlying sources you believe you have some competence to evaluate for yourself, and knowing that for any given referenced claim or source, there is some group of people out there, unaffiliated with the reviewer or speaker, who will have access to the source.

Hence, content on the Web can be independently verified by the user; unlike in the past, there is no static presentation of information because a user can substantiate or disagree with what he or she reads with easy-to-access, instant information. This new capacity, Benkler argues, is made possible through links. Interactive journalism embodies a "see-it-for-yourself" journalism through inviting discovery within the many layers of information and even promoting fun contained in the interactive. Users are actually able to investigate their own particular questions independently, offering a multiplicity of interpretations.

From a see-it-for-yourself perspective, though, interactive journalism provides an amplified potential beyond just linking within a news site to other articles or to external articles. Instead, users get to explore data and interactive storytelling on their own. Hard data or other forms of interactives, like multimedia engagement, offer an opportunity for users to check claims against those of the news organization. Beyond that, users can also explore questions of interest that may not be told by a specific narrative provided in a story or even be intended by the overarching interactive.

### See-It-for-Yourself Journalism at Work

One example of two contrasting stories told by data illustrates the premise of see-it-for-yourself journalism particularly well. The British government had collected in the 2011 census report figures about cycling to work. These figures were analyzed by both *The Financial Times* and *The Guardian* in 2013 with starkly different coverage tones, though each was using the same set of data, which was available for download and engagement via interactive features. *The Financial Times* in the first paragraph wrote about the obvious increase in cycling based on their interpretation of numbers:[56] "Anyone who spends time in the capital, where flocks of cyclists are a feature of life, will nod in recognition at the news that the number of people cycling to work in London has doubled over the last decade."[57] Seems like a solid conclusion based on the data—and a good one for cycling activists who are hoping that the cycle-to-work movement will yield increased safety measures and other advances for those using bikes.

However, *The Guardian* offered a much more negative tone, throwing cold water on this claim. While not explicitly disputing the London claim, *The Guardian*'s headline in its Datablog was:

No increase in proportion of commuters cycling: data breakdown
   The percentage of people travelling to work by bike was the same in 2011 as it was in 2001, Census analysis finds.[58]

*The Guardian* went on to explain that in 202 out of 348 areas, local authorities actually saw a decline. And while the blog posted an increase for London, we can see it is an incredibly modest rise of 1.6 percent.

What's a reader of these blogs to do if he or she wishes to figure out the actual situation for London bicycling commuters? While it's unlikely that an ordinary reader is going to download the data and start playing with it, he or she *could* because the data is in fact made available with a link to the census table. A community bicycling group could do these calculations and come to their own conclusions. And even without manipulating this data, the presentation of interactive charts and graphs can give the user some opportunity to examine the data and form an opinion, though *The Guardian* is indeed correct on the matter. The user can decide which to believe, judging for himself or herself in light of the actual data. The ability to manipulate data, search through evidence, and compare charts and graphs is rendered in an easily accessible way. The searching out of information, though available through Web browsing, is now available directly to the user.

### *"Fun" See-it-for-Yourself Journalism*

A more entertaining example of see-it-for-yourself journalism was the BBC's calculator, "Where are you on the Global Fat Scale?"[59] The calculator asks the user to enter his sex, age, weight, and height, and then compares the user against the average BMI's compiled by the UN for member countries. The interactive notes:

Using UN data on population size in 177 countries, together with estimates of global weight from the WHO and mean height from national health examination surveys, the team were able to calculate average BMI figures for each country.

Using the values that you input into the calculator, it works out your BMI as well as where you are in relation to the rest of the population in your country and the world for your gender and age.

A tab actually says "see it in action." The user inputs data and, thanks to the underlying code, finds something out about himself or herself. The user can seek out information on his or her own that renders a near/far result made possible only through an interactive. For instance, I tried this with my friend Chuck, who was eager to play with the calculator after I told him about it. He is a forty-six-year-old man from the United States who is five feet, ten inches tall and weighs two hundred pounds, and he was curious about how he would compare on the global fat scale, given that he works out almost every day. We saw that he is most like someone from the Bahamas, and has a lower BMI than 58 percent of U.S. males, which he was pleased about, given his athletic efforts. This self-discovery goes beyond just linking and is facilitated through more complicated coding, which is marshaled in the service of an interactive.

Bella Hurrel of the BBC explained that she thought the BMI calculator was just plain fun, allowing users to experience some enjoyment through discovering personalized information online:[60] "So we told the story in a new way. It was not data crunching. The Body Mass Calculator was a simple calculator. The [purpose] was to educate and inform—one tool might be quite silly but relevant." In this way, the BBC offered users a pathway to learn something about the world, on their own terms.

Interactives that aren't necessarily data-focused also demonstrate see-it-for-yourself journalism. *The New York Times* offers a wide range of interactives that do just that. Consider the interactive "46 places to go in 2013."[61] This was a simple interactive—no flashy videos or photos. But what made this fun and navigable was a bar that allowed the reader to search and scroll by area of the world: Europe, Africa, Asia and Pacific, Canada, and the United States. Clicking on the links would produce a list of destinations—say for example, The Kimberly, Australia. A sexy tagline was attached: in the case of The Kimberly, "A Soft Adventure in the Outer Reaches of the Outback."

A click would expose more, with a photo, a map, and a brief description. The options were limited to what *The Times* had decided were these top forty-six places, but the user could see for himself or herself where to go and what to see—this was user directed, and an opportunity to explore on his or her own the narrative of the story. This self-direction and the internal

"Where Are You on the Global Fat Scale?" *BBC News*

search features flexibility with added interactivity that until very recently was not prevalent in news—and still is not available on news sites that have not significantly upgraded their Web sites to be audience focused and interactive.

This see-it-for-yourself journalism I'm describing here does not even begin to touch on the interactives that offer immersive storytelling. As we have seen, "The Peril at Great Falls," "Snow Fall," and Matt Richtel's "Driven to Distraction" series of stories (which featured the cellphone video game) are all about see-it-for-yourself journalism. Their entire premise—perhaps their reason for existence as a new experiment in storytelling—is that people will engage with this content differently, that news consumers will explore and interact with the content on their own terms, moving through the story's myriad features in a way that provides a holistic experience of storytelling that goes beyond simply reading text, watching a video, or scanning through a photo slideshow. It brings the users to direct their experience of exploring multiple forms of content and allows them to self-guide through the storytelling experience.

### See-It-for-Yourself Journalism Roundup

See-it-for-yourself journalism is not solely a feature of interactive journalism. Online journalism today is embracing some of these core values of allowing a user to search outside the bounds of the traditional story. But see-it-for-yourself journalism is built into the very fabric of every interactive—every single interactive is created with the intention of allowing user exploration at his or her own pace to discover new ideas and to interpret a particular narrative independently. The idea of interactivity *builds in* the process of discovery. While there is often a bounded universe to what can be discovered, the user can indeed see the answers to the questions for himself or herself. Interactive journalists bring with them this abstract knowledge of how to *best* marshal the discovery potential of the Web and introduce it in a more sophisticated way to journalism because they are the experts who do it the best and can do it over and over again with the kind of results that may make a substantial impact on the future livelihood. They go far beyond linking and simple online engagement, changing the way users consume news.

## Narrative Nut-Grafs

Though stories may begin with code, and often with data, there is a narrative tale that emerges from the presentation of interactives. This focus on the narrative reflects how interactive journalists accept the dominant norms of journalism, ultimately telling a story through their work. The narrative is what helps define these projects *as* journalism. The narrative offers a nonlinear experience but still has a nut-graf according to the journalists charged with creating these interactives. If the nut-graf in traditional journalism is the core thesis of a story, the interactive nut-graf is a clear point that interactive journalists wish to get across through the presentation of stories through code.

Interactive journalists order and structure their work in a bounded environment; there's still a limited set of choices available to the user, despite the tremendous potential for exploration. Text guides the narrative. In addition, the interactive journalists can make design choices to lead a user through a

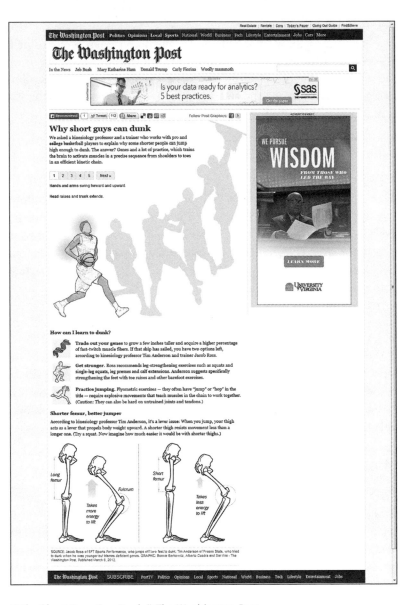

"Why Short Guys Can Dunk," *The Washington Post*

particular pathway designed to help the narrative emerge. A headline and descriptive text can also provide a guide to the subject at hand. Consider *The Washington Post*'s playful interactive, "Why Short Guys Can Dunk":[62]

> We asked a kinesiology professor and a trainer who works with pro and college basketball players to explain why some shorter people can jump high enough to dunk. The answer? Genes and a lot of practice, which trains the brain to activate muscles in a precise sequence from shoulders to toes in an efficient kinetic chain.

The paragraph explains exactly what the reader should find, and the intention of the graphic. The interactive is a nonlinear experience for users to navigate, but interactive journalists can put forward an underlying message through their interactive storytelling.

Design choices can also help direct users through an interactive—particularly helpful for multifaceted data projects, like *The New York Times*' project on generational income inequality across geography.[63] The interactive aims to illustrate income mobility, or the chance that a child would be able to rise from the bottom fifth of the income bracket to the top fifth over his or her lifespan. The map was divided regionally, with almost every major population center in the United States included. Design choices helped clarify how the reader was supposed to navigate this interactive; the boldest color, blue, showed the best chances; the worst areas were in red. Red worked in this case, given our associations with red and failure (being "in the red," "seeing red," "redlining," and so on). From this, the users could clearly see the story that the South was the worst place to try to overcome income inequality. The overwhelming amount of red helped underscore just how difficult it actually was to move up income brackets in the United States. This simple design choice made the difference for helping users discover a nut-graf.

### How Journalists Talk about Finding the Nut-Graf

Interactive journalists, particularly programmer journalists, remain certain that their work indeed has a clearly defined narrative for the reader. Jack Gillum at the AP argued, "You can approach projects on what's the nut graph—what's the point? If we can't figure it out, there's not a general conclusion." He explained that it was a mistake to think about interactives as just some sort of "notebook you just post on line." Instead, "you can search data with a purpose and now look for things."[64] Journalist Sara Sloane of *The Wall Street Journal* explained that while the data she worked with was often nonlinear, the ultimate product of her work was a "front end . . . a linear story [narrative]."[65]

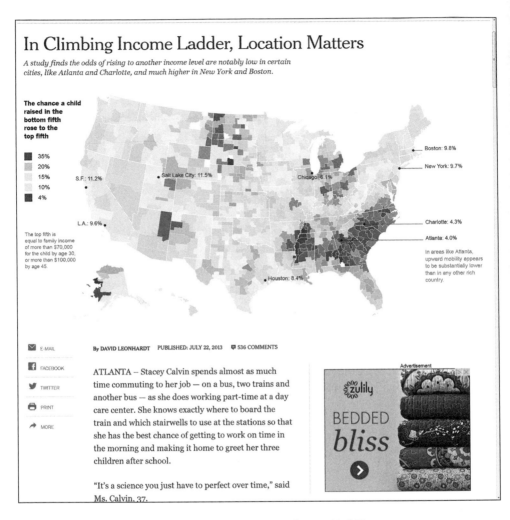

# In Climbing Income Ladder, Location Matters

*A study finds the odds of rising to another income level are notably low in certain cities, like Atlanta and Charlotte, and much higher in New York and Boston.*

**The chance a child raised in the bottom fifth rose to the top fifth**

- 35%
- 20%
- 15%
- 10%
- 4%

The top fifth is equal to family income of more than $70,000 for the child by age 30, or more than $100,000 by age 45.

S.F.: 11.2%
Salt Lake City: 11.5%
Chicago: 6.1%
Boston: 9.8%
New York: 9.7%
L.A.: 9.6%
Charlotte: 4.3%
Atlanta: 4.0%
Houston: 8.4%

In areas like Atlanta, upward mobility appears to be substantially lower than in any other rich country.

✉ E-MAIL
f FACEBOOK
🐦 TWITTER
🖨 PRINT
➔ MORE

By DAVID LEONHARDT    PUBLISHED: JULY 22, 2013    🗩 536 COMMENTS

ATLANTA – Stacey Calvin spends almost as much time commuting to her job — on a bus, two trains and another bus — as she does working part-time at a day care center. She knows exactly where to board the train and which stairwells to use at the stations so that she has the best chance of getting to work on time in the morning and making it home to greet her three children after school.

"It's a science you just have to perfect over time," said Ms. Calvin, 37.

"In Climbing Income Ladder, Location Matters," *The New York Times*

At *ProPublica*, interactive journalists also participate in actually reporting the story. Journalist Sisi Wei worked on a project to investigate the 990 forms of nonprofits. She ended up calling a number of experts to help her find out key aspects of what the underlying story might, in fact, be. Wei explained that as a nontraditional reporter, she was always amazed that someone would call her back or speak to her. But her underlying point was that these were stories—even if they were presented in new ways through code. They had central points, key ideas and takeaways, and explicit information to impart to people.[66] Her editor, Scott Klein, explained how these stories indeed emerged through code. "They go through academic clip searches to see what has been done before, diving deeply into data. They may develop sources; sometimes it is very similar to when a reporter quotes a source in the story, but the output in their head is always an interactive database or a visualization."[67] Narrative nut-grafs and a focus on the story remain central to how *ProPublica* thinks about its journalism.

### Narrative in Sum

While it is easy to think about what is different with interactive journalism, it is also important to remember that one of the essential aspects of journalism that unites interactive journalism with what has come before is narrative. The product of interactive journalism is indeed telling a story—the presentation is different, the tools to do so are different, and the experience for the reader is different. But the goal is to communicate information that may lead readers to a more informed understanding—either about how short men can dunk or about income inequality. Code conveys a story and provides a pathway to tell this story. The skills required may be different, but we see stories emerge through code. Each coding opportunity brings together information that was otherwise unassembled, much like a traditional story might sort mostly qualitative information into an order and then render it presentable for an audience to read.

Interactive journalists are making conscious choices about how to present information. They emphasize that their work does have a nut-graf. They are not simply presenting information without offering guidance. The decision that they make about the design of interactives takes the user through a particular pathway for understanding this information. Users are guided along an immersive experience, and while they have more options to explore, there is a central point articulated through the subject matter, text, and construction of the graphic. Narrative storytelling is a fundamental connection between interactive journalism and traditional journalism, underscoring its connection to the larger journalistic project.

## Abstract and Professional Knowledge

This chapter has shown how interactive journalists bring new kinds of knowledge to journalism in ways that expand the profession. In this case, knowledge is a way of thinking (and, ultimately, doing) that affects the ultimate process and product of work. On the most basic level, interactive journalists acquire practical knowledge that is far different from what most journalists have had—even specialty journalists like photographers or videographers. Job postings underscore the different requirements for interactive journalists and traditional journalists. In some cases, having any prior journalism experience is unnecessary: experience with code is what matters. Interactive journalists know code, or at least how to work with code, and with this knowledge they are able to create interactives that help bolster journalism's attempt to respond to the digital age. Code as editorial has come into its own.

There's also the more abstract knowledge that interactive journalists bring to newsrooms. Abstract knowledge suggests new ways of thinking about doing work. For instance, journalists have abstract knowledge about how to go about reporting a story, what news sense might be, how to wield editorial judgment, and perhaps how to incorporate objectivity into their work. But interactive journalists also offer another way of looking at journalism—what they build is constructed in the context of the internet age and is embedded with overtones of hacker culture and larger understandings about how we experience the Web.

We see new orientations toward journalism emerge. Journalism can actually be built and made; the metaphor for doing news work is literally a physical one where tools are constructed to improve both process and product. Interactive journalists take these ideas about making from hacker culture, which draws on a background of experimentation, problem solving, and seeing how things work to improve their functions. Traditionally, journalism has not focused much on improving the process of making it easier to do journalism, nor has journalism focused on making products that help people seek out their own information.

The near/far perspective that interactive journalists bring with their work illustrates the radical potential of data to offer literally personalized results for any particular problem (though the scale may vary), from the income inequality at your local high school to the accessibility options at the playground near your house. And contained within these interactives is still the larger story about how this issue affects us all. The ability to radically condense and expand storytelling is the direct result of interactive journalists knowing how to present data in interactive ways.

Openness and the idea of see-it-for-yourself presentations are integral elements of Web culture. Openness builds on the connections that interactive journalists have to a larger hacker culture that is committed to open source. But open source goes beyond just coding: it also suggests an attitude of how journalists should regard their work. These journalists offer up a new way of thinking about journalism as collaborative and as a process that can be shared with the world.

Similarly, as Benkler has written, the very nature of the Web encourages discovery. Exploration is possible because information is now all radically accessible and linked together. An interactive offers that see-it-for-yourself experience, bringing a focus on self-discovery to journalism as readers navigate through news on their own, experiencing, exploring, and learning according to their needs and desires. There is a bounded universe, but there is also a multitude of ways that the user can learn from what is presented, and interactive journalism recognizes the potential for experiencing content this way.

As we have seen, though, literature about subgroups in professions suggests that the subgroup will ultimately be forced to take on the dominant group's norms. In some ways, we can see this happening through interactive journalism's insistence on narrative: every interactive, though not traditionally linear, must have some sort of story embedded in it. Interactive journalism is not trying to upend the way journalism thinks about communicating information to the public; instead, the foundation is still a story: it just looks different. On the other hand, these interactives communicate a different set of assumptions about how readers should come to experience news work and also suggest distinct ways of approaching news work. So far, these new "norms" put forward by interactive journalists remain fully present as embodied by the work they create and the stories they tell about themselves.

Interactive journalism expands the profession by incorporating new ways of thinking into journalism. The work products illustrate the new "tasks" of journalism, underscoring how journalism has expanded to include new ways of creating and rendering content. These new "tasks" underscore how journalism now incorporates skills like coding and different approaches to news work. While underlying key features of journalism, such as the narrative, are still important, we see how interactive journalism expands traditional journalism. Interactive journalism, then, broadens the type of people, work, and knowledge found across the profession and inside newsrooms.

# Conclusion

## Interactives and the Future of Journalism

*The Des Moines Register*'s 2014 interactive project, dubbed "Harvest of Change," offered a 360-degree virtual-reality experience to the user. Using a mouse or an Xbox controller, a user could download software and experience a story about a farm dealing with the impact of climate change, immigration, genetically modified crops, rural depopulation, and general economic uncertainty.[1] There were opportunities to read, watch, and scan photos telling the story of change spanning four generations of farming. The experience was slow, as well as difficult to download and navigate, but the news had suddenly become an informative, interactive video game, with graphics and the potential engagement of the same quality as what one might find in Call of Duty or Grand Theft Auto, minus the explosions.

*Mashable* put the experiment this way: "Here are some words that don't seem to cohere: newspaper and virtual reality."[2] *Fast Company* wrote, "It feels like a documentary with a non-linear narrative. You are encouraged to explore."[3] *Business Week* called the experiment "the very start of what will likely be a wave of journalistic experiments with virtual reality in the next few years."[4]

This experiment may herald the future of interactive journalism, or it may not, but what it makes clear is that even cash-strapped newspapers like *The Des Moines Register* are betting on interactivity as a new form of news that can capture readers. Interactive journalism provides a way to tell stories as never before, relying on code-enabled multimedia created as *software* to enhance how audiences understand public information. The capacity for self-discovery, the potential for a richer engagement with content, and at times the enhancement of data presentation can help readers get a better sense of social phenomena at hand. Interactive journalism, then, offers a new way to claim authority over sharing and creating public knowledge for journalism through new skills and new approaches to news work.

Interactive journalism is a *visual presentation of storytelling through code for multilayered, tactile user control.* The product is *not* a text-based story. A narrative unfolds, albeit in a nontraditional way—one that often relies on the user to fill in the gaps. Specialized coding knowledge is required to create these additional layers of content upon existing frameworks. The interactive has a plasticity, creating a sense of engagement, and the user can select and make choices about pathways through content within a bounded universe, all in the context of a single user's experience.

Journalism is evolving in response to the multitude of pressures on the profession: external, internal, social, and technological. It is useful to revisit some of the arguments about the expansion of the profession, underscoring how it has changed in light of interactive journalism. The case studies involving the people invested in interactive journalism, the work that gets done, and the knowledge that interactive journalists have, offer insight into the dynamics of this new subfield.

## Professionalism

Ultimately, professionalism, according to Abbott, emerges out of a system of competing claims as occupations negotiate to do certain kinds of work. Professions are defined through their jurisdiction over work and have a special claim of conceptual knowledge ("abstract knowledge"). In this book, I made a few choices about how to talk about journalism as a profession. My aim was not to discuss professionalism writ large, or to assess how journalism as a totality was evolving in this system of professions. I sidestep the question of whether journalism is a profession and accept that it *is* one, given how it exacts its claim to authority through expertise in conveying public information. And I assert that within journalism there are agreed-upon conceptions of what the occupation means in the traditional sense. At the same time, as Abbott suggests, it isn't in the end particularly interesting if journalism is a profession or not: what matters is that it emerges out of interprofessional competition, journalism's ability to control work and types of knowledge, and journalism's responses to these pressures. So even if you disagree that journalism is a profession, the underlying argument is nonetheless valid because the *dynamics* of professionalism are at work.

I have argued a case for how a profession expands through new entrants who provide a different kind of needed expertise within the profession. In the past, there has been much focus on journalism as a profession and less so on the subspecialties within journalism. Throughout the book, I have shown how interactive journalism arises as a subspecialty of journalism and expands the profession's capacities. There are a number of conditions for the emergence of interactive journalism that I have outlined, namely:

1. Subspecialties may emerge uncontested, rather than out of contested external professional competition
2. Sociocultural external pressures, such as technology and economics, influence the rise of subspecialties
3. Subspecialties emerge out of a need to reclaim relevance
4. Subspecialties define and arrange their role using systems of measurement
5. Subspecialties offer a distinct claim to knowledge within a profession's larger jurisdictional aspiration

My argument is about interactive journalism but can also help underscore how scholars may begin to think about subspecialties within journalism and beyond.

First, we see how subspecialties can, in fact, be the product of uncontested forces rather than the usual competing system of professional forces that generally underlie professional change. The profession from which interactive journalists adapt most of their practices is programming (in so far as it can be called a profession), yet programming does not seem to actually contest journalism's jurisdiction over doing public-service work. Looking beyond programming, though, to other forms of information providers, we do see various professions working with interactives and creating data visualizations: historians are retracing battles through GIS, scientists are looking at bloodflow through the human body and the human genome, and art historians are reorganizing collections using interactive databases.

Companies are also using interactives to share information—GE, for example, maintains a data-visualization blog. And while these efforts are indeed adding public information from different realms, they are not competing on a daily basis (or hourly, or 24–7) to respond to news events to offer in one place a large variety of opportunities to investigate social phenomena. In short, there is little external professional contest on journalism as the subspecialty expands. And as we have seen, there is similarly little evidence of conflict between normative assumptions or backgrounds as interactive journalists become better known in the newsroom. The expected ideas of conflict (stated or not) when professions expand are not present.

We have seen how external pressures have influenced the rise of interactive journalism. The way people are using the Web is different than ever before, and the speed and rapid development of Web technologies is unprecedented. Users have access to better infrastructure for the Web and simply expect a better (and more interactive) user experience. The rise of more data than ever before and both the need and the capacity to harness this data puts pressure on journalism as an intermediary between this vast amount of information and the public. And as coding has become more sophisticated, journalism has to keep up with the latest advances as programmers push the boundaries. To this end, the experiences of people as they use developing technology put increased pressure on journalism: consider the felt need for speed, better user experience and design, the experience of information abundance, the results of better coding, and more data places. Other pressures from within the industry include the need to respond to economic challenges and, perhaps more significant, the need to exert a claim to authority and expertise in a world where journalists' domain over specialized knowledge appears threatened.

Uncertainty over journalists' authority is deeply connected to their desire to remain relevant. In a world of participatory media, blogging, data, information abundance, digitalization, and continued and increasing skepticism over bureaucratic professions, journalists face a challenge in asserting their ability to be *the* resource to tell us what is true. To continue to keep their relevance as authoritative providers of information with special expertise, journalists need to find a way to respond to these pressures. In this environment, journalists see interactive journalism as a key practice. Interactive stories provide information in a way that offers an authoritative means for dealing with new types of information rendered in both enhanced visual form and more sophisticated data. Interactive journalism also may bring fun back to journalism, providing another incentive for readers to come to news. Through interactive journalism, journalists make an argument for their relevance.

As we have seen, the subspecialty of interactive journalism has defined its success through internal and external measurement. Through clicks and shares, newsrooms from *The New York Times* to *Al Jazeera English*, from *The Wall Street Journal* to the BBC, are keeping careful track of how well these interactives are meeting the needs of users. These interactives may indeed be the most successful stories on any particular Web site, as in the case of *The New York Times'* Dialect Quiz. Those numbers are often guarded closely by newsrooms, and when the data is made public, the impact is quite clear: the traffic, thanks to interactives, is extraordinary. The justification for the importance of interactive teams within newsrooms emerges in part out of these successful traffic measurements, though of course it would be far too reductive to make this the causal reason for their existence.

And as Abbott has contended, subspecialties often develop their own internal groups to help define their expertise. NICAR serves as the primary group for these journalists, and it provides the kind of extended learning and commitment to specialized knowledge that, Abbott argues, help form a distinctive occupational group. The strength of NICAR is one indication of the rise of interactive journalism. NICAR serves as professional association that enables journalists to develop and expand their professional knowledge and to come together to solidify abstract knowledge.

Finally, the specialized knowledge that these journalists bring offers a key reason for the emergence of the subspecialty. With their different backgrounds and ways of thinking, these journalists have a perspective on how to do journalism that has never before been part of news work. They ascribe values to news work that come from programming and extend them to the interactives they create. And interactive journalists' more practical coding skills help further define them as specialists within the profession, as they possess skills other journalist do not have.

The arc of the book is focused on people, work, and knowledge in order to trace the dimensions through which interactive journalism was developing as a subspecialty. To this end, I relied on the theory of professionalism, specifically Abbott's, to trace how professions grow and change from the *inside*. Looking at people allows us to understand who actually does interactive journalism—what their backgrounds are and how they think and approach their work—thereby offering insight into how the subspecialty brings new kinds of journalists into newsrooms. We have seen how interactive journalists actually produce content—what they do—and can understand precisely what the jurisdictional claim they have is through their output. Chapter 5 underscores how interactive journalists bring new skills and new ways of thinking to journalism—professional and abstract knowledge to news work that has not traditionally been present.

Interactive journalists can be thought of as hacker journalists, programmer journalists, or data journalists. Hacker journalists come from a preexisting programming background; programmer journalists are journalists first and have subsequently taught themselves how to program; and data journalists may not have sophisticated coding skills but are fully engaged in the quantitative analysis of data for interactive work. These backgrounds help expand the profession: hacker journalists bring with them previous orientations and practices from the programming world; programmer journalists underscore how one can code in the service of journalism; and data journalists are the next evolution of computer-assisted reporters. These categories do overlap, as journalists will tell you, but the self-description of these journalists reveals empirically how different they are from the types of journalists who have previously populated the newsroom—from how hacker journalists think about problem solving to how programmer journalists think about stories and code as one.

The work these journalists do reveals how interactive journalists on the whole can create explanatory news work through software. Their creation of interactives is firmly embedded in the work culture of the newsroom, but it also creates distinct outputs. Looking at the process and product, we see how routinized at times the process seems to be and how different the actual artifacts of the work are from traditional news. Inside the newsrooms, from the AP to *The New York Times* to *The Wall Street Journal*, we saw how interactive journalists were initially and then on a continuing basis integrated into the larger efforts of the newsroom. There were variations across newsrooms that depended on the backgrounds of leaders, the process inside the newsroom, and the degree of independence granted to each team.

In some newsrooms, like at the AP, *The Times*, and *Al Jazeera English*, it was all but assumed that journalists would indeed have interactives as part of their offerings. This underscores the extent to which the profession has expanded to make interactive journalism so thoroughly part of news work. The products, though, are distinct from what has come before: from calculators to quizzes, from stories with inlaid videos and maps and databases to engaging charts, these news applications go far beyond the traditional text, photo, or graphic story. This change represents a new offering for journalistic work online.

The abstract and professional knowledge that interactive journalists bring to the profession augments and expands how journalists can think about doing journalism. While interactive journalists work within the traditional norms of professional journalism, the underlying values that they set forth through their different approaches help push and expand journalism. Traditional journalism has not seen ways of thinking such as openness, see-it-for-yourself journalism, build-it journalism, and near/far journalism—and even the approach to the narrative has similarities but offers some distinctive opportunities for news. In the next section, I will discuss what these modes of approaching news work can do to expand the profession—not only are they different, but they challenge professional normative understandings of what journalism can do.

## Expanded Ways of Thinking about Journalism

What does build-it journalism, near/far journalism, openness, see-it-for-yourself journalism, and the interactive's version of the narrative nut-graf bring to traditional journalism? Chapter 5 outlined these ways of thinking as distinct from traditional journalism, but it did not talk about how interactive journalism influences traditional journalism from within. So much of interactive journalism is influenced by a culture of technology, and these overtones in turn are distinct from the traditional norms of journalism, from objectivity to even immediacy.[5] Interactive journalism does indeed extend journalism by working within a set of dominant professional norms—if it did not, there would be far more contest between interactive journalists and traditional journalists—but this new form of news nonetheless challenges journalism to push beyond its preexisting conceptions about how to create news.

Build-it journalism brings maker culture into the newsroom as journalists think about news work as a process of construction. But how can build-it journalism, which considers how journalism can be made through tools, influence the newsroom as a whole? For one, build-it journalism is focused on the most elemental points of news as software—everything begins with code. Build-it journalism can help journalists begin to think about news *as code.*[6] For example, news can be thought of as specific chunks that can be dealt with in discrete ways. These small chunks can be fact checked on their own. If news is code, that code can be open to the public, and the public can be invited to contribute to the elements that make up stories. Thus, the story becomes a participatory platform built from small elements into a larger, collectively shaped story. Thus, the story is "made" or constructed.

Build-it journalism also suggests that journalism itself should be a tool. One way to think of journalism as a tool is to consider how the news organization can act as a knowledge manager for information,[7] not just a distributor of information but also a collection point for information. A news organization can collect all information pertinent to a story—all of the reporter's findings that could not go into the story, any documents related to the story—and essentially organize the sum of the journalist's work to be shared with the public in one place. This would be a tool to allow readers to experience news beyond the story and serve as one central gathering place to find out information about an issue or event.

The news organization could serve as a tool for knowledge management in another way—as the source of information for the news ecology related to a story by hosting the data of other actors related to a story, linking to comments and community resources, and providing access to sources—both in the story and in other news organizations. In these ways, the news organization literally builds a storehouse for public information and serves as a tool for information gathering and compilation rather than just a singular source of information distribution.

Interactive journalism also invokes a way of thinking about journalism as near and far at the same time. By near, it is not just the local that is imagined, but actual data relevant to a person—data that is individually specific. Far journalism speaks back to the larger picture of the story, which may be international, national, and local. The important difference of near/far journalism and current approaches is that near/far journalism embraces both the absolute personal focus *and* a larger focus at the same time. It's much harder to do this in the construct of how most journalism stories get told at present.

There's a scene in *The Paper*, a 1994 movie starring Michael Keaton about a New York tabloid, of a news meeting, wherein all national or international events mentioned conclude either with "with no one from New York" or "with someone from New York"—with the implication being that if it can be localized, it can be written about in a metropolitan newspaper. This is all too true in local news organizations; with the Ebola scare, *The Fort Worth Star-Telegram* localized a story and ran a full report on a couple who had been on the same cruise as a Dallas health worker who had handled Ebola samples.[8] This is the near and far at once as it is currently practiced (in its most egregious form, too).

But it's critically important for readers to feel connected to news organizations as the source not only for world, national, and local news but for news about themselves. This personal news builds a case for the newspaper's relevance in a world of social media and citizen journalism. So how can newspapers add this highly personalized near news into traditional formats?

The easiest way is to rely on interactive journalism to provide data. Instead of rendering interactives with only personal data, like the BBC Global Fat Scale calculator or the Opportunity Gap at *ProPublica*, journalists need to find ways to plug the personal into stories directly—for example, to situate calculators within text stories so that content can be personalized and the language actually modified through an algorithm to offer something that directly responds to an individual's experience. We may not be too far off from the ability to actually manipulate the words in a text story based on such direct input (and companies like Narrative Science are already paving the way of "robot journalism.") Algorithmic personalization would be a fantastic way to directly create engagement with readers and keep the news clearly relevant to their lives. We are already seeing algorithmic story selection from news aggregators and on social media, from Apple News to Facebook.

The "far" is what journalists do all the time. News is intended to give a window on the world, to provide a sense of the world that you cannot see for yourself because you cannot be everywhere at once.[9] And certainly, as Carey says, one can get caught up in the drama of news events, experiencing the rituals of everyday news through the comfort of one's own home.[10] Faraway news reminds us that journalists can tell us stories no one else can, but too far away divorces us from a personal connection. Near/far journalism suggests a radical possibility of personalization within the experience of all kinds of news. And in a world that is increasingly personalized through algorithms, why shouldn't the experience of actually reading the content of news (not just the selection) be personalized as well, albeit still placed within this larger social construct?

What can openness do for journalism? The openness that comes out of interactive journalism presents a model for showing work and for collaborating with others. This can share with readers the process of news work, which often appears to be a mysterious and secretive process. Openness can bring journalism toward a culture of transparency, such that consumers of news are able to see what is actually happening within a news organization. Too often, journalists have talked about transparency as exposing institutions external to news institutions, such as the government.[11] Rarely have newsrooms turned the mirror onto themselves to expose their own practices. In fact, it is only in the case of egregious missteps such as plagiarism or fabrication that we see a news organization reveal how stories are written.[12] Exposure to the news process can have dangerous consequences for sources, and regular engagement with audiences may challenge perceptions of journalistic authority over editorial judgment.

Openness suggests a culture of radical sharing. The open-source culture informing the "openness" that interactive journalists are bringing to their work suggests a cooperative process wherein individuals collaborate for some greater good. Openness in more traditional forms of journalism would involve the audience in the creation of news far beyond just trite participation via social media. Instead, the audience becomes part of the process of actually crafting the news, and the way that the sausage gets made within journalism is revealed.

The Guardian has led the way in trying to open the journalism process to ordinary people. The newsroom has begun publishing its newslist of noncompetitive stories that it will publish for the day.[13] Similarly, Alan Rusbridger, former editor-in-chief of The Guardian, has pushed for the paper to embrace "open journalism," which is a way to think about journalists as no longer the "only experts in the world."[14] In addition to a coffee shop in downtown London, *The Guardian* will open up a giant public space—thirty thousand square feet—as a "hub for events, activities and courses."[15] Other news organizations have tried similar efforts. *The Register Citizen*, a newspaper in Connecticut, opened a newsroom café where citizens could drink coffee and contribute to local news. Other newsrooms have begun to open their doors to news meetings; *The New York Times* had a brief experiment called TimesCast, wherein a very limited (and for-the-camera) news meeting was videoed for distribution online midday.

OpenFile embraces audiences as part of the story-creation process. The Canadian news organization uses reader suggestions to help inform what gets covered. The process goes something like this: "Coverage and subsequent community response unfolds on the site for all to see, sometimes resulting in 'files' with multiple layers: photo slideshows and video accompanying the text article, and, for some stories, extensive community input in the story's forum."[16] In this way, the audience is actually contributing to the very underlying process of generating a story.

Interactive journalism's openness also values collaboration. Newsrooms in the past have rarely collaborated with each other, but interactive journalism has shown that collaboration can be a means for newsrooms to create better products that are not at the expense of other news organizations.

*The Guardian*, *The New York Times*, and *Der Spiegel* collaborated on the WikiLeaks revelations, though each newspaper did its own analysis. Still, this was a fairly unprecedented effort. And the results were tremendous. Furthermore, investigative nonprofits, such as *ProPublica* and *The Texas Tribune*, partner with bigger news organizations such as *The New York Times* to distribute their reporting. In a time of limited resources, we need to see more collaboration between news organizations—not just with nonprofits—pooling resources for investigative projects, sharing bureaus, and cooperating on stories.

But this is not enough. Openness is not just about collaboration; it's also about process. As we know from open-source culture, the process is unmasked. The mantra of "show your code," "show your work," and "code in the open" are repeated on everything from t-shirts to hacker convention banners to coding academy Web sites. But journalists do not like to show their work. The process of writing a news ethnography is difficult, but one of the barriers is that journalists simply do not like the process—they feel concerned that something might be exposed if someone investigates how the news gets made. Yet, other than news ethnographies and journalists' autobiographies, as well as some Hollywood movies, we have little insight into how journalists actually do their work.

Openness in journalism would mean inviting readers to look at the process. Maybe, as Aron Pilhofer of *The New York Times* pointed out in chapter 5, it would be too much to share a reporter's notebook. But surely, for some stories, it might be possible to include the reader in the steps that a journalist might be taking to research a story, or there might be explainers about how journalists come up with ideas for a story. Journalists could do far more to explain their ethical system to the public and could also do more to spell out the seemingly unwritten rules of how interviewing works and the systematic method journalists use to garner information. Data journalism has begun providing some of these steps with explainers about where data comes from, but all too often this is reduced to a short paragraph. Some journalists might argue that this is not practical with regard to investigative reporting or that it might take too much time, but at a time when the authority of journalism is already compromised, rebuilding trust and emphasizing the special nature of professional skills is warranted.

Interactive journalists lead the way to openness by example. They collaborate with other journalists across different newsrooms, working together to solve common problems. They put their work out in the open for all to see. And they expose the process of how they do what they do. Interactive journalists are leading the way toward creating a recognition that openness matters with the audience and with other newsrooms, and this is encouraging for the future.

Another fundamental aspect of Web culture, as Benkler has argued, is this see-it-for-yourself property of exploration. Ideally, through the networked potential of information communication technologies, users have the opportunity to go from one site to another with few barriers between. Everything is connected by the linked structure of the Web, and the only thing stopping further investigation is one's own curiosity.

Certainly this is an idealistic way to think about the Web, as Matthew Hindman asserts.[17] But traditional journalism has been quite lousy at linking people across the web and within their outlet's own Web sites as well. One early fear was that linking out to other sites might cause people to navigate away from a news story, thereby taking people off the original news site.[18] Others weren't sure what to do with links—what to link and what not to link—a problem that still remains. The discovery process within text and multimedia was limited.

Steen Steensen argues that the general assumption among hypertext researchers in journalism studies has been that hypertext would provide direct access to sources, personalization, infinite ways to use space and deadlines, and targeting.[19] Some of the studies he reviews suggest that newspapers have not been adept at providing the kind of external links that would enhance such a practice; a 2000 study that investigated one hundred online newspapers, including sixty-two from the United States, revealed that only 33 percent of outlets offered links within news stories.[20] Others have argued that hyperlinks were the least-well-developed feature of online journalism, though a more optimistic study from 2008 reported that of sixteen hundred articles studied within a ten-country sample, 24.7 percent had external links pushing people out beyond the newspapers' Web sites.[21]

Interactive journalism doesn't do this, but it does offer something critical to this spirit—the ability to investigate. Contained within interactives are myriad pathways of multilayered text and images for the user to explore. A person can go in his or her own direction, experiencing *controlled freedom*, as users still have that opportunity for self-discovery on their own terms and in their own time. This ability to choose to navigate for more information goes beyond just the superficial level of moving from one story to the next. Instead, it offers the capacity to dive deep into a specific subject—or just to take a cursory look.

How can journalism get into a more see-it-for-yourself experience while alleviating some of the concerns about departures from the site? Journalists can do a far better job linking to other internal articles related to the topic at hand. *The New York Times* is leading the way among traditional news organizations because embedded into its content management system is code that actually creates links to "topics" pages about various big "words" in the article (for instance, diabetes, or crude oil), thus giving people a chance to see all *Times* articles written on the subject. Similarly, *The Times* has built an early tool to help link similar articles on the Web together. There might be five articles on an awards show, but one might be in news, another in business, and perhaps others in entertainment. The tool would show that these articles based on this event now exist and need to be linked, generating more clicks within the site. But this is evidence of *The New York Times*' prowess, and other news organizations need to think how they too can begin to improve recommendation systems for articles, which requires developers to do so.

But there's more to see-it-for-yourself journalism than just following links. This process of discovery is about truly witnessing things on one's own terms. This "witnessing" is endemic to the participatory Web.[22] Users can see for themselves the underlying documents that have helped contribute to the story. They can see the raw data and sources, even the names and email addresses of the reporters. Some of this is current practice, especially with some of the tools mentioned, but users should have the opportunity to experience stories not just as the stories are told but also as they can be explored. From linking to sharing the underlying guts of a story, see-it-for-yourself journalism can emerge from the practices of interactive journalism to inform practices in the rest of the newsroom.

Interactive journalism does have a distinct similarity that shows just how much it fits in with traditional journalism's practices: the focus on the narrative nut-graf. There is fundamentally some sort of story to tell (or that will eventually be told after analysis) with the interactive. This is ultimately what makes interactives not just something to click on but actual journalism, providing content with stories and information. The difference is this: the narrative is one where the user can explore on-demand—there is no preset order to the narrative, though the narrative will eventually be told. The narrative structure is not forced on the reader but is, rather, a process of discovery, freeing the reader to have this see-it-for-yourself experience.

How can journalism offer a more open narrative? Surely it is important for news organizations to continue to tell clear and authoritative stories. Linearity has a place and purpose within the context of journalism. But it would be fascinating to bring some of the flexibility of this unique narrative experience to the present linear experience of news. Perhaps news stories could use multimedia even more fully to place videos of sources offering their perspectives outside of the main story. And perhaps there is a way to set up the structure of a story so that a reader can more easily flip through from beginning to end or middle to end, perhaps by entering a search term or a name. Turning linear stories into stories with nonlinear capacities is coming—beyond just the news app—and perhaps this signifies just how distinct a role interactives have in providing an alternative way of telling stories.

I've put forward some radical ways that these new modes of thinking might intersect with more traditional journalism. Interactive journalists are embedded in a culture that is inspired by a close affiliation with technology practice. These journalists are the new entrants into the newsroom, and they offer new energy and a chance to influence the newsroom in nontraditional ways. Their influence has the potential to spur further change as they lead by example, as they demonstrate how they share their work with the public and other journalists, and how they collaborate across newsrooms. Interactive journalists are showing how users can be trusted in a pathway of self-discovery while those users remain on a news site—teaching themselves as they navigate an interactive. Interactive journalists are underscoring how the distant can be made radically personal, and they emphasize the potential for telling stories in nontraditional, nonlinear ways. As other journalists see the success of interactives in the newsroom, they may become motivated to think further about how to incorporate these tools into larger newsroom practices.

## A Step-Back Limitation

There are a number of problems that emerge, however, if we go too far in glorifying interactive journalism. One of the most significant is that interactive journalists may not do enough to investigate thoroughly the massive data sets before them. Data appears to be inert, after all: it has hard numbers attached to it and comes from official sources collecting this information—or from journalists who have gathered the data on their own. Journalists can now reveal all the data instead of just anecdotes, giving individual users a chance to experience the data on their own. And journalists can tell stories through the entirety of data sets beyond what they could do before, when data was more self-contained and tools were far less sophisticated.

Yet as Quartz points out, there are a number of problems that can emerge with data journalism. As Allison Schrager writes, "I worry that data give commentary a false sense of authority since data analysis is inherently prone to bias. . . . Even data-backed journalism is opinion journalism."[23] Her point is that data can be used to justify a particular hypothesis; journalists may have a story they are seeking out, and rather than inductively seeking out data, they seek out data that confirms what they hope they will find.

Other issues include the importance of being skeptical about the data itself. This involves understanding the implicit assumptions that go into the creation of the data set. For example, the Centers for Disease Control performs the largest phone data survey in the world about health. Their Behavioral Risk Factor Surveillance System collects information from all over the country about people's health behaviors. But the CDC makes decisions about how it will evaluate what constitutes risk. Thus, these assumptions are built into the data, and unless journalists are aware of these assumptions, question them, and define them in their analysis, the data is essentially taken on face value rather than as a *constructed set* of collected information. Even demographic statistics need to be adequately examined. Crime data provides a good example of how institutions can build their own bias into data; police might have certain ways of recording domestic disturbances and, in an effort to keep crime stats lower, may fail to report some of these disturbances unless police officers believe the events escalate to a certain level. *The Chicago Tribune* needed to investigate the data it received from the police about shootings, as multiple shootings in the same place were recorded as only one incident.

Journalists rely on institutions for much of their data, and it may not always be possible to investigate all of the underlying assumptions built into that data; as well, it's often tempting (and easy) to take these numbers at face value. Recently, we have seen the rise of daily data journalism blogs that aim to produce multiple offerings of data journalism each day—*The Guardian*'s DataBlog was perhaps a forerunner. *The New York Times*' Upshot and Nate Silver's *FiveThirtyEight* do daily data journalism often without questioning the numbers. *The Times* will often render polling data without asking how the data was collected. Other data stories underscore how difficult it is to collect data and how easy it is to make assumptions about data. A story about taxi medallions "plummeting" in price due to car-sharing service Uber is one example. Then-graduate student Benjamin Toff wrote a response to the story, arguing that "the article offers a few other data points mostly in the form of anecdotal evidence and isolated instances of [the] difficulties medallion owners and taxi commissions have faced selling and auctioning medallions in recent months."[24] In other words, journalists need to be careful about how they collect data and then draw conclusions from that data.

There is a larger point, though, in which we have to question this quantification of news from a larger social perspective. Quantification may yield particular forms of power to institutions; the ability to create, define, and classify social phenomena is incredibly potent. As Wendy Espeland and Mitchell Stevens suggest, we begin to see social reality through the lens of the categories through which we quantify them.[25] News organizations are now in the position to begin to quantify social data, from telling us how to think about social inequality to analyses of immigration and politics, and critique of this power is warranted.

Journalists on the whole are not social science experts or statisticians, though there are a few, such as data journalist wunderkind Nate Silver, who have backgrounds in statistics. While some journalists do have advanced statistical knowledge, we need to be aware of the limitations of journalists using these methods to find stories. Schrager quotes the economist/journalist Michael Mandel, who argues that journalists may not be ready to do enough analysis, noting "Making sense out of raw data requires more analytic firepower and more willingness to do independent research than journalists have traditionally been comfortable with."[26] Journalists may not have the *analytic firepower* yet to do this. Much of the statistics journalists learn may be on their own rather than from anything they have been traditionally taught in journalism schools.

The NICAR list goes back and forth with journalists requesting assistance with statistics, journalists instructing each other about how to solve problems. As one journalist wrote in an email:

Folks,

I'm puzzling over a way to correlate a couple of measures. One of them is, well, it's summer so let's go with baseball scores. Lots of baseball scores. You can make up the other variable.

My problem is this: I'm trying to correlate my other variable to the scores, some of which are losing—that is, negative, and some winning (positive).

No, they're not really baseball scores, but they really are positive and negative numbers, and I need to determine if there is a significant relationship between the scores on the one hand and the other variable.

My tentative idea is to square the scores, making the negative numbers positive solely to test for correlation. Am I in danger of wandering over a statistical cliff? Is there another, more sensible approach when dealing with mixed positive and negative values?[27]

Another journalist replied:

So what happens if you crosstab item 1 for item 2 > 0 and ≤ 0? Does that suggest a relationship? I mean if it was games won/lost vs profit/loss on snack bars, that might tell you something, and a scatter plot with a line fit might suggest a formula for tying close games to high profits or decreased losses. *This is probably all wrong but it might help you clarify.*

In other words, journalists are trying to lead each other through unfamiliar pathways about how to analyze data through statistical methods and software. Putting too much faith in the ability of journalists to generate sound data analysis is dangerous, simply because they might not know how.[28] This is not to deny that some journalists do have these very good statistical skills and very much do know how to conduct statistical analysis. Many newsrooms employ journalists with statistical expertise. In the legacy of *Precision Journalism*, statistical techniques are more advanced than ever before, and expertise is needed and warranted as data sets become ever larger.

Yet there's still a sense that working with data can solve problems with journalism that traditional journalism simply cannot. While qualitative journalism is considered important, quantitative forms of journalism are seen as giving the "hard answer," taking away uncertainty. I heard this theme from some of the data journalists and programmer journalists I interviewed. For instance, Chase Davis of *The New York Times* summarized this point: "Data journalism is different from regular traditional journalism. It's a difference between probability and uncertainty; with traditional journalism there might be a shadow of a doubt. With data journalism, you can say there were 92 campaign contributions. You can get absolute correctness with data journalism. You can get that hard precision." This idea of the *absolute correctness* may signal the unwillingness to question the data adequately. This is not to say that interactive journalists working with data don't question the data. They are journalists, after all. But the assertion that data can prove something may be far too tempting for journalists looking to make truth claims about the world.

What may be most infuriating to more qualitative journalists may be the insistence by some that data journalism is superior to other forms of journalism. Silver, the founder of the *FiveThirtyEight* blog, once hosted at *The New York Times* and now hosted at ESPN, earned his reputation by his near-perfect forecasting (forty-nine out of fifty states) of the 2008 presidential election based on substantial analysis of polling data,[29] and he argues that the two journalisms do complement each other but also points out that data journalism can tell us something that qualitative forms of journalism never would be able to offer. Almost everything can be data-fied and made better.

Silver has professed the significance of bringing data journalism to the center, arguing that it provides the potential for neutrality and precision that is not guided by emotion and qualitative anecdote, as in traditional qualitative journalism. As he rightly points out, "Almost everything from our sporting events to our love lives now leaves behind a data trail."

The obligation of journalism is to pick up where other institutions—government, science, academia, the private sector—have had difficulty understanding by charting through the data (the signal from the noise, as his book is titled). And from this data is a desire to bring together rigorous quantitative assessments. Silver offers that even emotions can be measured; he argues that the perseverance of a hockey player can be broken into key performance indicators and given a quantitative score.[30]

While qualitative journalism is important, and journalism would not be complete without it, Silver attests that the problem is that these journalists employ anecdotal use of statistics, which leads to improper assertions. He notes, "The problem is not the failure to cite quantitative evidence. It's doing so in a way that can be anecdotal and ad-hoc, rather than rigorous and empirical, and failing to ask the right questions of the data." This triumphalist approach to data journalism as having the answer, provided there is good analysis behind the data, reminds us that it is far too easy to fetishize data journalism.

In addition to getting overly excited about data, interactive journalism can compel journalists writ large to get overly focused on the potential of code. From the perspective of those who know little about code, those who can code are mysterious creatures with skills that no journalist has ever had before. Recall the *New York Magazine* article where Aron Pilhofer and his

*New York Times* interactive team were credited as "maybe saving" journalism. Interactive journalists are being hired when other positions are cut. At *The New York Times*, for instance, there were postings for interactive journalists while the newsroom was going through a one-hundred-person restructuring. In many struggling metropolitan newsrooms, from *The Detroit Free Press* to *The Minneapolis Star Tribune*, interactive journalism jobs have been advertised while projections for the news organizations have been dismal.

Perhaps, though, the greatest indication of the awe journalists have about coding is the debate over whether journalists should learn how to code. As one journalist said in an interview with *The American Journalism Review*, "Coding is the new grammar. If students don't know, at the very least, what web pages are and how they are built, they won't last long in this game."[31] Joshua Benton, head of the future of journalism blog Nieman Journalism Lab, penned a tweet in response to this question, arguing, "Look, not every journalist should learn Python! But if you want to ensure future employment, it's prob as good an investment as is available."[32] He noted that anyone who didn't see coding as a must-learn would be a historical joke, just as those who suggested word processors, spreadsheets, social media, and video editing were unnecessary for journalists to know.

Miranda Mulligan, a professor at Medill, in an article titled "Want to Produce Hirable Grads, Journalism Schools? Teach Them to Code," noted: "Learning how to make software for storytelling and how to realize news presentations into code are currently the hottest, most pressing skillsets journalists can study." Her solution to improving journalism on the Web: "*Journalists should learn more about code.*"[33]

The movement to teach journalists to code is happening not just in higher education but also on the professional level. As I have noted, there is now a proliferation of journalism schools offering classes in programming or specialized degrees. While most journalism students do learn some basic HTML, enough to navigate a Web page, schools are offering courses in far more complicated coding languages. But such efforts are not regarded as sufficient. As *Mediashift* contributor Ronald Legrand writes, "Programming means going beyond learning some HTML. I mean real computer programming."[34] Journalism schools have clearly bought into the premise that coding is indeed a critical part of preparing journalists for the future.

In addition, there is a major focus among professional organizations to help practicing journalists develop their skills. The Online News Association conference offers a bevy of sessions designed to help journalists gain facility with programming. One track of the conference was titled "Tools and Tracks for Developers." Sessions included a boot camp for beginning programmers, with the promise, "We'll help you sort it all out in a one-hour crash course in basic programming languages, including what kinds of tasks they are commonly used for, as well as their limitations."[35] Another was explicitly devoted to teaching journalists the Ruby programming language.[36] It would not be exaggerating to say that NICAR now offers as many courses in investigative reporting techniques as the conference does in teaching programming.

There are those who dissent from this journalists-must-code mantra. In response to the question "Should journalism schools require reporters to learn code?" Atlantic writer Olga Khazan answered "No," setting off a huge chorus of disagreement on Twitter. She argued that coding wasn't for all journalists and, in fact, that it might be a detriment to future advancement for a journalist who wasn't going to be good at coding to bother learning how. She wrote:

> Aside from a small percentage of journalism students who actually want to be newsroom developers, most j-school enrollees, in my experience, want to be reporters, writers, and editors (or their broadcast equivalents). Meanwhile, reporting and writing jobs are growing increasingly competitive, and as media outlets become savvier on the web, they are building teams dedicated solely to web programming and design work.
>
> What I took from my experience was this: If you want to be a reporter, learning code will not help. It will only waste time that you should have been using to write freelance articles or do internships—the real factors that lead to these increasingly scarce positions.[37]

In other words, code is distracting many journalists from getting ahead in what they really want to do.

Perhaps a more moderate version of the journalists-should-learn-to-code argument is warranted. As some have suggested, journalists do not need to know how to code, but they should be proficient in being able to talk about code. This is perhaps a good way to think about the translation opportunities between journalists and those who can code in the newsroom. If journalists can understand the potential of code, they can more intelligently talk about the projects they envision. There may be even greater integration between the interactive teams and the rest of the editorial department. But the danger is that an insufficient knowledge of code—this generalized awareness—may actually create more communication problems than it is worth.

As a whole, there are drawbacks to making too much of the role of interactive journalists as heroes of the newsroom of the future. We need to take what they bring to journalism with some caveats, and be sure not to hold them up on a pedestal of promise without adequately assessing the problems that also come with their work. Fetishizing both data and code will ultimately not help newsrooms move forward. At the same time, without interactive journalism, much remains to be lost if newsrooms do not get on board and watch the profession expand without them along for the ride.

## Mobile, Sensors, Drones, and More

Anyone who claims to predict the future of journalism is likely to be wrong—or, for that matter, to have a bit too much hubris for their own good. However, there are signs that point to where interactive journalism is going. The world beyond interactive journalism is bright, and even though interactive journalism is still so new, it will be further augmented by the continuing rise of mobile journalism and the increasing use of sensor journalism and drone journalism.

Many of the interactives still perform best on a desktop computer and, if done right, on an iPad. Most of this book focused on interactives developed for bigger screens, though this is changing. Yet longform storytelling of the "Snow Fall" variety, for example, is not what you might want to read on an iPhone, at least not yet. And screens are small—I had friends test out a number of data interactives to see how they felt about using them on their mobile phones, and a least three-quarters were frustrated by the inability of interactives to be responsive to mobile technology. Or as my friend Adam put it, "I think my fingers are too big to use this."

On the other hand, it is undeniable that the mobile revolution is coming—or it's come already. As Aron Pilhofer explained, early efforts at mobile in the late 2000s were clunky and difficult. He said, "At first, we approached mobile as a kind of nice-to-have, the sort of thing you'd throw in at the end of a big project to surprise users with something they didn't expect."[38] And mobile development might double or triple the complexity of interactives, especially given news organizations' mandates to develop on inflexible native apps, as browsers inside native apps worked differently from internet browsers on a phone or a desktop. Pilhofer, who had moved to *The Guardian* from *The Times* as the final stages of the book were completed, noted that some *Guardian* projects were developed for mobile first—including a data-driven interactive on the lack of affordable housing in the United Kingdom[39] and an interactive for the Manchester music festival.[40] But he noted, "Truth be told, we still struggle sometimes with mobile because it can be so constraining. But those constraints can also be quite liberating in a way because it does ensure you are laser beam focused on the user in ways we might not have been when we were designing for the desktop. It forces you to strip things back to just the essential elements of storytelling, and sometimes that works better in the end." Notably, then, mobile is still difficult for one of the most prominent newsrooms in the world. Mobile was mentioned very little by research participants during the research for this book, but I expect were I to repeat this work in three to five years, mobile might be a much bigger concern.

Sensor journalism is also making an impact as it rises to prominence. A major report out of Columbia University's Tow Center for Journalism, titled (quite appropriately) "Sensors and Journalism," is the best work so far detailing these new ways of gathering news and literally building sensors for collecting data.[41] The report proclaims just how far sensor journalism is beyond what we are seeing in computational journalism today. "When it comes to labels, 'sensor journalism' isn't even as understood as data journalism."[42] Sensor journalism takes advantage of the fact that not only is there more data, but there are also more hardware components collecting information: cellphones have cameras, accelerometers, GPS, microphones, and radio. The outgrowth of the maker movement, also reflected in the interactive journalism subspecialty, has helped spur DIY sensor hardware made from cheap, accessible technology. And, as the report contends, this is fundamentally connected to computational advances: "Sensors can produce data demanded by computer-aided journalistic processes."[43]

A number of newsrooms have begun to experiment with sensors for journalism. *The Houston Chronicle* embarked on an investigative project to look at the environmental costs of Houston's oil industry on poor neighborhoods. In the city, there were areas where residents were complaining about burning lungs, black plumes of smoke, and even chemical rain. But all of this was anecdotal. The reporter working on the story thought EPA data, measured once every six days, would not be enough, so she sought to collect her own data. She was able to get residents to use industry-standard chemical monitoring badges called organic vapor monitors at one hundred to two hundred dollars apiece. Using data from the sensors, in cooperation with the community, *The Houston Chronicle* found that the levels of benzene in the environment were over the threshold for cancer risk, including more than twenty-seven times the threshold level in one community.

Other examples of sensor journalism at work include an effort by *The South Florida Sun-Sentinel* to track police recklessness, including disregard of speeding limits. Through help with public-records laws and the "sun pass" used for toll roads, the journalists were able to track, through time stamps, serious speeding violations. *USA Today* also worked on a sensor project, dubbed "Ghost Factories," which collected soil samples at 430 abandoned factory sites across the country, looking for heavy-metal contaminants that had been left behind.

But one of the most ambitious efforts at sensor journalism was the project at WNYC, New York's public radio station, to have people make their own sensors to gather data. The project, called the Cicada Tracker, tracked what portended to be the largest invasion of cicadas in the New York City area in recent memory.

Head of the WNYC data team John Keefe learned that soil temperature was a good predictor of when the cicadas would arrive. Using parts from Radio Shack, the WNYC team built a prototype that ordinary people could copy to build their own sensors for eighty dollars. An improved prototype dropped the cost of the sensor, and a hacker collective was able to sell the kit for twenty dollars. WNYC began giving the kits away at public events. The project garnered more than 1,750 temperature readings from eight hundred different locations. Another forty-three hundred reports came in when listeners started recording when they saw cicadas.

The results of sensor journalism, as seen so clearly in the Tow Report, can of course be displayed through rich multimedia and—obviously—interactives. Sensor journalism is one new way of gathering data and involving the community. And as sensor journalism expands, the demand for journalists to analyze and present information in ways relevant and useful to the community continues to grow.

Another emerging form of journalism that complements interactive journalism is drone journalism, which relies on small unmanned aerial systems (sUAS) that are remotely piloted. Drones can provide all-encompassing views of places that might be too dangerous for journalists to visit on the ground, or of events that could not be captured except for an aerial vantage point.

So far, the use of drones in the United States for journalism has been limited by FAA restrictions. But there have been some notable examples. As the *Sensors and Journalism* report details, NPR's Planet Money was able to hire highly trained specialists to obtain aerial views to help them document the expansive cotton trade in the U.S. The report describes the coverage, through which "small incredibly maneuverable craft that could give viewers an exhilarating sense of the vast scale of cotton fields."[44] The drone video gathered six hundred thousand visitors, an external measure of the journalistic success.

Other drones are more basic. Journalists imagine using less expensive drones as a way to avoid renting news helicopters for breaking news events, such as large-scale protests or fires. Newsrooms have begun to take footage from ordinary citizens with drones for views of weather, explosions, and fires. Drone journalism has been more successful across the world, where there are fewer restrictions. The German media outlet *Ruptly* was able to send a drone into Kiev's Independence Square. El Salvador's *La Prensa* used drones to cover the scale of voter turnout for a recent presidential election.[45] And Brazil's *Globo* has used drones to cover protestors, underscoring the ability of drone journalism to help journalists get better estimates of crowd size.[46] Drones can go where journalists can't—indeed, one journalist flew a drone over the still-toxic Chernobyl site.[47] This expansion of hardware and technology goes beyond just programming to further intersect the potential of journalism as it becomes increasingly wedded to a future of technological capabilities. Drone journalism, along with sensor journalism, shows new ways of collecting data and viewing journalism. And journalists who gather their own data from scratch do not have to rely on interpreting the assumptions built into institutional data collection, which helps journalists truly understand what is behind the data.

## Interactive Journalism, Authority, and Integration

From virtual-reality journalism to drone journalism, the future of journalism on the Web and across digital platforms promises to be nothing if not exciting. But looking just at the output, rather than the people and the process, doesn't tell us enough about the fundamental changes taking place within the news industry. This book has attempted to look at process and product of interactive journalism from the inside—from the people, the work, and the knowledge that they have about what they do within the newsroom. Through an in-depth analysis of people's backgrounds to the workflow to the interactives themselves, we learn how interactives and interactive journalists are reshaping journalism as we know it.

There are so many pressures on traditional journalism today. What's clear is that journalism is at an inflection point—traditional journalism cannot stay as it always has been. The business model must change, but it's not as simple as just changing the price of the product. It's also clear that traditional journalism must assert its relevance in a time of personalization, participatory media, and citizen content, whereby it can show that professional journalists do play a critically important civic role. But the old standby investigative stories that journalists have relied on may no longer be enough to convince people to pay attention.

Enter new practitioners and a new subfield of the profession. These interactive journalists are behind changing the process and product of journalism in a significant way through the work they do. To some degree, these interactive journalists come out of a deep history in the newsroom: the photographers, the graphic artists and designers, the computational specialists are now emboldened as they take up new forms of technology to create different forms of journalism in a distinctly digital medium. But these journalists are also different: they bring with them a legacy of immersion in technological practices—and their skills, processes, and thinking strategies come into the newsroom in ways that have not been present in the past. In short, we have a convergence of some of the most forward-thinking practices of programmer culture meeting the realities of the newsroom, brought to the newsroom by interactive journalists.

Journalism faces a crisis of authority. Now, more than ever before, traditional journalists have to account for new forms of journalism and an increasingly active public. There is no longer a one-to-many distribution of news. Journalists are challenged as the sole arbiters of knowledge. But interactive journalism is one way to reestablish journalists as experts. No one else is doing interactive work with data on the scale of journalists, and no single institution is tackling the wide array of social phenomena before the American public. In making data more accessible and more easily understood, particularly through interactives, journalists give people a chance to learn about the world, and they remain a destination for and source of public knowledge. The sophistication of code displayed by the output of interactive journalists establishes news organizations as firmly embedded in the larger social experience of obtaining information through Web- and mobile-centric experiences. Journalists can claim authority through interactives by providing working software to tell stories in ways that expand the ability to explain social reality, thereby creating a greater claim to their social importance.

Journalists are reshaping the way society understands news itself. The boundaries between news and code are increasingly fuzzy as news becomes told through software. The way data has become critically important to thinking about the world gets articulated through daily news coverage, aided and pushed into daily news creation by interactive journalists. News takes on a new shape as software tells stories, often with data rather than (or in addition to) anecdotes that explain social reality. News becomes more than just a linear explanation, but how people understand what news *is* may change as news takes new forms and the profession expands.

A lingering question for some readers is that *if* interactive journalism is indeed reshaping the profession, how is it that interactive journalism has not been met with much resistance within journalism as a whole? While on one level interactive journalism is reshaping how journalism looks and feels and is prompting journalism to focus more on data, the larger questions of journalism are not being fundamentally challenged. What constitutes an important news story? What makes something newsworthy? Who are the powerful people? What problems and people ought to be paid attention to? What is news sense and news judgment?—these aspects of journalism have not been contested by interactive journalists. How this all gets communicated—through interactives, many with data at their core, with software as their form—is different. But the fundamentals are not changed.

And interactive journalism is viewed as a necessity for the future. Interactive journalists are welcomed as helpful renegades who do things differently—as innovators who think differently about how to create news (without questioning what news *is*) and who have the skills no one else has. The resistance we once saw with online journalists is not present in this case, perhaps because most newsrooms well acknowledge at this point that innovation is a prerequisite to survival. Interactive journalists are the potential saviors who can bring the newsroom into the future, who can drive traffic to a site, and who can spur a rethinking of how to tell stories. Interactive journalists can make journalism relevant and exciting in ways that those inside the newsroom may no longer feel confident in themselves to do on their own.

Interactive journalists bring a world of code and software applications to journalism. They journalists make it possible to turn journalism into interactive quizzes, ballots, maps, charts, videos, and more. Journalism through software can take advantage of and respond to new technological innovations. The profession expands because journalists learn to tell stories in new ways across a new medium. Old practices can combine with new ones to help the potential of journalism be filled with the promise of the digital age.

Ultimately, one underlying question of professions writ large is whether they can contribute something to the public good. This is a trait all professions have, and a much larger question is just how interactive journalists can indeed contribute to the public good. They can, in part because what they do adds to public knowledge in new ways. The ability to tell stories through news as software unleashes a fresh potential for audience understanding, one consistent with the potential for user experience, exploration, and knowledge building now possible with a more sophisticated technical platform online and across mobile platforms. Interactive journalists help make a specific claim to knowledge about news and help traditional journalism as it struggles to maintain its authoritative voice. This possible strengthening of journalism as a continued authoritative—and respected—information provider contributes quality information to the public domain.

Interactive journalists are not going to be the answer to "saving journalism," but they do spur the profession to move forward. These journalists challenge how traditional journalism does its work and introduce ideas about openness, self-discovery, making, narrative, and the personal that have not existed before. From what we learn about the profession, we can see how a variety of factors help pave the way for the rise of a subfield: relationships within the profession and with others, external pressures, a need to claim relevance, and special claims to knowledge. Interactive journalism pushes us to think more broadly about how professions may grow and change more generally, especially as they face the challenges of this postmodern information society.

# Methodology

## Introducing Hybrid Ethnography

This project was a multi-sited ethnography that relied on observation and interview. Unlike my first book, which relied on five months of immersive field research at a single site (*The New York Times*), this book sought to gather data from across the industry. As a result, I personally visited thirteen newsrooms, with some visits lasting more than two weeks (*Al Jazeera English*), while others consisted of repeat visits, and still others were simply a few hours' commitment.[1] This is not the traditional ethnographic practice that some sociologists might hold as standard, but it instead represents what I will call "hybrid ethnography," or the kind of ethnographic research that can be accomplished while trying to go beyond a single case and still carrying out some form of sustained observation.

Hybrid ethnography is a practice through which one combines interviews and ethnographic observation for the purpose of extended case-study comparison. Hybrid ethnography is not traditional ethnography, as there is no expectation of sustained monthly or yearly observation when one is seeking to research multiple cases. Instead, hybrid ethnography pulls together the best of interviewing and the best of ethnographic field research in a timeframe that makes sense for a series of case studies. Hybrid ethnography recognizes that research takes time, but for a broad view for qualitative research, time is of the essence.[2] How, then, can you maximize time and still gain ample data for making assessments of the case at hand?

Clifford Geertz explained that in order to interpret culture, a researcher has only to gain access to a particular group.[3] He does not suggest a requisite time or define this access, but others suggest a way to think about whether access has actually been obtained in a meaningful way. Ruth Frankenberg, in her critical ethnography *White Women, Race Matters*, suggests that access means being able to understand cultural grounding—the "unintended, unperceived consequences of behavior and understanding."[4] To evaluate whether one has achieved enough access is a subjective process, but the researcher must ask: Can I actually understand the cultural context of my research subjects? Am I able to consider, as Annette Markham proposes,[5] the ideological markers of the participants as they negotiate and build their social constructs? Katherine Lebsco puts it differently: Have I gained through my ethnographic practice an understanding of the meanings that this community I have investigated generates through conversation?[6]

The process of hybrid ethnography can do this. It first begins with the selection of a set body of cases. To justify this method, one should have a project that aims to look at a qualitative question across multiple sites so as to look broadly rather than deeply, though the goal of hybrid ethnography is to offer a deep view as well. There should be a justification for the cases—either expected similarities or dissimilarities—that accords with the overall research question at hand. For me, the focus was on looking at as many large newsrooms as I could, in order to assess their interactive journalism teams, and I wanted to look at print, radio, and TV. These vectors suggested that I needed more than one case of each type, and that I would need at least a few cases of each to begin to make comparisons across and within. My case selection did not have to be complete at the outset; I could add cases based on what I found in the field, especially as emergent themes began to suggest new directions for data gathering.

Hybrid ethnography as an actual work practice tries to maximize ethnographic observation within a compressed time. Ethnographic observation in newsrooms (and likely other organizations) is enhanced by the collection of documents, photos, emails, and other records of organizational process. The researcher should approach his or her case site with the goal of collecting as much internal documentation from the site itself, being careful to take note of how the documents may be used. Other suggestions for document collection include asking for copies of statements of standards or policies that employees might need to adhere to in their work—this could range from a best-practices in interactives design guide to a social media ethics guideline or even a list of union regulations. Thus, the hybrid ethnographer should approach each site with the intention of gathering as much document-based evidence about the organization as possible.

The hybrid ethnographer aims to combine ethnography and interviewing, which means balancing sustained observation with interviewing a single individual at a time. Time management and dexterity within the field site become critical. Hybrid ethnography necessitates an intensity of investigation, rapid-fire interviewing, and completely immersive field inquiry. At times, I conducted fifteen interviews in a single day. Stamina might be the most basic requirement.

A cardinal rule seems contrary to what one might expect: conduct the interviews in the field setting. Often, interviewees are given a set "safe" space to explain their viewpoints. But if it is possible to carve out a space for conversation that is not easily overheard while still being in the main space or setting of the field, this is critical. This may mean interviewing in a cubicle instead of a room, or at a series of empty desks instead of a private setting. But the objective is also to watch and listen while interviewing.

In fact, if the interviewee is left close to the field site during questions (in this case, his or her workspace), it becomes easier to gain some external validity about the way the interviewee is perceived or positioned within the newsroom. Any interruptions, any questions asked, any time the interview participant's name is called out—all of this provides insight into how the interviewee is situated within the frameworks of an organization.

The terms of this "out in the open interview" are set a bit differently. The interview participant should still be given a choice of whether to have a conversation in private. The kinds of conversations that can work out in the open are conversations that have less to do with internal personal beliefs and assessments of identity and more to do with roles, organizational behavior, the state of the site being observed, and so on. In other words, interviews out in the open are not ideal for trying to research personal issues. The interviewer needs to be quite alert to signs that there is more to a response that cannot be said out in the open, and, taking note of this, can suggest "Perhaps we talk about this later" in order to follow up the potentially difficult-to-share thought in a more private setting.

But interviewing in the open may set the interviewee at ease. If a series of colleagues have just been interviewed from their desks, it becomes easier to build a trust relationship after colleagues have also taken part. The interviewing is transparent—each participant has a clear view that the way he or she has been treated is the way all interview participants are being treated. And interviewing out in the open suggests that the questions being asked are not likely to create retribution because the questions are not divisive enough to be asked in private.

Some question whether interviews really constitute ethnographic work. In some contexts, interviews are accepted under the domain of ethnography, in part because interviewing is one of the best ways to gain access to the subject. Pertti Alasuutari argues that "what is called ethnographic study often amounts to qualitative interviews of a group of people."[7] Interview work presents an important contribution to qualitative work, regardless of one's opinion whether it ought to be considered part of the ethnographic oeuvre.

*Learning from Strangers*, my favorite book on the subject of interviewing, offers some insight into the depth of data that interviews may provide.[8] One can gain insight into the interior experiences of the participant as well as grasp information about an organization's set goals. The interview participant offers, through his answers, observations about the interactions of others. "How events occur or what an event produces"[9]—in other words, process—may be better understood. In this case, interviews are used to form a backbone for understanding workflow in the newsroom. As interview data is combined across a variety of participants, the researcher can obtain the depth of multiple perspectives and understand how events and people are interrelated. A respondent's internal and external observations of the subject under investigation, then, are illuminated through interviews.

It is important to interview in the open during hybrid ethnography because it maximizes the time spent in the field. The interviewer should be attuned to conversations taking place outside the interview taking place. The interviewer should use the time between interviews to watch how the organization works—listening closely to conversations and other interactions between staff, walking through an organization and looking at what is on people's computers, making note of the books and material on people's desk, attending meetings. The goal is to do as much watching as possible while being in the position of getting ready to do an interview or in the process of conducting an interview. Going to meetings is not always possible, but one is often able to observe small standing meetings when interviewing out in the open. Observing and interviewing at the same time may be difficult, but this is necessary in order to maximize time. This is difficult to do and requires practice, but observing interaction when there is little time to spend in the field is critical. The observation process of hybrid ethnography comes in the spaces between interviews, and situating oneself in the field (at a central desk, at a key table, next to a lead editor) helps with this process.

Hybrid ethnography is a solution to many of the contemporary issues with newsroom access. Instead of in-depth time in the newsroom—weeks and months—I often had days or even hours offered by newsroom management. Today, the conditions for access may be harder than they once were in a less litigious, competitive, and anxious time for traditional institutions. Asking a newsroom to allow a media sociologist to spend weeks or months inside a newsroom may be perceived as a threat. Today, newsrooms in particular are uncertain places with processes in flux, attempts at innovation that may fail, and hardships that create morale issues. Convincing institutions to reveal the sausage being made, with the eye of the researcher geared toward exposing patterns as well as inconsistencies is scary, and newsroom gatekeepers are particularly sensitive to the 24–7 social-media broadcast potential of what they might see as weaknesses perceived in the world.

Negotiating access for weeks or months was a no-go on these teams, but team leaders seemed entirely comfortable allowing me to visit for a few hours, a day, or a few days. My trip to *Al Jazeera English* did spread over two weeks, a lucky coincidence, thanks to a contact well versed in academic research. Hybrid ethnography, with its multiple case selections, helps go beyond the reliance on a single case to gain greater breadth.

Hybrid ethnography, then, is a way to think about getting the lay of the land as quickly as possible. Within the constraints of time, one must do all things at once: observe the setting and context, observe interactions, and conduct interviews. This is quite a lot to accomplish, and suggesting that this can be done in hours over days may seem an impossible task. But the attempt to combine the key needs of an ethnography into one setting to get *as much as possible within the constraints* is simply a reality of ethnography in today's newsroom settings.

In the case of my research, I found saturation. I saw repeating themes over and over again. I was able to extract patterns and signs of differentiation from the body of data I had collected. If these conditions can be met, where one can construct from one's data this understanding of cultural meaning, behaviors, observations of others, descriptions, perspectives, and the experiences of respondents through the data collected, then ethnographic goals have been achieved. Hybrid ethnography, as with all ethnography, means the researcher will eventually seek saturation, but saturation may still be achieved in a shorter time so long as the quality of the data offers a way to say honestly that the "lifeworld" of these participants may be understood, to use a Giddenesque term.

## A Hybrid Ethnography Set of Cases

The scope of my research focused on thirteen newsrooms across the United States, the United Kingdom, and the Middle East. I relied on one set of interview data for a fourteenth newsroom (from *The Chicago Tribune*) gathered by my fellow researcher Seth C. Lewis, who accompanied me on earlier interview trips. I thank him for sharing this *Tribune* interview data. I chose to investigate mostly large newsrooms to gain a sense of the industry, and only in two cases, at *The Seattle Times* and *The Miami Herald*, did I look at metropolitan newsrooms, though I did spend time at WNYC, the New York public radio station, and also gained insight from visits to *The Des Moines Register* and *The Star-Telegram* (Fort Worth).

I visited NPR, the BBC, *The Guardian*, *The New York Times*, the Associated Press (D.C. and N.Y.), *The Wall Street Journal*, *ProPublica*, *The Seattle Times*, *The Miami Herald*, WNYC, and *Al Jazeera English*. I spoke with *Zeit Online* over Skype. I sought out radio newsrooms and television newsrooms in addition to newspaper newsrooms, though I had extreme difficulty trying to get into any commercial broadcast newsrooms. In this book, I use the titles and organizations of people where they were employed when I interviewed them; many have changed jobs, but given the demand for interactive journalists, this happens almost constantly. I made my choices from this combination of internal journalism meta-discourse, snowball samples and contacts, and convenience opportunities. Some data is older than other data, and it is important to note that this does not mean the data is not useful for drawing out key concepts and ideas, even though circumstances may have changed.

Though cross-cultural comparisons are always important to consider, even though I journeyed to *Al Jazeera English* in Qatar and the BBC and *The Guardian* in London, what I found was a decidedly consistent approach to interactive journalism. Though there were some minor definitional terms and some historical differences, the work and work products were the same, backgrounds and perspectives were quite consistent, and the abstract knowledge offered was remarkably similar.

One might ask how I could attempt to gather the portrait of an industry from these large newsrooms. First, one can see these large newsrooms as linked to each other through the NICAR conference and other conferences on data journalism and online journalism they attend throughout the year. They are connected on Twitter, and they further communicate and share ideas across their blogs. As Katherine Fink and C. W. Anderson pointed out, it is incredibly difficult for smaller newspapers to devote time and resources to interactive journalism.[10] It's hard for these newspapers to retain talent. And the teams are often quite small—perhaps one person working alone. I did not investigate these small news organizations, even though some do produce excellent interactive journalism. I looked to the giant newsrooms because they are widely regarded as the leaders in interactive journalism.

In addition, big newsrooms set the standard for the industry; what they do has a large effect on how other newsrooms pursue their work. The talent that these newsrooms were able to attract, despite the small salaries relative to the tech world, meant that I would be getting to talk to some of the best individuals working in this domain. And it was also simply easier to concentrate time and money on a few key cities with major media offerings: New York and London; Doha was a lucky turn of events aided by a generous start-up package from George Washington University.

In all, I interviewed 183 people (if not more) across fourteen newsrooms and assorted conferences and events, and I interviewed some key informants a half-dozen times, in addition to regular email and Twitter contact between 2011 and 2015. I complemented my work with extra-newsroom events: various Hacks and Hackers meet-ups, Online News Association gatherings, the Knight-Mozilla News Technology Partnership Learning Lab, MozFest (where I hosted a "focus group" of sorts that included more than thirty people, not included in the interview count), Transparency Camp presented through the Sunlight Foundation (another "focus group"), the 2014 NICAR conference in Baltimore, and other events. The historical chapter 2 relied on a snowball sample of key figures in the field. Actually, 183 is just a rough, minimum estimate of the people I met and talked to while researching this book, but I do not feel that the interviews themselves are what constitute hybrid ethnography.

## Difficulties Facing the Researcher

There is a movement in critical ethnography to investigate the ethnographic practice—something called "auto-ethnography," whereby the researcher considers his or her position relative to the research participants.[11] This perspective is then embedded into the analysis. While I do not do this in this book, I find it important to explain some of the difficulties and uncertainties I faced when researching and writing this book.

The hardest part of this research was my unfamiliarity with programming. I have been studying changes in journalism since 2006, but I had not been exposed to programming until I began this research. I did not know much about programming culture, and I did not know about practices in software development; I didn't even know how or where people wrote code on their computers. As a result, I have had to learn about the larger programming practice and culture. This has been quite difficult. I have tried to teach myself to code in order to understand what my research subjects do—and I am happy to report some very elementary gains. I don't often know the programming languages my research subjects talk about, and so I was frequently lost when they began speaking about the exact technical programming specifications of what they do.

Now, to do ethnographic work, one does not need to *do* what research participants do. A study of working-class white women need not require that the researcher be a working-class white woman, for example. But there must be an attempt to reach familiarity with the life practices of the research subjects, and since so much of this work happened through programming and software development, I needed to understand what this meant.

I became afraid of mixing up terms and getting things wrong. This is because the interactive journalism world is quick to criticize those who try to speak in the language but don't have it quite right, particularly on social media, and in particular on Twitter. For instance, I mixed up the meaning of front-end design in a *Washington Post* article I wrote, and I was subsequently trolled with dozens of comments across a week by programmer journalists on Twitter. I often found that if I asked questions, I was met with the presumption that I should already know the answer. The attitude by some of the people I interviewed was that I shouldn't bother interviewing them or asking questions unless I already understood exactly what they were doing. And I felt easily discredited when I did not know something regarded as basic by the person I was speaking with. People were for the most part friendly and helpful, but others I interviewed were at times dismissive, intimidating, and often made me feel that I should know more than I did.

So I took an approach that fits much more to my strengths and competencies as a researcher. Since I have immersed myself in nearly a decade of newsroom-change studies, the way that I could work the best was through an analysis of how journalism was transforming. Throughout the book you'll see very little discussion of the actual technology or code behind the interactives. The decision to focus less on technical terms is, in part, because I understand my audience is primarily journalism scholars, journalists more generally, and students. Writing about specific technology was not necessary because I was interested in broader themes and changes, and as a result, I do not feel that the manuscript is incomplete.

To maintain the integrity of the technical aspects I did write about, I have had journalists and technology experts read sections of this book for feedback. For big-picture research and verification, as I wrote up my data, I continued to talk to my research participants. I went back into the field midway through the project to get fresh data as I saw themes emerge in previously collected data. I validated my write-ups with this additional material fresh from the field. As a result, I could feel increasingly confident that my work was being confirmed.

I found it useful to talk about my conclusions with other academics and practitioners who had also written about interactive journalism or data journalism, and I was generally pleased to see that, based on what they knew of the subject, my work resonated as sound. I am confident that what I found here reflects what Janice Radway calls the "cultural grounds" or the "unintended, unperceived consequences of behavior and understanding."[12] It is precisely this deeper level of analysis that will render some of the findings foreign to the daily experiences of interactive journalists, but valuable for a step-back, analytical, academic approach.

## Gender

I am not sure how to account for the imbalance of gender in this work. I am also unsure to what extent my gender influenced the responses that I got from the majority-male makeup of interactive journalists. I recruited subjects by snowball and convenience sample based on my field visits. I would go to a site, meet with the leads of a team, and then gain permission to speak with and observe members of the staff, so long as they were willing. When I used this method, I found that the majority of people I encountered in the field were male. Sometimes, though, the few women on the staff were not available to speak because they were caught in the busy news day, so these limitations made it even harder.

I made the decision not to deliberately seek out additional women in this sample. However, there are women represented here—at least some of the best-known female interactive journalists are quoted and profiled, as well as some less-well-known journalists. Some of those reading early versions of the manuscript actually were surprised by what they thought was a more equitable gender distribution in the field due to my data, but in the field, the reality was that there were predominantly male interactive journalists. It may actually have been the case that I spoke to more female interactive journalists, thanks to my gender position.

The question of gender in tech was simply not a research question I sought to engage, but I admit there could be more about gender and interactive journalism in this book—it's just that my data did not lead me in this direction.

Women *as* female interactive journalists is absolutely a subject worthy of research. It's a big problem that women are so poorly represented in programming (for example, Google's revelation that 83 percent of its technical staff are men, though there is no central database to assess the gender distribution of interactive journalists).[13] The women I have spoken with say that newsrooms are among the most gender diverse and welcoming places for women who want to work in tech. This structural issue deserves more research. I could spend more time trying to parse out possible implications of gender, and the intersubjectivity of my gender on this research remains a lingering question.

## An Endpoint to Methods

In this methods section, I have attempted to address the ways to gather a vast amount of data within access-restricted research opportunities. I have proposed an alternative of "hybrid ethnography" that works within the limitations of access to seek full immersion through strategies such as multiple cases and maximal field engagement. I have pointed out that one may gather "enough" data so long as the cultural meanings of the participants can be meaningfully extracted and analyzed.

In addition, I address the impostor syndrome of the researcher, which was made worse by engagement on social media. I struggled with whether to admit this in writing. But the insecurities created as a result strengthened my resolve to take the approach that I did. These experiences encouraged me to find footing in my strengths as a journalism researcher rather than as a technology expert. My hope is that by voicing the experiences of difficulty with subjects, others might also be forthright as well.

Finally, I leave open a question that I hope will provide an important jumping-off point for future research. As the specter of the technology industry grows ever more important, the fact that women are so poorly represented within it is quite scary. We need to consider what interventions might change this pattern. Newsrooms need to be vigilant to enhance diversity; just as the subfield of interactive journalism expands, so too should the role of women in an increasingly technology-oriented newsroom.

# Notes

*Preface*

1. Some of this work does not appear here but does appear in other articles.

*Introduction*

1. Haughney, "Times Wins Four Pulitzers."
2. Branch, "Snow Fall."
3. Greenfield, "New York Times's 'Snow Fall.'"
4. Romenesko, "More than 3.5 Million Page Views."
5. Boczkoski, *Digitizing the News*.
6. Freelon, *Crimson Hexagon*.
7. Anderson, Bell, and Shirky, "Post-Industrial Journalism," 2.
8. Usher, "Newsroom Moves."
9. Weissmann, "Decline of Newspapers," and suggested by Jay Rosen.
10. Chris Anderson, Emily Bell, and Clay Shirky, "Post-Industrial Journalism: Adapting to the Present" (whitepaper, Columbia University Graduate School of Journalism, New York, 2014).
11. Neilsen, "Ten Years."
12. Carlson, *Journalistic Authority*.
13. Reilly, "Respect." For complete polling and analysis across professions, see http:// www.pewforum.org/2013/07/11/public-esteem-for-military-still-high/#journalists.
14. Shafer, "Beware."
15. Kaiser, untitled memo.
16. Usher, *Making News*, 41.
17. Needle, "Roger Fidler."
18. Boczkowski, *Digitizing the News*, 20–35.
19. Anderson, "Between Creative and Quantified Audiences."

20. "Full New York Times Innovation Report."

21. Raju Narisetti, email message to author, July 8, 2015. Emphasis added.

22. Joe Pompeo, "SXSW Round-up."

23. Torchinsky, "Information in America."

24. Gold, "U.S. Internet Connection Speeds."

25. Personal communication, David Boardman, July 16, 2014.

26. Weinberger, *Too Big to Know*, xiii. Weinberger acknowledges that not all knowledge is right and that there is vast misinformation, but there has been too little focus on what we can know now—as more inclusive than ever before.

27. Hargittai, Neuman, and Curry, "Taming the Information Tide."

28. Boczkowski, see chap. 7, 171.

29. O3b Networks, "What Is Network Latency?"

30. Alex Smolen, "Lag Time."

31. Google Developers. "Mobile Analysis."

32. "Talk to the Newsroom."

33. Nielsen, "Response Times."

34. Benton, "How NYTimes.com Cut Load Times."

35. Edge, "'Responsive Philosophy.'"

36. Lewis, "Journalism," 322.

37. Silverman, "Day in the Life."

38. Rogawski, "GovLab Index."

39. Turner et al., *Digital Universe of Opportunities*.

40. Walmart, "Picking Up the Pace."

41. Babcock, "Amazon, Microsoft, IBM, Google."

42. Smith, "DMR."

43. Masnick, "U.S. Government."

44. King, "Dealing with Data."

45. Flew, Spurgeon, Daniels, and Swift, "Promise of Computational Journalism."

46. Young and Hermida, "From Mr. and Mrs. Outlier."

*Chapter 1. Interactive Journalism*

1. Tse and Quigley, "Is It Better to Rent or Buy?"

2. Bostock, Carter, and Tse, "Is It Better to Rent or Buy?" is the more current version of the calculator we used in 2011.

3. van Dijk, *Network Society*.

4. Rafaeli and Sudweeks, "Networked Interactivity."

5. Steuer, "Defining Virtual Reality."

6. Stromer-Galley, "Interactivity-as-Product," 391.

7. McMillan, "Exploring."

8. Bucy, "Interactivity in Society," 374.

9. Bucy, "Second Generation Net News."

10. Sundar, "Multimedia Effects."

11. Rogers, Sharp, and Preece, *Interaction Design*.

12. Code is only one tool used to enable interactivity. Other tools have afforded interactivity in the past, from phone lines to the mail service—even grammar. Code here is the specific tool that enables interactives to function this way.

13. Diakopoulos, "Functional Roadmap."

14. Cairo, *Functional Art*, 195.

15. Tidwell, *Designing Interfaces*, 125.

16. Park, "News as a Form of Knowledge."

17. Waisbord, *Reinventing Professionalism*, 227.

18. Atherton et al., "Secret Life of the Cat."

19. Kaufman, "To Spur Traffic."

20. Howard, "Art and Science," 4.

21. Ibid, 4.

22. Anderson, "Between the Unique and the Pattern."

23. Journalism and Computer Science (SEAS) Dual-Degree Program. Columbia Journalism School. Available at http://www.journalism.columbia.edu/page/306/7.

24. Hamilton and Turner, "Accountability through Algorithm," 2.

25. Diakopoulos, "Algorithmic Accountability."

26. Bucher, "'Machines Don't Have Instincts.'"

27. Schudson, *Discovering the News*.

28. Carlson, *Journalistic Authority*.

29. Lowrey, "Mapping."

30. Lewis, "Tension," 836.

31. Ibid.

32. Powers, "New Boots on the Ground."

33. Reich, "Journalism"; Ettema and Glasser, *Custodians of Conscience*, 22.

34. Reich, "Journalism," 32

35. Lewis, "Tension." Lewis's review offers a comprehensive discussion of professionalism, which I lean on heavily here.

36. Abbott, "System of Professions," 225.

37. Schudson and Anderson, "Objectivity."

38. Waisbord, *Reinventing Professionalism*.

39. Hanitzsch et al., "Mapping Journalism Cultures"; Weaver, et al., *American Journalist*.

40. For example, see Reich, "Journalism as Bipolar."

41. Waisbord, *Reinventing Professionalism*, 7.

42. Freidson, "Changing Nature."

43. McLeod and Hawley, "Professionalization among Newsmen"; Weaver et al., *American Journalist*.

44. Abbott, *Systems of Professions*, 225.

45. Ibid., 93.

46. Bloor and Dawson, "Understanding," 276.

47. Zelizer, "Journalism's 'Last' Stand," 89.

48. Ibid., 78–92.

49. Singer, "More Than Ink-Stained Wretches."

50. Ibid., 838.

51. From Erzikova and Lowrey, "Seeking Safe Ground," 353.

52. Lowrey, "Word People."

53. Ibid., 415.

54. Abbott, *Systems of Professions*, 149.

55. Lowrey, "Word People," 428.

56. Ibid.

57. Powers, "Forms," 24.

## Chapter 2. The Rise of a Subspecialty

1. Johnson, "Cyberstar."

2. Rob Curley, telephone interview with the author, June 25, 2015.

3. Barnhurst and Nerone, *Form of News*.

4. Monmonier, *Maps with the News*.

5. John Grimwade, telephone interview with the author, June 26, 2015.

6. Monmonier, *Maps with the News*, 154.

7. Ibid., 15–16.

8. Friendly, "Brief History."

9. Cairo, *Functional Art*, 185.

10. Ibid.

11. Ibid.

12. Compaine, "Newspaper Industry."

13. Andrew DeVigal, telephone interview with the author, June 23, 2015.

14. DeVigal, "1995 Chicago Homicides."

15. Fordahl, "Comdex Cancels."

16. Geoff McGhee, phone interview, June 23, 2015.

17. Boczkowski, *Digitizing the News*, 113.

18. Ibid.

19. Ibid., 135.

20. Ibid., 133.

21. Ibid., 187.

22. Derek Willis, in email to the author, January 27, 2016.

23. See https://github.com/dwillis/shboom.

24. Holovaty, "Fundamental Way."

25. See http://www.nytimes.com/packages/html/politics/2004_ELECTIONGUIDE_GRAPHIC.

26. Bilton, "Adobe."

27. Carter, Cox, Quealy, and Schoenfeld, "How Different Groups."

28. Garrett, "Ajax."

29. Ethan Zuckerman, email with the author, July 21, 2015.

30. Coleman, *Coding Freedom*; and Preston-Werner, "Open Source."

31. Nathan Ashby-Kuhlman, telephone interview with the author, June 8, 2015.

32. Adrian Holovaty, telephone interview with the author, June 9, 2015.

33. Brian Boyer, conversation with the author, Amsterdam, June 16, 2015.

34. James, "Open Source."

35. Nathan Ashby-Kuhlman, personal communication with the author, June 8, 2015.

36. Adrian Holovaty, personal communication with the author, June 9, 2015.

37. Holovaty, "Announcing chicagocrime.org."

38. Ibid.

39. O'Connell, "Do-It-Yourself Cartography."

40. Johnson, "Cyberstar," 1–2 (emphasis added).

41. Glaser, "Web Focus."

42. Knight Proposal (2006, 2007) provided by Rich Gordon to the author via email, June 24, 2015.

43. "Lede Program."

44. Benton, "Columbia's Year Zero."

45. Holovaty, "Post Remix."

46. Holovaty, "Announcing."

47. Holovaty, "New at washingtonpost.com."

48. Jacob Harris, interview with the author, *New York Times*, September 9, 2012.

49. "2010 Pulitzer Prize Winners."

50. Author's field notes, April 12, 2010.

51. Kaufman, "To Spur Traffic."

52. "Year's Most Visited."

53. Moses, "Narcissism."

54. Ibid.

55. Ibid.

56. Much of this early history has been chronicled by Scott Klein in a lecture for the March 2014 conference "Big Data Future" at Ohio State's Moritz College of Law. See Scott Klein, "Antebellum Data Journalism: or, How Big Data Busted Abe Lincoln," available at the *ProPublica* Nerd Blog, www.propublica.org/nerds/item/antebellum -data-journalism-busted-abe-lincoln

57. Anderson, "Between the Unique."

58. Hamilton and Turner, "Accountability through Algorithm."

59. Cox, "Development."

60. Reavy, "How the Media Learned."

61. Meyer, "New Precision Journalism."

62. Lewis and Usher, "Open Source and Journalism."

63. Cox, "Development."

64. Jaspin, Facebook message chat with the author, June 26, 2015.

65. "NICAR: About."

66. Garrison, "Tools," 113.

## Chapter 3. Hacker Journalists, Programmer Journalists, and Data Journalists

1. *Boing Boing*.

2. US$667,000.

3. Brian Boyer, personal communication with the author, November 5, 2011.

4. Fink and Anderson, "Data Journalism."

5. Ibid.

6. Flew, Daniel, and Spurgeon, "Promise."

7. Parasie and Dagiral, "Data-Driven Journalism."

8. Royal, "Journalist as Programmer."

9. Weber and Rall, "Data Visualization."

10. Gynnild, "Journalism Innovation."

11. Coddington, "Clarifying."

12. "Knight News Challenge."

13. Boyer, "Brian Boyer."

14. "Knight News Challenge."

15. Defining this group as male, and as wearing a certain wardrobe, has notable symbolic issues.

16. Gordon, "Programmer-Journalist."

17. Kelty, *Two Bits*.

18. Stray, "Identity Crisis."

19. Ryan Mark, personal communication with Seth C. Lewis, July 20, 2012.

20. Joe Germuska, personal communication with Seth C. Lewis, July 20, 2012.

21. Tsan Yuan, personal communication with the author, October 21, 2013.

22. Alastair Dant, personal communication with the author, November 2, 2011.

23. Ibid.

24. Mohammed el Haddad, personal communication with the author, June 7, 2012.

25. Graff, "*Al Jazeera*'s Mohammad Haddad."

26. Stray, "Journalism for Makers."

27. Coleman, *Coding Freedom*, 423.

28. Lewis and Usher, "Open Source."

29. Stijn Debrouwere, personal communication with the author, February 27, 2014.

30. Ransome Mpini, personal communication with the author, October 21, 2013.

31. Reed and Coester, "Coding for the Future."

32. Usher, *Making the News*.

33. Reed and Coester, "Coding for the Future."

34. Jon Keegan, personal communication with the author, September 4, 2013.

35. Ibid.

36. Sara Slone, personal communication with the author, September 4, 2013.

37. Ibid.

38. Ibid.

39. Mohammad el-Haddad, personal communication with the author, June 11, 2012.

40. Ibid.

41. Brian Boyer, personal communication with the author, August 8, 2013.

42. Hacker journalist, personal communication with the author, October 23, 2013.

43. Michelle Minkoff, tweet, August 19, 2014.

44. Minkoff, "Teaching at Medill!"

45. Minkoff, "Letter."

46. Fowler, Beck, Brant, Opdyke, and Roberts, *Refactoring*.

47. Michelle Minkoff, personal communication with the author, July 23, 2013.

48. Ibid.

49. Minkoff, "What's It Like?"

50. Sisi Wei, personal communication with the author, September 19, 2014.

51. Sisi Wei, personal communication with the author, September 17, 2014. Wei thinks this has changed since we spoke, as now journalists may be more confident as coders.

52. Emily Chow, personal communication, August 23, 2013.

53. Jeremy Bowers, personal communication with the author, August 15, 2014.

54. John Keefe, personal communication with the author, July 9, 2013.

55. Danny DeBelius, personal communication with the author, March 26, 2014.

56. Scott Klein, personal communication, August 7, 2013.

57. Jeremy Bowers, personal communication with the author, August 15, 2014.

58. Sisi Wei, personal communication with the author, September 17, 2014.

59. Michelle Minkoff, personal communication with the author, July 23, 2013.

60. Howard, "Art and Science."

61. Tracy, "Nate Silver."

62. Daniel and Flew, "Guardian Reportage."

63. Jonathan Stray, personal communication, October 27, 2011.

64. Powers, "In Forms."

65. Aron Pilhofer, personal communication with the author, November 11, 2011.

66. Matt Stiles, personal communication, July 30, 2013.

67. Scott Klein, personal communication, August 7, 2013.

68. Ibid.

69. Derek Willis, personal communication with the author, October 24, 2012.

70. Bradshaw, "Introduction."

71. Ibid.

72. Ibid.

73. Ibid.

74. Field notes, September 3, 2013.

75. Sascha Venohr, personal communication with the author, August 29, 2012.

76. Fink and Anderson, "Data Journalism."

77. Simon Rogers, personal communication, November 2, 2011.

78. Ibid.

79. Matt Stiles, personal communication with the author, July 30, 2013.

80. Matt Stiles, personal communication, March 10, 2014.

81. Mona Chalabi, personal communication, October 23, 2013.

82. "Schedule Details."

83. Ibid.

*Chapter 4. Inside the Interactive Journalism Newsroom*

1. Emily Chow, personal communication with the author, August 23, 2013.
2. Al-Jamea, Berkowitz, Chow, Karklis, and Lindeman, "Perils at Great Falls."
3. Youmans, *Media Economics*.
4. Usher, "Al Jazeera," 337.
5. Mohammad el-Haddad, personal communication with the author, June 7, 2012.
6. Ibid.
7. Ibid, June 5, 2012.
8. Author's field notes, June 11, 2012.
9. Haddad and Bollier, "Interactive."
10. Basma Atassi, personal communication with the author, June 7, 2012.
11. "Timeline."
12. As an interesting side note here, Atassi had to have her graphics tested for security, just in case the Syrians tried to conduct some sort of cyberattack on her work product—something no other newsroom had to do with their work.
13. Dar Jamal, personal communication with the author, June 11, 2012.
14. Basma Atassi, personal communication with the author, June 6, 2012.
15. Nanabhay and Farmanfarmaian, "From Spectacle to Spectacular."
16. Brian Boyer, personal communication with the author, February 28, 2014.
17. Howard, "NPR."
18. Field notes, September 4, 2013.
19. "WSJ Jet Tracker Database."
20. "Street Fashion."
21. Bostock, Carter, Quealy, and Ward, "NFL Draft."
22. Roberts, Carter, and Ward, "In 3-D."
23. Katz, "How Y'all."
24. Meyer, "*New York Times*' Most Popular Story."
25. Field notes, November 2, 2011.
26. Rogers, "Recycling Rates."
27. Rogers, "Welcome to the Datablog."
28. Rogers, immediately prior to the publication of this book, was working at Google and knows far more than he did in 2011.
29. Field notes, September 26, 2012.
30. Stray, "Editorial Search Engine."
31. Jonathan Stray, personal communication with the author, September 26, 2012.
32. Oreskes, "AP Reporters."
33. Ibid.
34. Brian Boyer, personal communication, August 8, 2013.
35. Ryan Mark, personal conversation with Seth C. Lewis, September 27, 2012.
36. Minkoff, "Letter."
37. Jonathan Stray, personal communication with author, October 17, 2012.
38. Abbott, *System of Professions*, 64.
39. Ibid.

## Chapter 5. Interactives and Journalism's Systems of Knowledge

1. Groeger, Ornstein, Tigas, and Jones, "Dollars for Docs."
2. Abbott, "Order of Professionalization," 355.
3. Abbott, *System of Professions.*
4. Ibid., 9.
5. Abbott, "Order of Professionalization," 355.
6. Lowrey, "Word People," 413.
7. Waisbord, *Professionalism*, chapter 9.
8. Lowrey, "Word People."
9. Ibid., 419.
10. See, for example, Sylvain Parasie's analysis ("Data-Driven Revelation") of the Center for Investigative Reporting in San Francisco, where he found that investigative reporters, data journalists, and programmers came together around different norms to develop one coherent approach to conducting journalism.
11. Anderson, Bell, and Shirky, "Post-Industrial Journalism," 79.
12. Merrill, "Heart of Nerd Darkness."
13. Notably, here I am not interrogating the underlying premises behind what it means to work with data.
14. Lewis and Westlund, "Big Data and Journalism."
15. "Dow Jones, REPORTER-NY."
16. "We're Hiring."
17. Sarah Ryley, email communication to NICAR-L, September 3, 2014.
18. Dougherty, "We are Makers."
19. Rheingold, *Virtual Community.*
20. Turner, *From Counterculture to Cyberculture.*
21. Tanenbaum, Williams, Desjardins, and Tanenbaum, "Democratizing Technology."
22. Graham, "Hackers and Painters."
23. Nagle, "Responsive Charts."
24. Eads, "Nuts and Bolts."
25. Ray, "Improving." Emphasis added.
26. Stray, "Video."
27. "Overview."
28. McDaniel, "Missouri."
29. "PANDA Project."
30. Brian Boyer, email message to author, September 30, 2014.
31. Pilhofer, "In Two Years."
32. Ibid.
33. "Chicago Shooting Victims."
34. Cohen, Hamilton, and Turner "Computational Journalism."
35. Ibid.
36. This idea of near and far was conceptualized with the help of *ProPublica.*
37. John Keefe, personal communication with the author, July 9, 2013.

38. "WNYC Bike Share Stations."

39. John Keefe, correspondence with the author, February 14, 2014.

40. Hinds and Bernstein, "Ten Percent."

41. LaFleur, Shaw, Coutts, and Larso, "Opportunity Gap."

42. Scott Klein, personal communication with the author, July 8, 2013.

43. Coleman, *Coding Freedom*, 3

44. Raymond, *Cathedral and the Bazaar*.

45. Balka, Raasch, and Herstatt, "Open Source"; Benkler, *Wealth of Networks*, 60.

46. Jordan, *Hacking*, 100.

47. Levy, *Hackers*; Sinker, "Hacker Journalism 2011."

48. Bruns, *Blogs*, 59.

49. Lewis and Usher, "Open Source."

50. John Keefe, personal communication with the author, July 9, 2013.

51. Aron Pilhofer, personal communication with the author, June 13, 2012.

52. Andrew Liemdorfer, personal communication with the author, October 21, 2013.

53. Alastair Dant, personal communication with the author, November 2, 2011.

54. Chase Davis, personal communication with the author, September 3, 2013.

55. Benkler, *Wealth of Networks*, 218.

56. Cadman, "Cycling."

57. "2011 Census Analysis."

58. Sedghi, "No Increase."

59. "Where Are You?"

60. Bella Hurrell, personal communication with the author, October 21, 2013.

61. "46 Places."

62. "Why Short Guys Can Dunk."

63. Leonhardt, "Climbing Income Ladder."

64. Jack Gillum, personal communication with the author, July 23, 2013.

65. Sara Sloane, personal communication with the author, September 4, 2013.

66. Sisi Wei, personal communication with the author, July 8, 2013.

67. Scott Klein, personal communication with the author, July 8, 2013.

## Conclusion

1. Brustein, "Newspaper's First Trip."

2. Santus, "Newspaper Experiments."

3. Gayomali, "Iowa Newspaper."

4. Brustein, "Newspaper's First Trip."

5. Deuze, "What Is Journalism?; Schudson, *Discovering the News*.

6. Lewis and Usher, "Open Source."

7. Ibid.

8. Clark, "Arlington Couple."

9. Park, "News."

10. Carey, "Cultural Approach."

11. Phillips, "Transparency."

12. Carlson, *Condition of Anonymity*.

13. Roberts, "*The Guardian*."

14. Rusbridger, "Open Journalism."

15. *Guardian* News Media Press Office. "*Guardian* News."

16. Santo, "Experiments."

17. Hindman, *Myth of Digital Democracy*.

18. Weber, "Newspapers."

19. Steensen, "Online Journalism," 313.

20. Kenney, Gorelik, and Mwangi, "Interactive Features."

21. Quandt, "(No) News," 717.

22. Allan, Sonwalkar, and Carter, "Bearing Witness."

23. Schrager, "Problem."

24. Toff, "NYC Taxi."

25. Espeland and Stevens, "A Sociology of Quantifications."

26. Schrager, "Problem."

27. Ronald Campbell, email correspondence to NICAR-L ("Statistical Question"), August 25, 2014.

28. Tim Henderson, email correspondence to NICAR-l, August 25, 2014.

29. O'Hara, "Nate Silver."

30. Silver, "What the Fox Knows."

31. Spinner, "Big Conundrum."

32. See https://storify.com/macloo/should-journalists-learn-to-code.

33. Mulligan, "Hirable Grads."

34. Legrand, "Why Journalists."

35. "De-Coded."

36. "[For Journalism] Ruby."

37. Khazan, "Should Journalism Schools."

38. E-mail with author, January 28, 2016.

39. See http://www.theguardian.com/society/ng-interactive/2015/sep/02/unaffordable-country-where-can-you-afford-to-buy-a-house.

40. See http://www.theguardian.com/stage/ng-interactive/2015/jul/16/street-dance-storytelling-flexn-strut-their-stuff-interactive-dance-video.

41. Pitt, *Sensors and Journalism*.

42. Ibid., 17.

43. Ibid., 18.

44. Ibid., 107.

45. Diep, "Salvadorian Newspaper."

46. Ibid.

47. "Q&A."

## Methodology

1. I used data from Seth C. Lewis's research on *The Chicago Tribune*.

2. For this reason, I rely strongly on online ethnography-methods articles and

audience-reception studies because these sources are concerned with attempting to concentrate vast amounts of data in constrained time.

3. Geertz, *Interpretation of Cultures.*

4. Frankenberg, *White Women, Race Matters.*

5. Markham, "Representation," 145.

6. Lebesco, "Managing Visibility."

7. Alasuutari, "Three Phases," 6.

8. Weiss, *Learning from Strangers.*

9. Ibid., 9.

10. Fink and Anderson, "Data Journalism."

11. Ellis and Bochner, "Autoethnography."

12. Radway, *Reading the Romance*, chap. 1.

13. Jacobson, "Google Finally Discloses."

# Bibliography

Abbott, Andrew. "The Order of Professionalization: An Empirical Analysis." *Work and Occupations* 18 no. 4 (1991): 355.

———. *The System of Professions: An Essay on the Division of Expert Labor*. Chicago: University of Chicago Press, 1988.

Alasuutari, Pertti. "Three Phases of Reception Studies." In *Rethinking the Media Audience: The New Agenda*, edited by Peretti Alasuutari. London: Sage, 1999.

Al-Jamea, Sohail, Bonnie Berkowitz, Emily Chow, Laris Karklis, and Todd Lindeman. "The Perils at Great Falls." *Washington Post*, August 10, 2013. Available at http:// www.washingtonpost.com/wp-srv/special/local/the-perils-of-great-falls.

Allan, Stuart, Prasun Sonwalkar, and Cynthia Carter. "Bearing Witness: Citizen Journalism and Human Rights Issues." *Globalisation, Societies and Education* 5, no. 3 (2007): 373–89.

Anderson, C. W. "Between the Unique and the Pattern: Historical Tensions in Our Understanding of Quantitative Journalism." *Digital Journalism*. Available at http:// www.tandfonline.com/doi/abs/10.1080/21670811.2014.976407?src=recsys&#.Vfs1 _J1VhBc.

———. "Between Creative and Quantified Audiences: Web Metrics and Changing Patterns of Newswork in Local U.S. Newsrooms." *Journalism* 12, no. 5 (2011): 550–66.

Anderson, Chris, Emily Bell, and Clay Shirky. "Post-Industrial Journalism: Adapting to the Present." Columbia School of Journalism: Tow Center for Digital Journalism, December 3, 2014. Available at http://towcenter.org/research/post-industrial -journalism-adapting-to-the-present-2.

Atherton, Steven, Chris Finch, Alex Ranken, Lucy Rodgers, Helene Sears, Marina Shchukina, and Noah Veltman. "The Secret Life of the Cat: What Do Our Feline Companions Get Up To?" *BBC.com*, June 12, 2013. Available at http://www.bbc .com/news/science-environment-22567526.

Babcock, Charles. "Amazon, Microsoft, IBM, Google Capture Cloud Market." *Infor-

*mation Week*, July 28, 2015. Available at http://www.informationweek.com/cloud/amazon-microsoft-ibm-google-capture-cloud-market/d/d-id/1321484 (accessed January 26, 2016).

Balka, Kerstin, Christina Raasch, and Cornelius Herstatt. "Open Source Enters the World of Atoms: A Statistical Analysis of Open Design." *First Monday* 14 no. 11 (2009). Available at http://firstmonday.org/ojs/index.php/fm/article/view/2670/2366.

Barnhurst, Kevin G., and John C. Nerone. *The Form of News: A History*. New York: Guilford, 2001.

Benkler, Yochai. *The Wealth of Networks: How Social Production Transforms Markets and Freedom*. New Haven, Conn.: Yale University Press, 2006.

Benton, Joshua. "Columbia's Year Zero, Aiming to Give Journalists Literacy in Data, Is Now Called the Lede Program." *NiemanLab*, March 26, 2014. Available at http://www.niemanlab.org/2014/03/columbias-year-zero-aiming-to-give-journalists-literacy-in-data-is-now-called-the-lede-program.

———. "How NYTimes.com Cut Load Times and Got Faster for Users." *NiemanLab*, September 23, 2014. Available at http://www.niemanlab.org/2014/09/how-nytimes-com-cut-load-times-and-got-faster-for-users/?utm_source=twitterfeed.

"Bike Share Stations." *WNYC*. Updated continually. Available at http://project.wnyc.org/bike-share-map.

Bilton, Nick. "Adobe to Kill Mobile Flash, Focus on HTML5." *Bits* [blog], November 9, 2011. Available at http://bits.blogs.nytimes.com/2011/11/09/adobe-to-kill-mobile-flash-focus-on-html5/?_r=0.

Bloor, Geoffrey, and Patrick Dawson. "Understanding Professional Culture in Organizational Context." *Organization Studies* 15, no. 2 (1994): 275–95.

Boczkowski, Pablo. *Digitizing the News: Innovation in Online Newspapers*. Cambridge, Mass.: MIT Press, 2005.

*Boing Boing: A Directory of Wonderful Things*. March 27, 2007. Available at http://web.archive.org/web/20070323002254/http://boingboing.net.

Bostock, Mike, Shan Carter, Kevin Quealy, and Joe Ward. "NFL Draft: How Good Are Teams at Picking the Best?" *New York Times*, April 25, 2013. Available at http://www.nytimes.com/interactive/2013/04/25/sports/football/picking-the-best-in-the-nfl-draft.html.

Bostock, Mike, Shan Carter, and Archie Tse. "Is It Better to Rent or Buy?" *New York Times*, 2014. Available at http://www.nytimes.com/interactive/2014/upshot/buy-rent-calculator.html.

Boyer, Brian. "Brian Boyer: Welcome to Hacker Journalism 101, Take Your Seats." *NiemanLab*, September 7, 2012. Available at http://www.niemanlab.org/2012/09/brian-boyer-welcome-to-hacker-journalism-101-take-your-seats.

Bradshaw, Paul. "Introduction: What is Data Journalism?" In *The Data Journalism Handbook*, edited by Jonathan Gray, Liliana Bounegru, and Lucy Chambers, 2–3. Sebastopol, Calif.: O'Reilly, 2012. Available at http://datajournalismhandbook.org/1.0/en.

Branch, John. "Snow Fall: The Avalanche at Tunnel Creek." *New York Times*, December 18, 2012. Available at http://www.nytimes.com/video/sports/100000001957178/the-avalanche-at-tunnel-creek.html.

Bruns, Axel. *Blogs, Wikipedia, Second Life, and Beyond: From Production to Produsage*. New York: Peter Lang, 2008.

Brustein, Joshua. "A Newspaper's First Trip into Virtual Reality Goes to a Desolate Farm." *BloombergBusinessWeek*, September 22, 2014. Available at http://www.businessweek.com/articles/2014-09-22/gannetts-first-virtual-reality-journalism-features-a-desolate-farm.

Bucher, Taina. "'Machines Don't Have Instincts': Articulating the Computational in Journalism." *New Media and Society* (2016), doi: 10.1177/1461444815624182 (published online before print).

Bucy, Erik P. "Interactivity in Society: Locating an Elusive Concept." *Information Society* 20 (2004): 373–83.

———. "Second Generation Net News: Interactivity and Information Accessibility in the Online Environment." *International Journal on Media Management* 6, no. 1–2 (2004): 102–13.

Cadman, Emily. "Cycling and the Gentrification of Inner London." *Financial Times*, March 26, 2014. Available at http://blogs.ft.com/ftdata/2014/03/26/cycling-and-the-gentrification-of-inner-london.

Cairo, Alberto. *The Functional Art: An Introduction to Information Graphics and Visualization*. New York: New Riders, 2012.

Carey, James. "A Cultural Approach to Communication." In *Communication as Culture: Essays on Media and Society*, 13–36. London: Routledge, 1988.

Carlson, Matt. *Journalistic Authority*. New York: Columbia University Press. Forthcoming.

———. *On the Condition of Anonymity: Unnamed Sources and the Battle for Journalism*. Champaign: University of Illinois Press, 2011.

Carter, Shan, Amanda Cox, Kevin Quealy, and Amy Schoenfeld. "How Different Groups Spend Their Day." *New York Times*, July 31, 2009. Available at http://www.nytimes.com/interactive/2009/07/31/business/20080801-metrics-graphic.html?_r=0.

"Chicago Shooting Victims." *Chicago Tribune*. Updated continually. Available at http://crime.chicagotribune.com/chicago/shootings.

Clark, Cammy. "Arlington Couple on Cruise that Included Ebola Scare." *Fort Worth Star-Telegram*, October 21, 2014. Available at http://www.star-telegram.com/2014/10/21/6218826/arlington-couple-on-cruise-that.html?rh=1.

Coddington, Mark. "Clarifying Journalism's Quantitative Turn: A Typology for Evaluating Data Journalism, Computational Journalism, and Computer-Assisted Reporting." *Digital Journalism* 3, no. 3. (2015): 331–48. Available at doi: 10.1080/21670811.2014.976400.

Cohen, Sarah, James T. Hamilton, and Fred Turner. "Computational Journalism." *Communications of the ACM* 54, no. 10 (2011): 66–71.

Coleman, E. Gabriella. *Coding Freedom: The Ethics and Aesthetics of Hacking*. Princeton, N.J.: Princeton University Press, 2013.

Compaine, Benjamin M. "The Newspaper Industry." In *Who Owns the Media?* edited by Benjamin M. Compaine and Douglas Gomery. Mahwah, N.J.: Erlbaum, 2000.

Cox, Melisma. "The Development of Computer-Assisted Reporting." Paper presented at the Association for Education and Mass Communication, Chapel Hill, N.C., 2000.

Daniel, Anna, and Terry Flew. "The Guardian Reportage of the UK MP Expenses Scandal: A Case Study of Computational Journalism." In *Record of the Communications Policy and Research Forum 2010*. Sydney: Network Insight, 2010, 186–94.

"De-Coded: An Overview of Basic Programming Languages for Beginners." *ONA 14*. Available at http://ona14.journalists.org/sessions/coding-language-overview/#.VD1_9ku6oqc.

Deuze, Mark. "The Changing Context of News Work: Liquid Journalism for a Monitorial Citizenry." *International Journal of Communication* 2 (2008): 18.

———. "What Is Journalism? Professional Identity and Ideology of Journalists Reconsidered." *Journalism* 6, no. 4 (2005): 442–64.

DeVigal, Andrew. "1995 Chicago Homicides on ChicagoTribune.com." Online video upload (0:20). November 2, 2009. Available at https://flic.kr/p/7cw1ZQ.

Diakopoulos, Nicholas. "Algorithmic Accountability: Journalistic Investigation of Computational Power Structures." *Tow Center for Digital Journalism Report*. New York: Columbia University, 2014.

———. "A Functional Roadmap for Innovation in Computational Journalism." *Nickdiakopoulos.com*, April 22, 2011.

Diep, Francie. "Salvadoran Newspaper Sends Drone to Cover Presidential Election." *Popular Science*, February 4, 2014. Available at http://www.popsci.com/article/technology/salvadoran-newspaper-sends-drone-cover-presidential-election.

Dougherty, Dale. "We Are Makers." *TED Talk*. 2011. Available at http://www.ted.com/talks/dale_dougherty_we_are_Makers.html.

"Dow Jones, REPORTER-NY." *Gorkana*, September 2, 2014. Available at http://www.gorkanajobs.com/job/43453/dow-jones-reporter-ny/?deviceType=Desktop&TrackID=33.

Eads, David. "The Nuts and Bolts of *Tribune* News Apps Event Listings." *News Apps Blog* [*Chicago Tribune*], February 17, 2014. Available at http://blog.apps.chicagoTribune.com/page/3.

Edge, Abigail. "Why Newsrooms Need a 'Responsive Philosophy.'" *Journalism.co.uk*, September 26, 2014. Available at http://www.journalism.co.uk/news/why-newsrooms-should-adopt-a-responsive-philosophy-/s2/a562590/?utm_source=API%27s%20Need%20to%20Know%20newsletter.

Ellis, Carolyn S., and Arthur Bochner. "Autoethnography, Personal Narrative, Reflexivity: Researcher as Subject." In *The Handbook of Qualitative Research*, edited by Norman Denzin and Yvonna Lincoln, 733–68. London: Sage, 2000.

Ensha, Azadeh. "How Fast Is Your Internet Connection?" *Lifehacker*, August 25, 2009. Available at http://lifehacker.com/5345301/how-fast-is-your-internet-connection.

Erzikova, Elina, and Wilson Lowrey. "Seeking Safe Ground: Russian Regional Journalists' Withdrawal from Civic Service Journalism." *Journalism Studies* 11, no. 3 (2010): 343–58. Available at http://www.tandfonline.com/doi/pdf/10.1080 /14616700903407411.

Espeland, Wendy Nelson, and Mitchell L. Stevens. "A Sociology of Quantification." *European Journal of Sociology* 49, no. 3 (2008): 401–36.

Ettema, James S., and Theodore L. Glasser. *Custodians of Conscience: Investigative Journalism and Public.* New York: Columbia University Press, 1998.

Fink, Katherine, and C. W. Anderson. "Data Journalism in the United States: Beyond the 'Usual Suspects.'" *Journalism Studies* 3, no. 3 (2015): 1–15.

Flew, Terry, Anna Daniel, and Christina L. Spurgeon. "The Promise of Computational Journalism." In *Proceedings of the 2010 Australian and New Zealand Communication Association, ANZCA.* Canberra. 2010.

Flew, Terry, Christina Spurgeon, Anna Daniels, and Adam Swift. "The Promise of Computational Journalism." *Journalism Practice* 6, no. 4 (2012): 157–71.

Fordahl, Matthew. "Comdex Cancels November 2004 Tech Convention." *RedOrbit*, June 24, 2004. Available at https://web.archive.org/web/20090823072906/http:// www.redorbit.com/news/technology/67462/comdex_cancels_november_2004 _tech_convention/index.html.

"[For Journalism] Ruby." *ONA14.* Available at http://ona14.journalists.org/sessions/ ruby-for-journalism/#.VD2ASEu6oqc.

"The 46 Places to Go in 2013." *New York Times*, January 11, 2013. Available at http:// www.nytimes.com/interactive/2013/01/10/travel/2013-places-to-go.html.

Fowler, Martin, Kent Beck, John Brant, William Opdyke, and Don Roberts. *Refactoring: Improving the Design of Existing Code.* Westford, Mass.: Pearson Education, 1999.

Frankenberg, Ruth. *White Women, Race Matters: The Social Construction of Whiteness.* Minneapolis: University of Minnesota Press, 1993.

Freelon, Deen. *Crimson Hexagon Search for Interactive Journalism Terms.* June 30, 2015.

Freidson, Eliot. "The Changing Nature of Professional Control." *Annual Review of Sociology* 10 (1984): 1–20.

Friendly, Michael. "A Brief History of Data Visualization." In *The Handbook of Data Visualization*, edited by Chun-houh Chen, Wolfgang Karl Härdle, and Antony Unwin, 15–56. Berlin: Springer, 2008.

"The Full New York Times Innovation Report." *Mashable*, May 16, 2014. Available at http://mashable.com/2014/05/16/full-new-york-times-innovation -report/#E2bhhanNAOq0.

Garrett, Jesse James. "Ajax: A New Approach to Web Applications." *Adaptive Path*, February 18, 2005. Available at http://www.adaptivepath.com/ideas/ajax-new -approach-web-applications.

Garrison, Bruce. "Tools Daily Newspapers Use in Computer-Assisted Reporting." *Newspaper Research Journal* 17, no. 1/2 (1996): 113.

Gayomali, Chris. "How an Iowa Newspaper Is Using Oculus Rift for Big, Ambitious Journalism." *Fast Company*, September 22, 2014. Available at http://www.fastcompany.com/3035851/world-changing-ideas/how-an-iowa-newspaper-is-using-oculus-rift-for-big-ambitious-journalism.

Geertz, Clifford. *The Interpretation of Cultures: Selected Essays*. New York: Basic, 1973.

Glaser, Mark. "Web Focus Leads Newspapers to Hire Programmers for Editorial Staff." *MediaShift*, March 7, 2007. Available at http://mediashift.org/2007/03/web-focus-leads-newspapers-to-hire-programmers-for-editorial-staff066.

Gold, Jon. "U.S. Internet Connection Speeds Still Lag behind Other Developed Nations." *Network World*, August 6, 2015. Available at http://www.networkworld.com/article/2959544/lan-wan/u-s-internet-connection-speeds-still-lag-behind-other-developed-nations.html.

Google Developers. "Mobile Analysis in PageSpeed Insight." Last modified April 8, 2015. Available at https://developers.google.com/speed/docs/insights/mobile.

Gordon, Rich. "A 'Programmer-Journalist' Contemplates Careers." *Idea Lab/MediaShift*, July 1, 2008. Available at http://mediashift.org/idealab/2008/07/a-programmer-journalist-contemplates-careers005.

Graff, Ryan. "Al Jazeera's Mohammad Haddad on His Journey from Computer Science to Data-Driven Storyteller." *Idea Lab/MediaShift*, July 3, 2013. Available at http://www.pbs.org/idealab/2013/06/al-jazeeras-mohammed-haddad-on-his-journey-from-computer-science-to-data-driven-storyteller151.

Graham, Paul. "Hackers and Painters." *Paulgraham.com*, May 2003. Available at http://www.paulgraham.com/hp.html.

Greenfield, Rebecca. "What the *New York Times*'s 'Snow Fall' Means to Online Journalism's Future." *Wire*, December 20, 2012. Available at http://www.thewire.com/technology/2012/12/new-york-times-snow-fall-feature/60219.

Groeger, Lena, Charles Ornstein, Mike Tigas, and Ryann Grochowski Jones. "Dollars for Docs: How Industry Dollars Reach Your Doctors." *ProPublica*, September 29, 2014. Available at http://projects.propublica.org/docdollars.

*Guardian* News Media Press Office. "*Guardian* News and Media Invites Readers to Shape the Future of *Guardian* Membership through Beta Programme." *The Guardian*, September 10, 2014. Available at http://www.theguardian.com/gnm-press-office/2014/sep/10/guardian-news-media-invites-readers-to-shape-the-future-of-guardian-membership-through-beta-programme.

Gynnild, Astrid. "Journalism Innovation Leads to Innovation Journalism: The Impact of Computational Exploration on Changing Mindsets." *Journalism* 15, no. 6 (2014): 713–30.

Haddad, Mohammed el-, and Sam Bollier. "Interactive: An Austere Trip through Europe." *Al Jazeera English*, June 2, 2012. Available at http://www.aljazeera.com/indepth/interactive/2012/06/20126127221845926.html.

Hamilton, James T., and Fred Turner. "Accountability through Algorithm: Developing the Field of Computational Journalism." Center for Advanced Study in the Behavioral Sciences Summer Workshop. Duke University in association with Stanford University. Stanford, Calif., July 27–31, 2009.

Hanitzsch, Thomas, Folker Hanusch, Claudia Mellado, Maria Anikina, Rosa Berganza, Incilay Cangoz, Mihai Coman et al. "Mapping Journalism Cultures across Nations: A Comparative Study of 18 Countries." *Journalism Studies* 12, no. 3 (2011): 273–93.

Hargittai, Eszter, W. Russell Neuman, and Olivia Curry. "Taming the Information Tide: Perceptions of Information Overload in the American Home." *Information Society* 28, no. 3 (2012): 161–73.

Haughney, Christine. "Times Wins Four Pulitzers; Brooklyn Nonprofit Is Awarded a Reporting Prize." *New York Times*, April 15, 2013. Available at http://www.nytimes.com/2013/04/16/business/media/the-times-wins-four-pulitzer-prizes.html.

Hindman, Matthew. *The Myth of Digital Democracy*. Princeton, N.J.: Princeton University Press, 2008.

Hinds, Kate, and Andrea Bernstein. "Ten Percent of Citi Bike Docks Appear to Fail Each Day." *WNYC*, June 11, 2013. Available at http://www.wnyc.org/story/298321-problems-what-problems-ny-officials-bat-citi-bike-complaints-away-adjustment-period.

Holovaty, Adrian. "Announcing chicagocrime.org." May 18, 2005. Available at http://www.holovaty.com/writing/chicagocrime.org-launch.

———. "Announcing washingtonpost.com's U.S. Congress Votes Database." December 5, 2005. Available at http://www.holovaty.com/writing/326.

———. "Covering Elections on LJWorld.com." February 24, 2003. Available at http://www.holovaty.com/writing/195.

———. "A Fundamental Way Newspaper Sites Need to Change." September 6, 2006. Available at http://www.holovaty.com/writing/fundamental-change.

———. "New at washingtonpost.com: Faces of the Fallen 2.0." April 13, 2006. Available at http://www.holovaty.com/writing/335.

———. "Post Remix: The *Washington Post*'s Official Mashup Center." November 22, 2005. Available at http://www.holovaty.com/writing/325.

Howard, Alexander. "The Art and Science of Data-Driven Journalism." Columbia University School of Journalism: Tow Center for Digital Journalism, 2014. Available at http://towcenter.org/wp-content/uploads/2014/05/Tow-Center-Data-Driven-Journalism.pdf.

———. "NPR News App Team Experiments with Making Data-Driven Public Media with the Public." Columbia University School of Journalism: Tow Center for Digital Journalism, August 30, 2013. Available at http://towcenter.org/blog/npr-news-app-team-experiments-with-making-data-driven-public-media-with-the-public.

Jacobson, Murrey. "Google Finally Discloses its Diversity Record, and It's Not Good." *PBS News Hour*, May 28, 2014. Available at http://www.pbs.org/newshour/updates/google-discloses-workforce-diversity-data-good.

James, Steve. "Open Source Social Platforms: 10 of the Best." *Mashable*, July 25, 2007. Available at http://mashable.com/2007/07/25/open-source-social-platforms.

Johnson, Steve. "Cyberstar." *Chicago Tribune*, August 17, 2008. Available at http://articles.chicagotribune.com/2008-08-17/features/0808110560_1_cyberstar-user-generated-programmers.

Jordan, Tim. "Hacking and Power: Social and Technological Determinism in the Digital Age." *First Monday* 14, no. 7 (July 6, 2009).

———. *Hacking: Digital Media and Technological Determinism*. Malden, Mass.: Polity, 2013.

Kaiser, Bob. Untitled memo to *Washington Post* about the rise of online content. *Recovering Journalist*, August 6, 1992. Available at http://recoveringjournalist.typepad.com/files/kaiser-memo.pdf.

Katz, Josh. "How Y'all, Youse and You Guys Talk," *New York Times*, December 20, 2013. Available at http://www.nytimes.com/interactive/2013/12/20/sunday-review/dialect-quiz-map.html.

Kaufman, Leslie. "To Spur Traffic at News Sites, Just Travoltify." *New York Times*, March 5, 2014. Available at http://www.nytimes.com/2014/03/06/business/media/to-spur-traffic-at-news-sites-just-travoltify.html?_r=0.

Kelty, Christopher M. *Two Bits: The Cultural Significance of Free Software*. Durham, N.C.: Duke University Press. 2008.

Kenney, Keith, Alexander Gorelik, and Sam Mwangi. "Interactive Features of Online Newspapers." *First Monday* 5, no. 1 (2000).

Khazan, Olga. "Should Journalism Schools Require Reporters to 'Learn Code'? No." *The Atlantic*, October 21, 2013. Available at http://www.theatlantic.com/education/archive/2013/10/should-journalism-schools-require-reporters-to-learn-code-no/280711.

King, Michael. "Dealing with Data: Be Very, Very Skeptical; Interviewing Data: Derek Willis, the *New York Times*." *American Journalism Review*, April 5, 2014. Available at http://ajr.org/2014/04/05/dealing-data-skeptical.

"Knight News Challenge Interim Review." *Redub*, June 22, 2011. Available at http://redubllc.com/knight-news-challenge-interim-review.

LaFleur, Jennifer, Al Shaw, Sharona Coutts, and Jeff Larson. "The Opportunity Gap." *ProPublica*. Last updated January 24, 2013. Available at http://projects.propublica.org/schools.

Layton, Julia. "How Amazon Works." *How Stuff Works*, 2006. Available at http://money.howstuffworks.com/amazon1.htm.

Lebesco, Katherine. "Managing Visibility, Intimacy, and Focus in Online Critical Ethnography." In *Online Social Research: Methods, Issues and Ethics*, edited by Mark D. Johns, Shing-Ling Sarina Chen, and G. Jon Hall, 62–79. New York: Peter Lang, 2004.

"The Lede Program: An Introduction to Data Practices." Columbia University Graduate School of Journalism. Available at http://www.journalism.columbia.edu/page/1058-the-lede-program-an-introduction-to-data-practices/906.

Legrand, Roland. "Why Journalists Should Learn Computer Programming." *MediaShift*, June 2, 2010. Available at http://mediashift.org/2010/06/why-journalists-should-learn-computer-programming153.

Leonhardt, David. "In Climbing Income Ladder, Location Matters." *New York Times*, July 22, 2013. Available at http://www.nytimes.com/2013/07/22/business/in-climbing-income-ladder-location-matters.html.

Levy, Steven. *Hackers: Heroes of the Computer Revolution*. New York: Penguin, 2001.

Lewis, Seth. "Journalism in an Era of Big Data: Cases, Concepts, and Critiques." *Digital Journalism* 3, no. 3 (2015): 321–30.

———. "The Tension Between Professional Control and Open Participation: Journalism and Its Boundaries." *Information, Communication and Society* 15, no. 6 (2012): 836–66.

Lewis, Seth C., and Nikki Usher. "Open Source and Journalism: Toward New Frameworks for Imagining News Innovation." *Media, Culture and Society* 35, no. 5 (2013): 602–19.

Lewis, Seth C., and Oscar Westlund. "Big Data and Journalism: Epistemology, Expertise, Economics, and Ethics." *Digital Journalism* 3, no. 3. (2015). Available at doi: 10.1080/21670811.2014.976418.

Lowrey, Wilson. "Mapping the Journalism–Blogging Relationship." *Journalism* 7, no. 4 (2006): 477–500.

———. "Word People vs. Picture People: Normative Differences and Strategies for Control over Work among Newsroom Subgroups." *Mass Communication and Society* 5, no. 4 (2002): 411–32.

Lowrey, Wilson, and Elina Erzikova. "Institutional Legitimacy and Russian News: Case Studies of Four Regional Newspapers." *Political Communication* 27, no. 3 (2010): 275–88.

Markham, Annette. "Representation in Online Ethnographies: A Matter of Context Sensitivity." In *Online Social Research: Methods, Issues and Ethics*, edited by Mark D. Johns, Shing-Ling Sarina Chen, and G. Jon Hall. New York: Peter Lang, 2004.

Masnick, Mike. "The U.S. Government Today Has More Data on the Average American than the Stasi Did on East Germans." *Techdirt*, October 3, 2012. Available at http://www.techdirt.com/articles/20121003/10091120581/us-government-today-has-more-data-average-american-than-stasi-did-east-germans.shtml.

McDaniel, Chris. "Missouri Swore It Wouldn't Use a Controversial Execution Drug. It Did." St. Louis Public Radio, September 2, 2014. Available at http://news.stlpublicradio.org/post/missouri-swore-it-wouldn-t-use-controversial-execution-drug-it-did.

McLeod, Jack M., and Searle E. Hawley Jr. "Professionalization among Newsmen." *Journalism and Mass Communication Quarterly* 41 (1964): 529–577.

McMillan, Sally J. "Exploring Models of Interactivity from Multiple Research Traditions: Users, Documents and Systems." In *Handbook of New Media*, edited by Leah Lievrouw and Sonia Livingstone, 205–30. London: Sage, 2006.

Merrill, Jeremy B. "Heart of Nerd Darkness: Why Updating Dollars for Docs Was So Difficult." *ProPublica*, March 25, 2013. Available at http://www.propublica.org/nerds/item/heart-of-nerd-darkness-why-dollars-for-docs-was-so-difficult.

Meyer, Philip. *The New Precision Journalism*. Bloomington: Indiana University Press, 1991.

Meyer, Robinson. "The *New York Times*' Most Popular Story of 2013 Was Not an Article." *The Atlantic*, January 17, 2014. Available at http://www.theatlantic.com/technology/archive/2014/01/-em-the-new-york-times-em-most-popular-story-of-2013-was-not-an-article/283167.

Minkoff, Michelle. "A Letter to Journo-Programmers: Teach Me, Inspire Me." *Michelleminkoff.com*, November 24, 2009. Available at http://michelleminkoff.com/2009/11/24/a-letter-to-journo-programmers-teach-me-inspire-me.

———. "Teaching at Medill!" *Michelleminkoff.com*. Available at http://michelleminkoff.com/2014/06/30/teaching-at-medill.

———. "What's It Like Looking for a Programmer-Journalist Job?" *Michelleminkoff.com*, July 30, 2011. Available at http://michelleminkoff.com/2011/07/30/what-is-it-like-looking-for-a-programmer-journalist-job.

Monmonier, Mark. *Maps with the News: The Development of American Journalistic Cartography*. Chicago: University of Chicago Press, 1989.

Moses, Lucia. "'Narcissism Works Really Well': Why *Time* Magazine Created a Site for Its Interactive Stories." *Digiday*, June 22, 2015. Available at http://digiday.com/publishers/narcissism-works-really-well-time-magazine-created-site-interactive-stories.

Mulligan, Miranda. "Want to Produce Hirable Grads, Journalism Schools? Teach Them to Code." *NiemanLab*, September 5, 2012. Available at http://www.niemanlab.org/2012/09/miranda-mulligan-want-to-produce-hirable-grads-journalism-schools-teach-them-to-code.

Nagle, Ryan. "Responsive Charts with D3 and Backbone." *News Apps Blog [Chicago Tribune]*, March 3, 2014. Available at http://blog.apps.chicagotribune.com/2014/03/07/responsive-charts-with-d3-and-backboneS.

Nanabhay, Mohamed, and Roxane Farmanfarmaian. "From Spectacle to Spectacular: How Physical Space, Social Media and Mainstream Broadcast Amplified the Public Sphere in Egypt's 'Revolution.'" *Journal of North African Studies* 16, no. 4 (2011): 573–603.

Needle, David. "Did Roger Fidler 'Invent' the iPad in 1994 at a Knight-Ridder Lab?" *TabTimes*, March 9, 2012. Available at http://tabtimes.com/did-guy-invent-ipad-back-1994-2745.

"NICAR: About." N.d. Available at http://www.ire.org/nicar/about.

Nielsen, Jacob. "Response Times: The 3 Important Limits." *Nielsen Norman Group*, 1993. Available at http://www.nngroup.com/articles/response-times-3-important-limits.

Neilsen, Rasmus Kleis. "Ten Years that Shook the Media World: Big Questions and

Big Trends in International Media Developments." Report. University of Oxford / Reuters Institute for the Study of Journalism. October 12, 2012. Available at http://reutersinstitute.politics.ox.ac.uk/sites/default/files/Nielsen%20-%20Ten%20 Years%20that%20Shook%20the%20Media_0.pdf.

O'Connell, Pamela Licalzi. "Do-It-Yourself Cartography." *New York Times Magazine*, December 11, 2005. Available at http://www.nytimes.com/2005/12/11/magazine/ doityourself-cartography.html.

O'Hara, Bob. "How Did Nate Silver Predict the US Election?" *The Guardian*, November 8, 2012. Available at http://www.theguardian.com/science/grrlscientist/2012/ nov/08/nate-sliver-predict-us-election.

O3b Networks. "What Is Network Latency and Does It Matter?" *O3bnetworks.com*, n.d. Available at http://www.o3bnetworks.com/media/40980/white%20paper _latency%20matters.pdf.

Oreskes, Michael. "AP Reporters Find Steroid Crackdown Ineffective." *AP*, January 4. 2013. Available at http://www.ap.org/Content/Press-Release/2013/AP-reporters -use-data-bases-to-show-HGH-crackdowns-ineffective.

"Overview: Completed Stories." *Overview.ap.org*. Updated continually. Available at http://overview.ap.org/completed-stories.

"PANDA Project." Available at http://pandaproject.net.

Parasie, Sylvain. "Data-Driven Revelation: Epistemological Tensions in Investigative Journalism in the Age of 'Big Data.'" *Digital Journalism* 3, no. 3 (2015). Available at doi: 10.1080/21670811.2014.976408.

Parasie, Sylvain, and Eric Dagiral. "Data-Driven Journalism and the Public Good: 'Computer-Assisted-Reporters' and 'Programmer-Journalists' in Chicago." *New Media and Society* 15, no. 6 (2013): 853–71.

Park, Robert E. "News as a Form of Knowledge: A Chapter in the Sociology of Knowledge." *American Journal of Sociology* 45, no. 5 (1940): 669–86.

Phillips, Angela. "Transparency and the New Ethics of Journalism." *Journalism Practice* 4, no. 3 (2010): 373–82.

Pilhofer, Aron. "In Two Years, DocumentCloud Becomes Standard." *KnightBlog*, September 8, 2014. Available at http://www.knightfoundation.org/blogs/knight-blog/2012/9/18/in-two-years-documentcloud-becomes-standard.

Pitt, Fergus. *Sensors and Journalism*. Columbia University School of Journalism: Tow Center for Digital Journalism, 2014. Available at http://towcenter.org/wp-content/ uploads/2014/05/Tow-Center-Sensors-and-Journalism.pdf.

Pompeo, Joe. "SXSW Panel Round-up: Remembering Carr, Digital Detox, and an Epic Panel Fail." *Capital New York*, March 16, 2015. Available at http://www .capitalnewyork.com/article/media/2015/03/8564091/sxsw-round-remembering -carr-digital-detox-and-epic-panel-fail.

Powers, Matthew. "'In Forms that Are Familiar and Yet-to-Be Invented': American Journalism and the Discourse of Technologically Specific Work." *Journal of Communication Inquiry* 36, no. 1 (2012): 24–43.

———. "The New Boots on the Ground: NGOs in the Changing Landscape of International News." *Journalism* (2015, published online before print). Available at http://jou.sagepub.com/content/early/2015/01/27/1464884914568077.abstract

Preston-Werner, Tom. "Open Source (Almost) Everything." November 22, 2011. Available at http://tom.preston-werner.com/2011/11/22/open-source-everything.html.

"Q&A with the Photographer Who Explored Chernobyl with a Drone." *Professional Society of Drone Journalists*, August 29, 2014. Available at http://www.dronejournalism.org/news/2014/8/qa-with-the-photographer-who-explored-chernobyl-with-a-drone.

Quandt, Thorsten. "(No) News on the World Wide Web? A Comparative Content Analysis of Online News in Europe and the United States." *Journalism Studies* 9, no. 5 (2008). 717–39.

Radway, Janice. *Reading the Romance: Women, Patriarchy, and Popular Literature.* Chapel Hill: University of North Carolina Press, 1991.

Rafaeli, Sheizaf, and Fay Sudweeks. "Networked Interactivity." *Journal of Computer-Mediated Communication* 2, no. 4 (1997).

Ray, Silas. "Improving the User Experience of Automated Integration Testing." *Open* [code blog of *The New York Times*], April 8, 2014. Available at http://open.blogs.nytimes.com/2014/04/08/improving-the-user-experience-of-automated-integration-testing.

Raymond, Eric S. *The Cathedral and the Bazaar: Musings on Linux and Open Source by an Accidental Revolutionary.* Sebastopol, Calif.: O'Reilly, 2001.

Reavy, Matthew. "How the Media Learned Computer-Assisted Reporting." Unpublished paper presented to the Newspaper Division, Association for Education in Journalism and Mass Communication Southeast Colloquium, Roanoke, Va., 1996.

Reed, Maryanne, and Dana Coester. "Coding for the Future: The Rise of Hacker Journalism." *MediaShift*, May 2, 2013. Available at http://www.pbs.org/mediashift/2013/05/coding-for-the-future-the-rise-of-hacker-journalism.

Reich, Zvi. "Journalism as Bipolar Interactional Expertise." *Communication Theory* 22, no. 4 (2012): 339–58.

Reilly, Katie. "Respect for Journalists' Contributions Has Fallen Significantly in Recent Years." *Pew Research Center*, August 24, 2015. Available at http://www.pewresearch.org/fact-tank/2013/07/25/respect-for-journalists-contributions-has-fallen-significantly-in-recent-years.

Rheingold, Howard. *The Virtual Community: Homesteading on the Electronic Frontier.* Cambridge, Mass.: MIT Press. 1993.

Roberts, Dan. "*The Guardian* Is Opening Up Its Newslists So You Can Help Us Make News." *The Guardian*, October 9, 2011. Available at http://www.theguardian.com/media/2011/oct/09/the-guardian-newslists-opening-up.

Roberts, Graham, Shan Carter, and Joe Ward. "In 3-D: How Mariano Rivera Dominates Hitters." *New York Times*, April 13, 2013. Available at http://www.nytimes.com/interactive/2012/04/13/sports/baseball/mariano-rivera-3d.html.

Rogawski, Christina. "The GovLab Index: The Data Universe." *Govlab.org*, August 22, 2013. Available at http://thegovlab.org/govlab-index-the-digital-universe.

Rogers, Simon. "Recycling Rates in England: How Does Your Town Compare?" *The Guardian*, November 4, 2011. Available at http://www.theguardian.com/news/datablog/2011/nov/04/recycling-rates-england-data.

———. "Welcome to the Datablog." *The Guardian*, March 9, 2009. Available at http://www.theguardian.com/news/datablog/2009/mar/10/blogpost1.

Rogers, Yvonne, Helen Sharp, and Jenny Preece. *Interaction Design: Beyond Human-Computer Interaction*. West Sussex: Wiley, 2011.

Romenesko, Jim. "More than 3.5 Million Page Views for New York Times' 'Snow Fall' Feature." *Jimromenesko.com*, December 27, 2012. Available at http://jimromenesko.com/2012/12/27/more-than-3-5-million-page-views-for-nyts-snow-fall.

Royal, Cindy. "The Journalist as Programmer: A Case Study of the New York Times Interactive News Technology Department." Paper delivered at the International Symposium in Online Journalism, Austin, Tex., April 23, 2010.

Rusbridger, Alan. "Open Journalism at *The Guardian*." *The Guardian*, February 29, 2012. Available at http://www.theguardian.com/media/video/2012/feb/29/alan-rusbridger-open-journalism-guardian-video.

Santo, Alysia. "Experiments in the Open Newsroom Concept." *Columbia Journalism Review*, November 17, 2011. Available at http://www.cjr.org/the_news_frontier/experiments_in_the_open_newsro.php?page=all.

Santus, Rex. "Newspaper Experiments with Virtual Reality in Remote Iowa." *Mashable*, September 25, 2014. Available at http://mashable.com/2014/09/25/virtual-iowa-farm.

"Schedule Details." NICAR. March 2, 2014. Available at http://ire.org/conferences/nicar-2014/schedule.

Schrager, Allison. "The Problem with Data Journalism." *Quartz*, March 19, 2014. Available at http://qz.com/189703/the-problem-with-data-journalism.

Schudson, Michael. *Discovering the News: A Social History of American Newspapers*. New York: Basic, 1981.

Schudson, Michael, and Chris Anderson. "Objectivity, Professionalism, and Truth Seeking in Journalism." In *The Handbook of Journalism Studies*, edited by Karin Wahl-Jorgenson and Thomas Hanitzsch, 88–101. London: Routledge, 2008.

Sedghi, Ami. "No Increase in Proportion of Commuters Cycling: Data Breakdown." *The Guardian*, March 26, 2014. Available at http://www.theguardian.com/news/datablog/2014/mar/26/no-increase-commuters-cycling-data-census.

Shafer, Jack. "Beware the Old Nostalgic Journalist." *Reuters*, March 3, 2014. Available at http://blogs.reuters.com/jackshafer/2014/03/03/beware-the-old-nostalgic-journalist.

Shaw, Jonathan. "Why 'Big Data' Is a Big Deal." *Harvard Magazine*, March-April 2014. Available at http://harvardmagazine.com/2014/03/why-big-data-is-a-big-deal.

Silver, Nate. "What the Fox Knows." *Fivethirtyeight*, March 17, 2014. Available at http://fivethirtyeight.com/features/what-the-fox-knows.

Silverman, Matt. "A Day in the Life of the Internet." *Mashable*, March 6, 2012. Available at http://mashable.com/2012/03/06/one-day-internet-data-traffic.

Singer, Jane B. "More Than Ink-Stained Wretches: The Resocialization of Print Journalists in Converged Newsrooms." *Journalism and Mass Communication Quarterly* 81, no. 4 (2004): 838–56.

Sinker, Daniel. "Hacker-Journalism 2011: A Year of 'Show Your Work.'" *Dansinker .com*, December 30, 2011. Available at http://dansinker.com/post/15050642729/hacker-journalism-2011-a-year-of-show-your-work.

Smith, Craig. "DMR YouTube Statistic Report (Year-End 2015)." Available at http://expandedramblings.com/index.php/downloads/youtube-statistic-report.

Smolen, Alex. "Lag Time and Cat Kickers and Star Wars . . . Oh My." *Alxsmolen. wordpress.com*, May 6, 2014. Available at http://alxsmolen.wordpress.com /2014/05/06/finalproject.

Spinner, Jackie. "The Big Conundrum: Should Journalists Learn Code?" *American Journalism Review*, September 24, 2014. Available at http://ajr.org/2014/09/24/should-journalists-learn-code.

Statistics. *YouTube.com*. 2014. Available at https://www.youtube.com/yt/press/en -GB/statistics.html.

Steensen, Steen. "Online Journalism and the Promises of New Technology: A Critical Review and Look Ahead." *Journalism Studies* 12, no. 3 (2011): 311–27.

Steuer, Jonathan. "Defining Virtual Reality: Dimensions Determining Telepresence." *Journal of Communication* 42, no. 4 (1992): 73–93.

Stray, Jonathan. "The Editorial Search Engine." *Jonathanstray.com*, March 26, 2011. Available at http://jonathanstray.com/the-editorial-search-engine.

———. "Journalism for Makers." *Jonathanstray.com*, September 22, 2011. Available at http://jonathanstray.com/journalism-for-makers.

———. "Video: What the Overview Project Does." *Overview*, April 7, 2014. Available at https://blog.overviewdocs.com/2014/04/07/video-what-the-overview-project-does.

———. "What's with this Programmer-Journalist Identity Crisis?" *Jonathanstray. com*, October 5, 2011. Available at http://jonathanstray.com/whats-with-this-programmer-journalist-identity-crisis.

"Street Fashion: From the Closet to the Pavement." *New York Times*, 2013. Available at http://www.nytimes.com/interactive/fashion/fashion-week-user-photos-interactive.html#index.

Stromer-Galley, Jennifer. "Interactivity-as-Product and Interactivity-as-Process." *Information Society* 20 (2004): 391–94.

Sundar, S. Shyam. "Multimedia Effects on Processing and Perception of Online News: A Study of Picture, Audio, and Video Downloads." *Journalism and Mass Communication Quarterly* 77, no. 3 (2000): 480–99.

"Talk to the Newsroom: Interactive News Collaborative." *New York Times*, January 17, 2009. Available at http://www.nytimes.com/2009/01/19/business/media /19askthetimes.html?pagewanted=all.

Tanenbaum, Joshua G., Amanda M. Williams, Audrey Desjardins, and Karen Tanenbaum. "Democratizing Technology: Pleasure, Utility and Expressiveness in DIY and Maker Practice." *Proceedings of the SIGCHI Conference on Human Factors in Computing Systems*, Paris, 2013, pp. 2603–12.

Tidwell, Jenifer. *Designing Interfaces*. Sebastopol, Calif.: O'Reilly, 2004.

"Timeline of Syria's Raging War." *Al Jazeera*. Last updated August 9, 2014. Available at http://www.aljazeera.com/indepth/interactive/2012/02/201225111654512841.html. This was different content than what I saw and was present in 2012.

Toff, Benjamin. "Are NYC Taxi Medallion Prices Really 'Plummeting'?" *Benjamintoff.com*, November 30, 2014. Available at http://benjamintoff.com/2014/11/30/medallions.

Torchinsky, Jason. "Information in America Moves 33,480,000 Times Faster than It Did 200 Years Ago." *Jalopnik*, January 11, 2013. Available at http://jalopnik.com/5975008/information-in-america-moves-33480000-times-faster-than-it-did-200-years-ago.

Tracy, Marc. "Nate Silver is a One-Man Traffic Machine for *The Times*." *New Republic*, November 6, 2012. Available at http://www.newrepublic.com/article/109714/nate-silvers-fivethirtyeight-blog-drawing-massive-traffic-new-york-times.

Tse, Archie, and Kevin Quigley. "Is It Better to Rent or Buy?" *New York Times*, 2007. Available at http://web.archive.org/web/20110226054855/http://www.nytimes.com/interactive/business/buy-rent-calculator.html. For current/updated calculator, see Bostock, Carter, and Tse, above.

Turner, Fred. *From Counterculture to Cyberculture: Stewart Brand, the Whole Earth Network, and The Rise of Digital Utopianism*. Chicago: University of Chicago Press, 2010.

Turner, Vernon, David Reinsel, John Gantz, and Stephen Minton. *The Digital Universe of Opportunities: Rich Data and the Increasing Value of the Internet of Things*. Issue brief. April 2014. Available at http://idcdocserv.com/1678.

"2011 Census Analysis: Cycling to Work." *Office for National Statistics*, March 26, 2014. Available at http://www.ons.gov.uk/ons/rel/census/2011-census-analysis/cycling-to-work/2011-census-analysis—-cycling-to-work.html#tab-conclusions.

"The 2010 Pulitzer Prize Winners: National Reporting." Available at http://www.pulitzer.org/citation/2010-National-Reporting.

Usher, Nikki. "Al Jazeera English Online: Understanding Web Metrics and News Production When a Quantified Audience Is Not a Commodified Audience." *Digital Journalism* 1, no. 3 (2013): 337.

———. *Making the News at the New York Times*. Ann Arbor: University of Michigan Press, 2014.

———. "Newsroom Moves and the Newspaper Crisis Evaluated: Space, Place, and Cultural Meaning." *Media, Culture and Society* 37, no. 7 (2015) (published online before print, June 18, 2015).

van Dijk, Jan. *The Network Society: Social Aspects of New Media*. London: Sage, 1999.

Waisbord, Silvio. *Reinventing Professionalism: Journalism and News in Global Perspective*. Malden, Mass.: Polity, 2013.

Walmart. "Picking Up the Pace of Change for the Customer." News release. June 6,

2014. Available at http://news.walmart.com/executive-viewpoints/picking-up-the
-pace-of-change-for-the-customer.

Weaver, David H., Randal A. Beam, Bonnie J. Brownlee, Paul S. Voakes, and G. Cleveland Wilhoit. *The American Journalist in the 21st Century: U.S. News People at the Dawn of a New Millennium*. London: Routledge, 2006.

Weber, Matthew S. "Newspapers and the Long-Term Implications of Hyperlinking." *Journal of Computer-Mediated Communication* 17, no. 2 (2012): 187–201.

Weber, Wibke, and Hannes Rall. "Data Visualization in Online Journalism and Its Implications for the Production Process." In *Proceedings of the 16th Annual Conference on Information Visualisation* (IV), June 2012, 349–56.

Weinberger, David. *Too Big to Know: Rethinking Knowledge Now That the Facts Aren't the Facts, Experts Are Everywhere, and the Smartest Person in the Room Is the Room*. New York: Basic, 2014.

Weiss, Robert S. *Learning from Strangers: The Art and Method of Qualitative Interview Studies*. New York: Simon and Schuster, 1995.

Weissmann, Jordan. "The Decline of Newspapers Hits a Stunning Milestone." *Moneybox* [blog]. *Slate*, April 28, 2014. Available at http://www.slate.com/blogs/moneybox /2014/04/28/decline_of_newspapers_hits_a_milestone_print_revenue_is_lowest _since_1950.html.

"We're Hiring: Code in the Public Interest, Make Your Mother Proud." *News Apps Blog*, *Chicago Tribune*, n.d. Available at http://blog.apps.chicagotribune.com/2011/09/08/ we%E2%80%99re-hiring-code-in-the-public-interest-make-your-mother-proud.

"Where Are You on the Global Fat Scale?" *BBC News*, July 12, 2012. Available at http:// www.bbc.com/news/health-18770328.

"Why Short Guys Can Dunk." *Washington Post*, March 7, 2012. Available at http:// www.washingtonpost.com/wp-srv/special/health/why-short-guys-can-dunk.

"WSJ Jet Tracker Database." *Wall Street Journal*, June 16, 2011. Available at http:// online.wsj.com/news/articles/SB10001424052748704904604576336194411640185.

"The Year's Most Visited: 2014." New York Times Company. Available at http://www .nytco.com/wp-content/uploads/NYT-Years-Most-Visited-of-2014.pdf.

Youmans, Will Lafi. *The Media Economics and Cultural Politics of Al Jazeera English in the United States*. PhD diss. University of Michigan, 2012.

Young, Mary Lynn, and Alfred Hermida. "From Mr. and Mrs. Outlier to Central Tendencies: Computational Journalism and Crime Reporting at the *Los Angeles Times*." *Digital Journalism* 3, no 3 (2015).

Zelizer, Barbie. "Journalism's 'Last' Stand: Wirephoto and the Discourse of Resistance." *Journal of Communication* 45 no. 2 (1995): 78–92.

# Index

129; Fusion, 96, 97, 106, 107, 109, 127, 128–29, 152; Gmail, 51; male staff, 217; Maps, 54–55, 56, 61, 107; page load times, 11; Refine, 151; Tableau, 151; technical staff, 217; tools, 129; user's flow of thought, 12
Gordon, Rich, 57–60, 71; News Challenge, 58
Graham, Paul, 153
*The Greensboro News and Record*, 56
Grimwade, John, 39, 40
*The Guardian*, 66, 77, 79, 82, 91, 102, 135, 136, 171, 202; DataBlog, 95, 96, 129, 142, 172, 197; data desk, 15; finances, 137; newsroom, 127–30, 140, 141, 214; open source, 191–2; Reality Check blog, 97; WikiLeaks revelations, 91, 192. *See also* Dant, Alistair; Rogers, Simon
Gynnild, Astrid, 73

hacker journalists 56–57, 59, 72–86, *75*, 88, 89, 90, 95, 98, 99, 112, 117, 118, 122, 134, 135, 138, 139, 150, 158, 168, 169, 187–88; are they journalists? 81–84; origin 74–76; reason for becoming 76–78; ways of thinking 78–81
hacker journalists, programmer journalists, and data journalists, 71–101; backgrounds and perspectives 75–76; are hacker journalists journalists?, 81–84; data journalists, 90–95; data journalists are not coders, 95–98; hacker journalists origin 74–76; hacker journalists ways of thinking, 78–81; programmer journalists 84–85; programmer journalists backgrounds and perspectives, 85–87; programmer journalists way of thinking about stories, 87–90; reason for becoming a hacker journalist, 76–78; turning coders into journalists, 71–74. *See also* data journalists; hacker journalists; programmer journalists
Hamilton, James, 24, 160
Hamilton, Jay, 24
Harris, Jacob, 61, 62
Hindman, Matthew, 194
Holovaty, Adrian, 38, 47–48, 52, 53, 54–58, 60–61, 73; "Congress Votes," 60; "Faces of the Fallen," 61
*Houston Chronicle*, 203; "At Sea," 45; Virtual Voyager, 45
Howard, Alexander, 22, 90, 91
Hurrel, Bella, 173

HTML (HyperText Markup Language), 49, 51, 82, 87, 96, 151, 200
hybrid ethnography, 16, 209–18; difficulties facing the researcher, 215–17; gender, 217–18; introduction 209–13; set of cases, 213–15
HyperText Markup Language. *See* HTML

IBM, 13; 360 mainframe, 67
interactive journalism: definition, 18–24
International Data Corporation, 13

Jamal, Dar, 110
Jaspin, Elliott, 67, 68
Jobs, Steve, 119
job skills, 149–52
Jordan, Tim 166
journalism: crisis, 5–10; demands, 10–14

Kaiser, Robert G., 7, 8
Keaton, Michael: *The Paper*, 190
Keefe, John, 86
Keegan, Jon, 50, 81, 118, 119, 120–21, 125, 170
Keller, Bill, 80
Khazan, Olga, 201
Klein, Scott, 21, 88, 93, 153, 157, 164, 165, 179
Knight-Batten award, 55
Knight Foundation: data visualization, 131, 155; DocumentCloud, 158; hacker journalist, 74, *75*, 76; News Challenge Grant, 57, 58, 71; PANDA, 156
Knight-Mozilla News Technology Partnership Learning Lab, 215
Knight Ridder, 7, 58; computers, 40; Research and Design Newspaper Lab, 8; Videotext technology, 42
knowledge, 26–28; abstract and professional, 15, 16, 27, 28, 30, 74, 84, 99, 104, 143, 145, 146, 148, 149, 152, 161, 170, 175, 179–81, 184, 187, 214; build-it journalism, 153–61; narrative nut-grafs, 175–79; near/far, 161–65; openness, 166–70 (*see also* open source); see-it-for-yourself journalism, 171–75; skills, 15, 27, 34, 35, 36, 43, 62, 117, 149–52; systems, 145–81
Koski, Ben, 122, 125

*La Prensa*, 205
Lavallee, Mark, 124
*The Lawrence Journal-World*, 37–38, 46–48, 54
Legrand, Ronald, 200

sis in Maps," 64; Upshot, 197; Videotext technology, 42; Website up to date, 10–11; "Where are the Hardest Places to Live in the U.S.?," 64; WikiLeaks revelations, 91, 192. *See also* Abramson, Jill; Ashby-Kuhlman, Nathan; Bilton, Nick; Bowers, Jeremy; Davis, Chase; Keller, Bill; Koski, Ben; Lavallee, Mark; Pilhofer, Aron; Richtel, Matt; Torok, Tom; Willis, Derek

NICAR. *See* National Institute for Computer Assisted Reporting

Nielsen, Jakob, 12

Northwestern University 57, 76, 86, 139; Medill School of Journalism, 58, 59, 71, 72, 86, 200

NPR, 15, 37, 48, 53, 82, 134; audience, 143; autonomy, 137; business model, 137; News Apps, 111–18, 153, 169; newsroom, 86, 102, 111–18, 135, 137, 139, 140, 141, 214; open source, 170; Planet Money, 204; public service, 137; slow speed, 136. *See also* Boyer, Brian; Curley, Rob; DeBelius, Danny; Folkenflik, David; Stiles, Matt

Obama, Barack, 60, 125

Oculus Rift, 11

Online News Association, 200, 215

online speed, 5, 10, 11, 12, 14, 40, 115, 186

open source, 73, 76, 80, 112, 152, 155, 166–70; challenges, 169–70; commitment from journalists 167–69; culture, 166–67, 170, 180, 191, 192; ethics, 67; hackers, 166, 180; libraries, 169; repositories, 53, 166; social, 52–53

*The Orange County Register*, 38

O'Reilly, Tim: *MAKE*, 153

*The Paper*, 190

Parasie, Sylvain, 73, 227n10

people, 24–26

Perl, 53

Pew Research Center, 7

*The Philadelphia Inquirer*, 45, 67. *See also* Bartlett, Don; Steele, James; Torok, Tom

Pilhofer, Aron, 61, 62, 86, 92–93, 95, 122, 124, 125, 158, 167, 169, 193, 199, 202

Planet Money, 204

Powers, Matthew, 32–33, 92

*ProPublica* ; DocumentCloud, 157; Dollars for Docs, 139, 145, 146, 147; near/far, 228n36; Nerd Blog, 223n54; News Apps 93, 153, 164; newsroom, 127, 214; non-profit, 4, 21, 192; nut-graf, 178, 179; open source, 169; Opportunity Gap, 164, 190; social problems database, 161. *See also* Klein, Scott; Wei, Sisi; Willis, Derek

professionalism, 26, 29, 30, 104, 184–88; through work, 140–43

programmer journalists, backgrounds and perspectives, 85–87; traditional background, 84–85; way of thinking about stories, 87–90

*Providence Journal*, 67

Python, 47, 61, 93, 96, 97, 115, 151, 152, 154, 200

Quartz, 1, 196

Rabaino, Lauren, 80

Radway, Janice, 217

Rall, Hannes, 73

Raymond, Eric: *The Cathedral and the Bazaar*, 166

Reavy, Matthew, 67

*The Register Citizen*, 192

Richtel, Matt, 62–63

*Rocky Mountain News*, 87

Rogers, Simon, 96, 127, 135, 226n28; DataBlog, 129

Royal, Cindy, 73

*Ruptly*, 205

Rusbridger, Alan, 191–92

Schrager, Allison, 196, 197

Schudson, Michael, 28, 29–30

*Scotusblog*, 6

*The Seattle Times*: News Apps, 80; newsrooms, 153, 214

see-it-for-yourself journalism, 27–28, 147, 171–75, 180, 181, 193, 194, 195; "fun" journalism 172–75; roundup 175; at work, 171–72

sensor journalism, 202, 203–5

Shafer, Jack, 7

Shirky, Clay, 4, 147

Silver, Nate, 91; FiveThirtyEight blog, 197, 199

Sloane, Sara, 177

Slobin, Sarah, 81

Society for News Design, 40

*The South Florida Sun-Sentinel*, 41, 203

speed, online. *See* online speed

Spurgeon, Christina, 73

Stallman, Richard, 52

NIKKI USHER is an assistant professor at The George Washington University's School of Media and Public Affairs. She is the author of *Making News at the New York Times*.

DATE DUE | RETURNED
10/7/17 |

The University of (
is a founding mem
Association of Ame

_____

Composed in 10.5/13
with Meta display
by Jim Proefrock
at the University of Illinois Press
Manufactured by Sheridan Books, Inc.

University of Illinois Press
1325 South Oak Street
Champaign, IL 61820-6903
www.press.uillinois.edu